Pakistan's Birth
&
Allama Mashraqi

Pakistan's Birth & Allama Mashraqi

Chronology & Statements
Period: 1947-1963

Edited & Compiled by:
Nasim Yousaf

Copyright © 2005 by Nasim Yousaf.

First Edition published in 2005

Library of Congress Control Number: 2005932487
ISBN: 0-9760333-4-8

All rights reserved. No part of this book may be reproduced or transmitted in any form or by any means, graphic, electronic, or mechanical, including photocopying, recording, taping, or by any information storage retrieval system, without the written permission of the author/editor.

This work is sold subject to the conditions that it shall not, by way of trade or
otherwise, be lent, re-sold, hired out, or otherwise circulated, without the author/editor's prior written consent, in any form of binding or cover other than that in which it is published and without a similar condition, including this condition being imposed on the subsequent purchaser.

This book is printed in the United States of America.

Published by:
AMZ Publications
P.O. Box 2802
Liverpool, New York, 13089-2802
USA

"Allama Mashraqi's life — his message to humanity"

-Nasim Yousaf

Acknowledgements

I extend my heartiest thanks to my mother, relatives, Khaksars, and others, who during my life have contributed to my knowledge on Allama Mashriqi and the Khaksar Tehrik, and have thus helped make this work possible.

I am also extremely grateful to those authors and publications whose works I have used in compiling this book. I have cited the sources used in this work to the best of my ability. I extend my cordial thanks to the authors of these sources. If inadvertently I have forgotten to cite or made an error in citing a source, I extend my deepest regret to the author or the organization of the source concerned.

Declaration

I, Nasim Yousaf, have produced this work to the best of my ability. All events and dates have been collected from credible sources. I have made every attempt possible to list all events in chronological order, however error(s) is possible. In some cases, the exact day and/or month of the event may not available. In case of quotes, any typographical errors have been preserved and may appear in this text. I cannot be held responsible for any error(s) or omission(s) due to any reason.

Clarification & Comments

I have added comments/clarification wherever it was needed.

If similar news is found in more than one source, I have included the other source or sources, but that does not necessarily mean that the exact same information is available in both sources mentioned.

Note

The following are spelled in several different ways including:

Mashraqi; Mashriqi; Mashraqui; Mashriqui
Al-Mashriqi; El-Mashriqi
Khaksar; Khaksaar
Tehreek; Tehrik; Tehrique

The Khaksar Tehreek is also known as the Khaksar Movement.

The people who joined the Islam League (including Khaksars) were known as Razakars.

Editor's Biography

This publication has been edited and compiled by Mr. Nasim Yousaf, a grandson of Allama Mashraqi. This document is the result of exhaustive study on Pakistan's history carried out by Mr. Yousaf and his personal knowledge of Allama Mashraqi and the Khaksar Tehreek (Khaksar Tehrik)[1].

Mr. Yousaf began his career as a Pilot Officer in the Pakistan Air Force. He left the cherished profession and became an exporter and a leader in the business community in Pakistan. The editor is a founding member of the Board of Directors that established The Pakistan Commercial Exporters of Towels Association (PCETA), one of the largest trade associations in Pakistan. He also held other important positions in the PCETA, including Vice Chairman (North Zone), Member of the Central Executive Committee, and Member of the Textile Quota Committee of the PCETA. As part of the Textile Quota Committee, he and other members disbursed textile quota to exporters of PCETA. Mr. Yousaf also represented the business community in front of various levels of the Government of Pakistan, including the ministerial level, to discuss and resolve trade issues. Mr. Yousaf has traveled extensively around the world, which according to him, has been a great source of learning and has opened his vision on global issues.

Since his move to the USA, he has continued to be in his own business, and has simultaneously pursued his passion (an inspiration he derived from Allama Mashraqi and Dr. Akhter Hameed Khan) of writing books and articles, particularly on Allama Mashraqi and the Khaksars' role towards the independence of Pakistan. He has spent many years on research on the Pakistan movement and has continuously devoted a considerable amount of time toward this project.

---

[1] The Khaksar Tehreek is also known as the Khaksar Movement.

The author's other published works include:

- *Allama Mashriqi & Dr. Akhtar Hameed Khan: Two Legends of Pakistan*
- *Pakistan's Freedom and Allama Mashriqi: Statements, Letters, Chronology of Khaksar Tehrik (Movement), Period: Mashriqi's Birth to 1947*
- *Import &Export of Apparel & Textiles; Part I: Export to USA, Part II: Import from Pakistan*
- *Import &Export of Hand Knotted Oriental Rugs; Part I: Export to U.S.A., Part II: Import from Pakistan*
- *Importing Gifts, Housewares & Decorative Accessories from Hong Kong*
- *Export Housewares, Gifts & Decorative Accessories to the United States of America* (under print)
- Articles on Allama Mashraqi and the Khaksar Tehreek. Extracts from his research have been published on the web sites dedicated to Allama Mashriqi and Dr. Akhtar Hameed Khan.

The following web sites have been dedicated to Allama Mashraqi (Mashriqi) and Dr. Akhter (Akhtar) Hameed Khan:

- www.allamamashriqi.info
- www.allama-mashriqi.8m.com
- www.akhtar-hameed-khan.8m.com

For more information and updates on the author/editor's works, visit the following web sites:

- www.nasimyousaf.info
- www.nasimyousaf.8m.com

Preface

It gives me immense happiness to have completed another chronology, *Pakistan's Birth & Allama Mashraqi: Chronology & Statements, Period: 1947-1963*. This book lists important events, activities of the Islam League (that Mashraqi founded soon after Pakistan's independence), and statements of Mashraqi and various other persons. It lists Mashraqi's efforts in regards to the freedom of Kashmir. It gives dates of government actions against Mashraqi and how he was prevented from playing any role in the political arena. It also documents court proceedings in which Mashraqi was implicated on fabricated cases. This work is a continuation of my previous chronology titled: *Pakistan's Freedom and Allama Mashriqi: Statements, Letters, Chronology of Khaksar Tehrik (Movement), Period: Mashriqi's Birth to 1947*.

***

The story of Allama Mashraqi and his Khaksar Tehrik (Movement) is an incredible one. He and his followers (over 4 million in number) dedicated their lives to work for the masses in the Indian-subcontinent. Pre-partition they worked endlessly and selflessly for the freedom of India. The details of this period can be found in my previous chronology and my other works.

Post-partition, Mashraqi and the Khaksars and continued to work for the good of the people. Soon after the creation of Pakistan, Mashraqi founded the Islam League in order to undo injustices in the partition plan, protect Muslims in India, and work for the liberation of Kashmir. To mobilize the world opinion for Kashmir, he even organized a one million man march to Delhi in 1957. This is just one example of his efforts.

Throughout the years, the government felt threatened by the power of Mashraqi and his followers as they had a different agenda from that of Mashraqi's; they were interested in personal gains, whereas Mashraqi's interest was solely the uplift of the masses. Hence, the government did everything to stand in Mashraqi and the Khaksars' way and to keep them from operating. Mashraqi, his sons, and his followers were arrested numerous times, and all of their families were harassed. Vindictive anti-Mashraqi elements kept Mashraqi behind bars based on flimsy and fabricated cases and attempted to falsely implicate him; they even tried to falsely incriminate him in one case that would have resulted in a death sentence. Those who had no interest in the masses but only in themselves eventually committed Mashraqi's political murder.

All the while, it was ignored that Mashraqi and the Khaksars had nothing on their minds except the nation's cause. They were selfless people and not the seekers of prominent positions or wealth. Mashraqi was one of the greatest statesmen and patriot ever born. My heart bleeds to see how a man of Mashraqi's stature was treated in the same land for the freedom of which he had given his life for.

***

It is regrettable that the Muslim League refused to recognize anyone else's contributions and concealed everyone else's role except its own. Hence, the role of Allama Mashraqi and the Khaksars has been distorted and deleted from Pakistan's history. The freedom of India was not obtained single-handedly by the Muslim League or the Indian National Congress. Hence, Mashraqi and the Khaksars' role needs to be highlighted in both Pakistan and India's history.

It is even worse to note that the purpose of obtaining Pakistan is yet to be accomplished. If one reads the history, there has been a shift in the real purpose of why Pakistan was created; hence no one seems to know the real purpose and the truth. The situation that prevails in Pakistan today and the ills that plague is society is not what the freedom fighters of the time envisioned for Pakistan. Only a small class of Pakistanis are benefiting from Pakistan's potential, while the masses lack education and even food. Further, it is a matter of grave concern that civil rights and freedom have been denied to the people of Pakistan from the onset of its creation. This bothers me significantly as my grandfather, Allama Mashraqi, gave his life to the country. This was not what Mashraqi had wanted; he worked for freedom and to lift the masses and crush the class system.

***

These publications are too small to cover the course of Mashraqi's life and all of the activities of his followers. All information and events surrounding this period, including the Khaksars Tehreek and Islam League's material, need to be collected, documented and made available in the libraries for public consumption. Based on the extensive information that is out there, I have written letters to the President and Prime Ministers of Pakistan to propose that an Allama Mashraqi Research Academy be established immediately. I have also apprised various Pakistani dignitaries of this; some of these letters have been reproduced in this publication.

My works provide evidence that Mashraqi and the Khaksars played an extremely important role to mobilize the public to rise for freedom. I am currently working on another publication that surrounds the correspondence of the Viceroy of India, Governors of various Provinces, and the British senior officers in the U.K. regarding the elimination of the Khaksar Movement (Khaksar Tehreek). This will further reveal the importance of the Khaksar Movement's role in the freedom of the Indian sub-continent and how the British felt threatened by it and thus pounced on it. The British's actions against Mashraqi and the Khaksars' rigorous efforts to demand the freedom of India, in fact, mobilized the nation to rise for freedom. This reveals who actually suffered to seek freedom from the British that resulted in the creation of Pakistan and India.

Truth Alone Will Survive

The dream of independence was not achieved single-handedly by the All India Muslim League or the Indian National Congress. The services of Allama Mashraqi and the Khaksars made the dream of independence become a reality.

Mashraqi envisioned the entire India to be Pakistan. He and the Khaksars infused the spirit of re-awakening among the people of India. Their efforts were of great importance in mobilizing the people for freedom and in re-building the nation. Those who have denied or ignored this are responsible for distorting the facts of Indo-Pakistan history.

Mashraqi's Vision

Allama Mashraqi had the vision to build a nation with high morals and values and without discrimination against anyone regardless of caste, color or creed. Mashraqi's philosophy – simplicity, discipline, brotherhood, and cleanliness of body and soul.

Mashraqi led a principled life which continues to inspire those who seek to become better humans and those who seek to build the future of mankind. His vision, ideas, principles, and works are of utmost importance.

1947

"Allama Mashraqi's legacy is immortal"

– Nasim Yousaf

1947

1947

Mashraqi warns the Government of Pakistan to secure Kashmir by any means necessary and not allow India to take the issue to the United Nations Security Council. Otherwise, it will never be resolved (Zaman 1987, 424).

Editor's comments: The source used does not list the date of this warning. Mashraqi's foresight proved to be correct, as the Kashmir issue still remains unresolved, even today. Mashraqi issued these warnings at various times over the years. See December 1950, September-November 1952, and many other dates throughout this book for his statements in regards to this issue.

1947 January 18

Allama Mashraqi meets with Dr. Shafaat Ahmed Khan (former Member of the Interim Government) to discuss the current political situation.

1947 February 18

The Free Press Journal, Bombay reports:
"The Khaksars stand for Hindu-Muslim unity, declared Dr. F.K. Abra, Chief of the Khaksar organisation in the Bombay Province in an interview to pressmen here.

Dr. Abra who has come to Poona to organise a camp of Khaksar officers from all over Bombay Presidency further stated that the policy adopted at present by the Muslim League would lead the Muslim masses nowhere. In fact, he said, it was suicidal.

Over 125 Khaksar leaders from the Province are attending the camp.

The object of this camp, said Dr. Abra, was to train the Khaksar officers to propogate Hindu-Muslim unity and communal harmony. Also it intended to train them up as to how to act during communal strifes. Dr Abra also revealed that at a recent meeting of Khaksar leaders from over the country convened by their leader, Allama Mashriqi at Lahore the question regarding the role to be adopted during such emergencies was discussed" (FPJ 1947 Feb. 18).

1947 February 23

Jinnah addresses a group of Bihar Muslims. He states, "The Muslim League will not yield an inch in their demand for Pakistan...Whatever the Hindus may do, we shall ever remain generous and good to all. Our demand is just and is the only way to liberate the ten crores [100 million] of Muslims in India" (FPJ 1947 Feb. 24).

Editor's comments: Here Jinnah's stance was not to yield even an inch of land that would have been part of Pakistan. However, the Muslim League changed their stance and on June 09, 1947, they accepted the Mountbatten Plan. The Khaksars protested the Muslim League's acceptance of a truncated Pakistan under the Mountbatten Plan. The Mountbatten Plan divided Punjab and Bengal, which were initially supposed to be part of Pakistan. Ultimately, the Khaksars were right, as 50 million Muslims were left behind in India when Pakistan was created.

1947 February 26

In Lahore, six Khaksars are arrested for parading and carrying belchas.

1947 March

Allama Mashraqi calls for 300,000 Khaksars to assemble in New Delhi on June 30, 1947 in order to decide the future of India.

1947 March 07

A discussion takes place between Gandhi and the Khaksars. The Khaksars offer their help to resolve the Hindu-Muslim riots of Bihar.

1947 March 30

Allama Mashraqi arrives in Peshawar to consult with Frontier Khaksar leaders and study the political situation.

1947 April 11

The Eastern Times reports that Allama Mashraqi is to arrive in Lucknow on April 14, 1947. The newspaper further states that Major General Dost Mohammad Khan and Col. Ehsan Qadir will accompany him (ET 1947 Apr. 11).

1947 May 03

13 Khaksars are arrested in Lahore while making speeches at a public meeting. Police disperse the crowd that had gathered for the meeting. Police pickets are also posted in the area.

1947 May 07

The Pakistan Times reports that "Allama Mashriqi is reported to have placed his views on the rehabilitation of Muslim refugees in the Province before the Bihar Government. He has expressed his views against levying of fines on affected villages, it is learnt, and has suggested instead the levying of a cess-tax of rupee one per adult, to be known as the Bihar Relief Tax to meet a portion of the heavy expenses involved in undertaking relief and rehabilitation measures" (PT 1947 May 07).

1947 May 10

Khaksars parade in Lahore in observance of "Bahadur Shah Day." Many Khaksars are arrested.

Mashraqi addresses the public at Banqipur, Putna.

1947 May 13

Allama Mashraqi issues a statement demanding the rehabilitation of Bihar refugees. According to Mashriqi: "We remain firm in this demand until Government actually concedes it. I am also satisfied that the Bengal Government has actually spent rupees eighty lakhs on the Noakhali refugees and that about 75 per cent of the refugees have come back and resettled. No resettlement worth the name has taken place in Bihar so far" (*Dawn* 1947 May 15).

1947 May 14

Mashraqi addresses over 50,000 people at a gathering at Banqipur, Patna.

1947 May 24

A discussion is held between Gandhi and the Khaksars.

1947 May 29

Mashraqi issues a statement asking the people to start a revolution against the British Government.

1947 May 30

M.Yunus writes from Patna to M.A. Jinnah, and encloses his correspondence with Mashraqi (see enclosures 1-4 below):
My dear Quaid-i-Azam,
I am enclosing my recent correspondence with Allama Inayetullah Mashraqi, the Khaksar leader, regarding the rehabilitation scheme in Bihar.
Yours sincerely,
M.Yunus

Enclosure 1

Inayetullah [Allama] Mashriqi to M.Yunus
KHAKSAR RELIEF AND REHABILITATION H.Q.,
CAMP PATNA,
29 May 1947

My dear Yunus,
The Government has accepted almost all the demands that the Khaksar Organisation had made with respect to the rehabilitation of Bihar refugees and the work of constructing thousands of houses will now begin.
In January last, Sir Shafaat Ahmed Khan, when he met me at Ichhra and we discussed the problem, was particularly keen on telling me that you had written to him that you were very interested in relief work and that your "joining" the Muslim League was not so much on account of leaning towards the League as on account of their claim to do relief work. He also suggested that you should be asked to cooperate in the work that the Khaksars will undertake. I am, therefore, asking you to join as a member of the Relief Committee to which I am entrusting the task of rehabilitation before I leave Patna. A meeting of this Committee is going to be held today at 6 p.m. at the above address. Please attend it.
I hope you are quite well now.
Yours sincerely,

INAYETULLAH

Enclosure 2

M. Yunus to Inayetullah [Allama] Mashriqi

DAR-UL-MALIK, FRASER
ROAD, PATNA,
29 May 1947

My dear Mr. Inayetullah,
Many thanks for your letter No. 42488 dated 29th May 1947. You have been kind enough to inform me that the Government has accepted almost all the demands that the Khaksar Organisation had made with respect to the rehabilitation of the Bihar refugees and the work of constructing thousands of houses will now begin. Its feasibility would depend on the nature of your demands and of your scheme, copies of which you have not been pleased to send me, and I shall be obliged if you will kindly do so to appraise in proper perspective the value of the rehabilitation scheme...

I am grateful to you for asking me to co-operate in the work that the Khaksars will undertake for relief work...
Yours sincerely,
M.YUNUS

Enclosure 3

Inayetullah [Allama] Mashriqi to M. Yunus

KHAKSAR RELIEF ANDREHABILITATION H.Q.,
CAMP PATNA
29 May 1947

Dear Mr. Yunus,
I have your letter. On the back you will find the conditions that have been accepted. There are some others which they are likely to accept gradually. At any rate, the work should start at once as people in Bengal and Sind are suffering terribly and it is absolutely impossible to rehabilitate them anywhere except on their own lands, otherwise four lakh (people) will perish and lose all honour. The condition in the camps is simply terrible.

You must come forward individually or otherwise. The funeral is of the Biharis themselves, perpetrated through the dirty politics of the present day, and if the Biharis themselves do not do it, it will be a regrettable thing. In a humanitarian work one should leave all politics. I shall explain to you further if you come this evening at 6 p.m. I have given invitation to Mr. Jafar Imam through Syed Abdul Aziz who says he cannot join as his condition is worsening

unfortunately. If you can ask him to join today's deliberations I shall be pleased.
Yours sincerely,
INAYETULLAH

Enclosure 4

PATNA,
29 May 1947

PRESS STATEMENT BY ALLAMA MASHRIQI

'Nearly five months' persistent haggling with the Bihar Government on the matter of resettlement of nearly 4 lakhs of Bihar refugees, I am glad to announce, has made the Government come to the conclusion that the problem has got to be tackled. My demand that one thousand rupees per adult be given at a flat rate for reconstruction of houses has not been met in full on financial grounds, but the final proposals which Mahatma Gandhi has placed before the Bihar Government concerning the conditions on which the Khaksar organisation would or should take up the work of rehabilitation, are as follows:
1. The Government will grant Rs.1,000 for every house rebuilt.
2. In addition, a rehabilitation grant of Rs. 500 for a family of 5 members will be made.
3. Building grants of more than Rs. 1,000 will be made in special cases.
4. Special grants of Rs. 1,500 or more will be given even to those who do not wish to resettle in Bihar on the recommendation of the Khaksar Organisation, (this being Mr. Gandhi's verbal suggestion may be taken to be the opinion of the Government).
5. Interest-free loans repayable in 5 yearly instalments will be given to artisans and agriculturists for the purchase of seeds and implements.
6. Free Education will be provided for refugees who settle.
7. Work will be given by the Government to those adults who need it.
8. During the recuperation period, free rations will be provided to those people who help in the work of reconstruction of houses by the Khaksar Organisation.
9. Orphanages and widows' homes will be provided for and built wherever recommended.

I have asked the Khaksar Negotiating Committee to start work on these lines at once as well as to keep up the negotiations with respect to the remaining demands. The work of rebuilding 10,000 houses in

Bihar that we contemplate is a tremendous work and it is primarily for the Biharis and not the Khaksars to complete it. I am, therefore, setting up a strong Committee of Bihari intelligentsia and have invited Mr. Yunus, Mr. Jafar Imam, President Muslim League, and the ailing Syed Abdul Aziz and others to join it most vigorously. A capable Rehabilitation Officer and an efficient paid staff will be and is being appointed. The whole scheme will be headed by the *Hakim-i-A'la* of the Relief Camp and his staff. I invite freely the help of every feeling person in India in this grand humanitarian scheme.

1947 June 02

The Mountbatten Plan is announced.

1947 June 09

The All-India Muslim League Council holds a meeting at the Imperial Hotel in New Delhi to make a decision regarding the acceptance of the Mountbatten Plan. Khaksars and other Muslims hold large protests outside the hotel to urge the Muslim League not to accept a truncated Pakistan. The Khaksars want other areas such as Ajmere, Delhi, and Agra to be a part of Pakistan. They are also opposed to the division of Punjab and Bengal. The Khaksars, who attempt to enter the hotel, are beaten up by the Muslim League National Guard. The Muslim League National Guard also uses lathis to remove the Khaksars from inside the hotel and from the room where the meeting is being held. Many of the Khaksars are picked up and thrown out of the hotel. The Muslim Leaguers also call police, who open fire, use tear gas, and arrest a large number of Khaksars.

The Star of India would report on June 10, 1947, "the New Delhi police this morning took into custody a number of 'Khaksars' and other Muslim demonstrators who paraded the vicinity where the Muslim League Council held its sessions raising slogans against the Plan and demanding a 'complete Pakistan'" (SI 1947 June 10).

Editor's comments: This event has been distorted in many history books to suggest that the Khaksars were against the creation of Pakistan and that they tried to attack the Muslim League leaders. However, the reality is that the Khaksars were only opposed to the *truncated* Pakistan, which the Muslim League wanted to accept. The Khaksars' only crime was that they protested against the unjust Mountbatten Plan, which gave a truncated Pakistan to the Muslims (who had ruled India for almost 1,000 years). The Hindus were much happier than the Muslims as they were able to attain a majority of the land as a result of the Partition Plan, whereas the Muslims had lost a major share of the land they had once ruled. It is the basic right of the citizens of a nation to be able to protest against any injustice or leaders who are making wrong decisions. To turn the story around and accuse the Khaksars of being against Pakistan is highly deplorable.

1947 June 10

In Patna (Bengal), police open fire on a Khaksar procession. Five Khaksars are killed and some are injured. The Khaksars had taken out the procession in observance of "Bahadur Shah Day." Following the clash, they raid the Khaksar camp at Sabzibagh and arrest two dozen Khaksars. Police also raid another Khaksar camp at Lodikatra in Purnea City. The police remain on full alert to control the Khaksars.

In Delhi, the Muslim League Council holds a secret session. *The Tribune*, Lahore of June 11, 1947 would report:
"The session being secret, strict watch was kept on those who were going in. Mr. Jinnah's tactics in having a 'purdah' session was motivated to keep a wet blanket on the dissentient voices raised from the Leaguers from the Muslim minority provinces — east Punjab and Bengal — against the [Mountbatten] plan.
Khaksars…suddenly highlighted the session against 'langra [lame] Pakistan,' their description of the truncated variety. Police removed them [the Khaksars] quickly…" (TT 1947 June 11).

1947 June 11

Allama Mashraqi is arrested in Delhi. Strong preventive measures are taken by the Government to ensure that Mashraqi doesn't organize a movement against the Mountbatten Plan. Mashraqi is later released to avoid any demonstrations from the Khaksars.

The bodies of five Khaksars (who were killed by police in Patna on June 10, 1947) are taken out in a procession. Syed Makhdoom Shah Banori (the Ahrar leader), Major General Shah Nawaz, Colonel Mahboob Ahmed, Balram Dubey, Shah Uzair Munimi, and others follow the funeral procession.

Two of the Khaksars (who were injured by the police in Patna on June 10, 1947) die in the hospital.

Khaksar arrests continue in Delhi.

1947 June 14

Approximately 24 Khaksars are arrested in Jullundur.

1947 June 17

Khaksar drills and parades are banned in Agra.

In Lahore, Allama Mashraqi issues the following statement to the Press: "The report that I have received today concerning the massacre of Khaksars at Patna on the occasion of the 'Bahadur Shah Day' on June 10 last, surpasses in cruelty and arrogance of all human imagination. Four Khaksars were left to die in a hospital with no one to attend to them. The Khaksars were absolutely innocent, their procession peaceful and symbolised Hindu-Muslim unity. It is certain now that the Bihar Ministry, because they were compelled to accept the demand of Rs. 1,500 per family of the Khaksars, through the intervention of Mahatma Gandhi, retaliated on them as soon as I left Patna. We put forward this demand for 50,000 refugees and 10,000 houses that we shall reconstruct. I hold the Congress responsible for the killing of 50,000 Bihari Muslims. I appeal publicly to Pandit Nehru to stop this wholesale murder of Mussalmans by Congress agents in the interests of public peace" (PT 1947 Jun. 18).

1947 June 27

A Khaksar meeting is held at Idara-i-Aliya (Khaksar headquarters in Lahore) to discuss the upcoming Khaksar Camp in New Delhi on June 30, 1947. In March 1947, Mashraqi had called for 300,000 Khaksars to assemble in New Delhi to discuss the future of India.

1947 June 28

Mashraqi sends the following letter to Nehru:
Dear Pandit Jawaharlal Nehru,
    Please refer to my letter No.43636 dated the 17th June to you concerning the shooting of five Khaksars by the Bihar ministry and the subsequent events.
    I have now received the report of interviews the Khaksar deputation had with you and others, also you letter of 26th June to Nawab Muhammad Hussain Khan in which you put down the result of your enquiries from the Bihar Government and say that 'certain

Khaksars attacked the police with belchas and also fired upon them, killing two, etc.' The story of the Bihar Government is, I venture to say, purely ficticious and is calculated to justify the wild doings of the ministry in your eyes. It is most regrettable that lies are passed as truths from responsible persons...

...I request you again in the name of good neighbourly relations between the Hindus and the Muslims and the future good of India not to treat the matter lightly as the Khaksars are agitated over my supposed inattention towards the matter and persons who were murdered were very well to do men. The deputation is awaiting your decision at Delhi and has proposed that a sum of Rs. 20,000 should be paid to the relatives per person through the Khaksar Organisation, that all arrested Khaksars should be released, that no obstacle should be put by the Bihar ministry in the way of rehabilitation as agreed to by Mahatma Gandhi with the Khaksar Negotiating Committee and that amicable relations with the Bihar ministry should be re-established.

These are not tough conditions in face of what has happened. It is only good relations between the two communities that can save India now. I would ask you and other Congress leaders to think more calmly about the events that are happening. I am disappointed with the hot words about the future treatment of the Congress with the Muslims spoken in the interviews of some Congress leaders with the deputation.

With best wishes,
Yours sincerely

Mashraqi sends the following letter to Gandhi from Lahore:
Dear Mahatma Gandhi,

A serious tangle has occurred in our relations with the Bihar ministry owing to the killing of several Khaksars in Patna on 10th June and the arrest of several Khaksars etc. I referred the matter to Pandit Jawaharlal but he has told the deputation that met him that the matter was a minor one in the face of what has happening eleswhere and he seems to have treated it lightly.

I have now asked the deputation to turn to you and appeal to you for making amends. I trust you will do the best you can. You can see the responsibility on my shoulders in the matter especially when these Khaksars tried their utmost to promote good relations among the two communities in Bihar for several months together at great personal inconvenience.

I am sending you a copy of the letter I have written to Pandit Sahib today in order to give you an idea of what has happened. The Khaksars are agitated over the affair and I hope the matter will be

amicably settled very soon. Please do the needful as much as you can immediately.
With best wishes,
Yours sincerely.

1947 June 30

Khaksars gather in New Delhi for a rally scheduled to begin in the evening (Allama Mashraqi had asked in March 1947 for 300,000 Khaksars to assemble in New Delhi). Police adopt strict measures, prevent the Khaksars from holding the rally, and arrest a large number of Khaksars. A ban on holding demonstrations or taking out processions continues to remain in place in Delhi. Delhi remains under Section 144.
Editor's Note: See editor's comments on July 04, 1947.

The Dawn, Delhi would report on July 02, 1947, "Khaksars were not allowed to hold their rally which was scheduled to take place today [June 30, 1947] in Delhi" (*Dawn* 1947 Jul. 02).

1947 July 01

A delegation of Khaksars meets with Gandhi to discuss the police firing on the Khaksars on June 10, 1947 in Patna. The delegation demands that the Bihar Government pay Rs. 20,000 as compensation for each Khaksar who was killed. The delegation also demands the release of the Khaksars who were arrested following the police firing. Gandhi assures the Khaksars that he would request the Bihar Government to consider the matter. The Khaksars had also met with Pandit Nehru regarding this matter.

1947 July 02

The Tribune, Lahore reports that the Khaksar publicity chief, Shaukatullah, has stated that if the Khaksar rally which is to be held in Delhi on July 03, 1940 fails to draw 300,000 volunteers, then Allama Mashraqi would disband the entire Khaksar Tehrik. He further stated that 70,000 to 80,000 Khaksars had already arrived in Delhi and that the program is to include flag hoisting, a mass rally, and a public address. According to Shaukatullah, many Khaksars have already been arrested.
Editor's Note: See editor's comments on July 04, 1947.

1947 July 04

Allama Mashraqi disbands the Khaksar Movement. *The Tribune*, Lahore would report on July 05, 1947 that Mashraqi stated:
"About three and a half months ago I announced that if three lakhs of Khaksars would not have rallied in Delhi there would be no revolutionary power left in the movement and, therefore, it would be necessary to disband it. Now with the establishment of Pakistan, which has been bestowed upon the Muslims by the British, the last hope that ten crores of Muslims who have been divided into various parts would continue their struggle for freedom has been lost. I, therefore, disband the movement" (TT 1947 July 05).
Editor's Note: The date of July 04, 1947 for the disbandment of the Khaksar Movement is taken from Sher Zaman Khaksar's book *Khaksar Tehrik Ki Jiddo Juhad Volume 2* (page 325).

Al-Islah publishes Mashraqi's statement regarding the disbandment of the Khaksar Movement. "Ah! After 17 years of intense and honest struggle to which I gave the best part of my life and resources, the nation has not been able to develop qualities which could enable it to re-establish its authority in India" (*Al-Islah* 1947 July 04).

Editor's comments: According to the Khaksar circle, the figure of Khaksars who had already arrived in surrounding areas of Delhi was much greater than 70,000 to 80,000. Many had reached the outskirts of Delhi but were facing difficulty in entering the city owing to rigorous government restrictions. There was a continuous influx of Khaksars from across the country, however continued arrests and massive government checks and restraints were hindering them from reaching the venue.
   Mashraqi had called 300,000 Khaksars to assemble in the city so that they could forcibly take over at least Delhi in order to remove the injustices in the partition plan toward the Muslims. He knew that these injustices were well planned and were a result of vested motives. Mashraqi was against the division of India and believed in the brotherhood of all communities. However, he had observed events closely as they had been developing over time and felt that he was left with no choice but to protect the Muslim interest. The idea of partition had not only taken the land that was once ruled by Muslims but had created hatred between the Muslims, Hindus, Sikhs, etc.; the riots were a result of this hatred. He was sorrowful that the leaders were ignoring the repercussions of this division. Today's circumstances of the sub-continent speak of his vision.

As a result of mass arrests, etc., 300,000 Khaksars were unable to assemble in New Delhi. Thus, Mashraqi decided to disband the Khaksar Movement. This was a not an easy decision for him, and he was highly saddened and disheartened when he made the decision to dissolve the Khaksar Movement. Mashraqi had spent the best part of his life working toward his goal and had faced a lot of personal sufferings. However, he came to the understanding that the Muslims were not yet ready to change their lives and lacked the spirit that was needed to revolutionize their lives.

Mashraqi's message to disband the Khaksar Movement was announced in Delhi in front of hundreds of thousands of people. Upon hearing this, the public cried, as people were completely shocked and saddened. They chanted slogans such as, "Dehli is Ours," "Lal Fort is Ours," "Allama Mashriqi Zindabad," "Khaksar-e-Azam Zindabad," and "Khaksar Tehrik Zindabad." Khaksars and the public pleaded to Mashraqi to reconsider his decision. Khaksar men and women continued to stay in Delhi, despite the disbandment, in the hope that Mashraqi would withdraw his decision under pressure. People sent thousands of messages requesting Mashraqi to reconsider, but Mashraqi did not withdraw his decision.

1947 July 05

Following the disbandment of the Khaksar Tehrik, Salar-i-Ala of the Muslim League National Guard asks the Khaksars to join the Muslim League National Guard forthwith.

1947 July 06

The Pakistan Times publishes an editorial regarding the Khaksar Tehrik. The newspaper states: "The Khaksars began and rose in the early Thirties — the period of blackest economic and spiritual depression throughout the world. The period was particulary black for the Indian Muslims who appeared to have fought and lost all their battles from the Mutiny to the Khilafat, with precious little left to hope or fight for" (PT 1947 Jul. 06).

1947 July 09

Khaksars raise slogans for the release of all Khaksars arrested in Delhi and Patna. 17 Khaksars are arrested in Delhi. Police use tear gas to disperse the Khaksars and the public.

1947 July 24

Even after the disbandment of the Khaksar Movement, many of the Khaksars remain in Delhi. Police open fire on the Khaksars at a mosque in Delhi. Some Khaksars are injured and many others are arrested.

1947 July 26

Gandhi writes to Sardar Patel regarding the Khaksars.

1947 August 06

Gandhi writes a letter to Vallabhbhai Patel regarding his meeting with the Khaksars.

1947 August 11

Sardar Patel writes to Gandhi regarding the Khaksars.

1947 August 14

Pakistan emerges on the world map.

1947 August 18

The Radcliffe Award is announced. Muslims lose many other areas that were supposed to be a part of Pakistan.

1947 October

Mashraqi sends a telegram to Gandhi.

1947 October 09

Nehru writes a letter from New Delhi to Vallabhbhai Patel:
My dear Vallabhbhai,
    Dr. Zakir Husain mentioned to me that he had received information about the ill-treatment of Muslim prisoners in the jail here. According to report they are being manhandled, are beaten severely and are kept in solitary confinement...
    Many of these prisoners are the old Khaksars...
    I am told that among the Khaksar prisoners there is Allama Mashriqui's son Asghar Inayatullah, aged eleven years. If this fact is

correct, the boy need hardly be kept in prison. His sister is in the Jamia.
Yours sincerely,
Jawaharlal Nehru

1947 October 16

The Pakistan Times publishes the headline "Pakistan opposed to mass migration of Indian Muslims." The newspaper also publishes Liaquat Ali Khan's statement (PT 1947 Oct. 16).

1947 October 31

The Islam League is formed.
Editor's comments: The exact date of the formation of the Islam League could not be traced. According to one source (Hussain 1994, 109), the date was October 31, 1947; another source (PT 1952 Apr. 15) reported that it was formed in July 1948, while a third source (PT 1951 Sept. 30) stated that October 1948 was the date of formation.
   The people who joined the Islam League (including Khaksars) were known as Razakars.
   Though partition had taken place, Mashraqi could not reconcile with the idea of accepting a truncated Pakistan. As a matter of fact, he could not forget the India that was once ruled by Muslims. Hence Mashraqi was compelled to start another organization. Mashraqi formed the Islam League to lift the masses within Pakistan, protect the interests of the Muslims in India, undo injustices in the Partition Plan, liberate Kashmir, etc.
   Soon after the creation of Pakistan, he started mobilizing his followers across India so that injustices in the Partition Plan and the liberation of Kashmir could atleast be achieved. The Criminal Investigation Department (C.I.D.) continued to monitor Mashriqi and his followers' activities on both sides (India and Pakistan) and reported the matter to the concerned governments. Unfortunately, the government of Pakistan, whose support he badly needed, did not aid him and in fact created many hurdles for him. Thus, Mashraqi could not achieve desired results.

1947 December 07

Mashraqi gives a warning to inform the nation and the Government about a brewing conspiracy between Gandhi and Lord Mountbatten regarding the Kashmir issue.

1947 December 07

Mashraqi issues a Press statement (Hussain 1994, 25).

1948

"Discard those leaders who live in luxury while the nation lives in poverty"

– Nasim Yousaf

1948

1948 February 10

The Civil & Military Gazette, Lahore reports that the Government of India has declared the Khaksar Tehrik to be unlawful in the Chief Commissioner's Provinces and Governors' Provinces. According to the newspaper, the Ministry of Home Affairs issued the following communique:

"The organisation of Khaksars has been equally wedded to communal hatred and violence. On several occasions members of the organisation have been guilty of violent acts.

It convened an all-India rally of their members at Delhi last year. Soon after the organisation was officially disbanded by its founder, but his followers have refused to abide by his mandates. They congregated in large numbers in various places, particularly in Delhi, and made no secret of their ambition of disintegrating the country. As a result the organisation was declared unlawful in the Delhi province.

They are, however, still carrying on underground propaganda on the same lines as the Muslim League National Guards. They have been circulating posters exhorting people to collect arms, to extricate certain parts of the country from the clutches of the Congress and to make preparations for jihad to this end. Members have been known to be also collecting arms.

The threat to the peace of the country from this source in the present crisis is obvious, and there is no place in India for an organisation of this kind. The Government have, therefore, decided to declare the Khaksar organisation to be unlawful in the remaining Chief Commissioners' province and similar action is being taken in Governors' province.

The Government wish to make it clear, and are certain that all right minded Muslims will recognise, that this action is not aimed at the Muslim community in any way. India has now gained independence and all sections of her people must now rely for the protection of their life, property and civic rights on the forces of the State, and not on any private armies.

The Government have repeatedly declared that India is to be a secular State in which all communities, irrespective of their strength, religion and culture, shall enjoy equal rights. The Government repeat their determination to afford to all minorities in India the fullest possible protection against any unlawful activities. They are confident that this future measure taken by them towards eliminating the evils of hate and violence would be regarded by the Muslim community as a decisive step towards ensuring that protection and not as a measure that will impair it" (C&MG 1948 Feb. 10).

The newspaper further reports that the Muslim League National Guards were also banned under the same communique (C&MG 1948 Feb. 10).

1948 February 23

The Government of West Bengal issues two notifications prohibiting drills or exercises of a military nature (except by the armed forces) (SI 1948 Feb. 24). The first notification reads as follows:

"In exercise of the powers conferred by Sub-sections (1) and (2) section 11 of the Bengal Special Powers Ordinance, 1946 (Bengal Ordinance VI of 1946) as enacted and continued in operation by and under the Bengal Ordinances Temporary Enactment Act, 1947 (Bengal Act I of 1947), the Governor is pleased to prohibit the performance, within the province of West Bengal of any exercise, movement, evolution or drill of a military nature with or without arms or articles capable of being used as arms.

With a view to securing that no unauthorised exercise, movement, evolution or drill of a military nature is performed at any place, the Governor is pleased further to prohibit the holding of or taking part in any camp, parade, meeting or Assembly in connection with any exercise, movement, evolution or drill of a military nature with or without arms or articles capable of being used as arms except as provided hereinafter.

Provided that the prohibitions hereinbefore imposed shall not apply to the performance of any such exercise, movement, evolution or drill or to the holding of or taking part in any camp, parade, meeting or Assembly: -

(1) By members of the Indian Naval, Military or Air Forces or of any official police force or of any force constituted under any law for the time being in force in exercise of their duty as such:

(2) By members of the association commonly known as the Boy Scouts Association in India or of the Association commonly known as the Girl Guides Association in India in their capacity as such:

(3) By members of
   (I) The St. John Ambulance Brigade Overseas, Bengal Branch.
   (II) The Bengal Bratachan Society or Associations constituent of or recognised by the Society.

(III) Village defence parties organized under the direction of the Superintendent of Police.

(IV) Any other organisation which may be specified in writing in this behalf by Government:

(4) Within the precincts or premises of any Government school or college or of any school or college recognised by Government in this behalf, by persons whose participation in such exercise, movement, evolution or drill is part of the ordinary curriculum of such school or college." (SI 1948 Feb. 24)

The second notification reads as follows:

"WEARING OF UNIFORM

Whereas the Provincial Government is satisfied that the wearing in public of any dress or article of apparel resembling any uniform or part of a uniform required to be worn by a member of the Indian armed forces or by a member of any official police force or of any force constituted under any law for the time being in force would be likely to prejudice the public safety or the maintenance of public order:

Now, therefore, in exercise of the powers conferred by Sub section (1) of Section 12 of the Bengal Special Powers Ordinance 1946 (Bengal Ordinance VI of 1946) as enacted and continued in operation by and under the Bengal Ordinances Temporary Enactment Act, 1947 (Bengal Act I of 1947) the Governor is pleased to prohibit the wearing in public of any such dress by any person who is not a member of the said forces or a member of an Association which has been authorised by the Central Government as respects the whole of the Dominion of India, or the Provincial Government as respects the province of West Bengal to wear a specified uniform." (SI 1948 Feb. 24)

Editor's comments: The Khaksar Movement was a novel and unique phenomenon, which awoke the nation from its deep slumber and prompted it to rise up and seek freedom. The sub-continent had been witness to the Khaksar Tehrik's discipline and dedication in obtaining independence and opposing the British. After the independence, India feared that the Khaksar Tehrik could become a threat to their sovereignty. Plus, Mashraqi had started re-mobilizing his followers for the Muslim cause. Therefore, approximately six months after the partition of India, they introduced a general ban prohibiting military style activities by any party.

1948 February 25

The Civil & Military Gazette reports that the Khaksar Tehrik was declared unlawful in Patiala (India) (C&MG 1948 Feb. 25).

1948 March 02

The Star of India, Calcutta reports, "An All-Pakistan Khaksar Salars and Officers' Conference has been convened here on March 15 and the two following days to explore ways and means for defending Pakistan in case of an emergency.
    The conference will also consider measures for removing misunderstandings about the Khaksars and will formulate a programme for establishing friendly relations with the Pakistan Government and the Muslim League" (SI 1948 Mar. 02).
Editor's comments: According to *The Civil & Military Gazette*, Lahore of March 23, 1948, this conference was actually held from March 19 to March 21, 1948.

1948 March 19 – March 21

An All-Pakistan Khaksar conference is held in Lahore. Khaksars from all over Pakistan attend the conference. The following decisions are unanimously adopted at the conference:
    "The ideals of the predominance of Islam, selfless humanitarian work, sacrifice and jihad and the organisation of Muslims so amply exemplified by the Khaksar movement in the 17 years of its working are the real backbone of Muslim thought and action, without which Pakistan can never become a strong independent Islamic country, and to revive which Allama Inayatullah Khan Al-Mashriqi should be urged to resume leadership of the movement.
    With the object of preparing the Muslims of Pakistan, for a truly Islamic life to provide a nucleus for these ideals and actions and to fight the various sinister and subversive forces still at work among Muslims, a fully constituted body in accordance with Islamic democracy – as completely free from the evils of so-called Western democracy – should be inaugurated under the name of All-Pakistan Khaksar League, and a Khaksar Mujahid Corps should also be raised.
    The All-Pakistan Khaksar League, true to its ideals, shall be loyal to Pakistan and shall have its defence and everincreasing strength, with all the means at its disposal, as one of its objectives.
    The Khaksars of Pakistan express their sincere gratitude to Qaid-e-Azam Mohammad Ali Jinnah, Governor-General of Pakistan,

and assures him of their un-tinted loyalty to this new country, where the Muslims are now in a position to fulfil them long cherished desire of making Islam and Koran the code of their lives.

They also express their confidence in the sincerity, sacrifice, and foresight of Allama Mashriqui" (C&MG 1948 Mar. 23).

Dr. Alam Chishti and Amir Habibullah Khan are elected President and General Secretary respectively of the newly formed party (C&MG 1948 Mar. 23; PT 1948 Mar. 23).

Editor's comments: One of the objectives of the Conference was to bring unity between the Muslim Leaguers and the Khaksars, however the League was not responsive to this effort. The participants offered their complete loyalty to the Muslim League. The Muslim League avoided the Khaksar Tehreek on purpose, because the elite of the Muslim League had a different agenda from that of the Khaksar Tehreek. The Khaksar Tehreek's agenda was to lift the masses, whereas the Muslim League's idea was to lift a certain class, which is evident from the circumstances that have prevailed since Pakistan's creation. Once again, Mashraqi's efforts to unite the Muslims were not supported by the Muslim League.

1948 July

The Islam League is formed.

Editor's comments: The exact date of the formation of the Islam League could not be traced. According to one source (Hussain 1994, 109), the date was October 31, 1947; another source (PT 1952 Apr. 15) reported that it was formed in July 1948, while a third source (PT 1951 Sept. 30) stated that October 1948 was the date of formation.

See additional Editor's comments on October 31, 1947.

1948 August 03

The Civil & Military Gazette, Lahore reports that Indo-Pakistan League literature was sent to prominent Indian Muslims (C&MG 1948 Aug. 03).

Editor's comments: The Indian government had arrested Muslims for receiving literature sent by Mashraqi. Mashraqi tried to mobilize support among the Muslims in India in order to regain Kashmir and other areas of India that should have been part of Pakistan.

1948 August 29

The Islam League holds a meeting in Lahore. Mashraqi attends the meeting (C&MG 1948 Sept. 01).

1948 August 30

The West Punjab Government issues a Press Note:

"The West Punjab Government have prohibited under the Public Safety Act 'the publication or distribution of any letter, leaflet or other material printed or issued by and on behalf of the Indo Pakistan Islam League, Ferozepore Road, Lahore or any member thereof' (C&MG 1948 Sept. 01).

The Civil & Military Gazette, Lahore of September 01, 1948 would further report:

"Following this order, the C.I.D. searched the premises of 22 persons in Lahore who were believed to be active workers of the Indo-Pakistan Islam League. Proscribed literature was recovered during the searches" (C&MG 1948 Sept. 01).

Editor's comments: Mashraqi was using various means including leaflets, etc. to mobilize his followers in India in order to annex Kashmir and other areas that were wrongly given to India. This would have been possible had the government supported Mashraqi. At that time, the Kashmir issue was new and injustices in the Partition Plan were very obvious, hence world opinion could have been mobilized in favor of Pakistan. Mashraqi was willing to do whatever it took to resolve these issues, including use of force. But the Pakistan Government, according to Khaksar circle, did not want to go through the struggle; and they resorted to negotiations and issuing statements, instead of actively fighting for what should have been their's. Meanwhile India increased its claims on Kashmir including moving in forces, and it became increasingly difficult to get the area back.

1948 September 12

Mashriqi regrets Quaid-e-Azam's death. Allama Mashraqi flies to Karachi to attend Jinnah's funeral (PT 1958 Oct. 24; Zaman 1987, 367).

1948 September 30

Mashriqi applies for a passport to travel to some European and Muslim countries (including Egypt) (Zaman 1987, 348).

1948 October

The Islam League is formed.
Editor's comments: The exact date of the formation of the Islam League could not be traced. According to one source (Hussain 1994,

109), the date was October 31, 1947; another source (PT 1952 Apr. 15) reported that it was formed in July 1948, while a third source (PT 1951 Sept. 30) stated that October 1948 was the date of formation.

See additional Editor's comments on October 31, 1947.

1948 November 06

The Deputy Commissioner of Lahore sends a letter to Mashriqi informing him that the Government has denied his application for an international passport (Zaman 1987, 348).

1949

"Allama Mashraqi's life is an inspirational book"

– Nasim Yousaf

1949

1949 February 10

Mashraqi writes to the Governor of Punjab regarding the denial of Mashraqi's application for an international passport (Zaman 1987, 350).
Editor's comments: The source lists the date of Mashraqi's letter to the Governor of Punjab as February 10, 1948, but the year seems to be a misprint.
There needs to be an inquiry on why, from the very early years of Pakistan's creation, the Government was hostile toward Mashraqi and denied travel for no legitimate reason. Mashraqi had to travel for an important purpose.

1949 April 08

The Government sends Mashraqi a letter informing him that his international passport application has again been denied (Zaman 1987, 350).

1949 May 15

Mashriqi sends a notice to the Government of Punjab for refusing to issue a passport to him (Zaman 1987, 347; Hussain 1991, 238 - 240).

1949 June 23

Mashraqi sends correspondence to Trygve Lie (Secretary General of the United Nations) regarding the denial of human rights to the Muslims of India (C&MG 1949 Aug. 23).
Editor's comments: Mashraqi also provided proof of the charges against India.

1949 August 22

Hussain Shaheed Suhrawardy gives his consent to act as Allama Mashraqi's counsel for Mashraqi's representation in the United Nations regarding the denial of human rights to the Muslims in India (C&MG 1949 Aug. 23).
Editor's comments: Hussain Shaheed Surhrawardy later became Prime Minister of Pakistan.

1949 August 23

The Civil & Military Gazette, Lahore reports that Trygve Lie (Secretary General of the United Nations) informed Mashraqi that his representation will receive due consideration by the Human Rights Commission of the United Nations. The newspaper further reports that Mashraqi replied to a questionnaire sent to him by the U.N. Secretariat (C&MG 1949 Aug. 23).

1949 August 24

The Tribune, Ambala reports that the Government refused to issue a passport to Allama Mashriqi. Mashraqi had intended to travel to address the United Nations regarding the rights of Muslims in India (Zaman 1987, 347).

1949 October 04

The Civil & Military Gazette, Lahore reports that Punjab Governor Sardar Rab Nishtar refused to issue a passport to Hussain Shaheed Suhrawardy to go along with Allama Mashraqi to the United Nations. They were to present the case of the denial of human rights of the Muslims in India. According to the newspaper, "In the petition put forward by Allama Mashriqi before H.E. the West Punjab Governor, it was urged that, in view of special circumstances arising from the favourable response given by U.N. early passports for Lake Success may be issued. H.E. Sirdar Abdur Rab Nishtar, however, after a lapse of about one month, has now communicated to the Allama that he 'sees no reason to revise the previous orders.'

The case of the Indian Mussalmans will now be heard by the Human Rights Commission without the Allama or his two counsels appearing before it.

The decision of the Government has been widely regretted." (C&MG 1949 Oct. 04).

1949 November 21

Mashraqi addresses the public in Lyallpur (now Faisalabad).

1950

"A leader who lives in luxury while his nation lives in poverty is an exploiter"

– Nasim Yousaf

1950

1950 May 02

Punjab Criminal Investigation Department (C.I.D.) police raid Mashriqi's house in Ichhra, Lahore. They conduct a thorough search and confiscate materials of the Islam League, including copies of a pamphlet called *Akhri Umeed* (Last Hope). On the same day, police also raid the offices of *Waqt* (newspaper) and Indo-Pakistan Kitab Ghar (bookstore) and the residences of Khawaja Yasin Butt (Editor of *Waqt*) and Maulvi Nasiruddin (PT 1950 May 03).
Editor's comments: Thus, freedom of speech and the basic rights of citizens were denied soon after the birth of Pakistan. The new country was supposed to ensure that basic rights were available to all indviduals without discrimination of any sort. But *alas*, real freedom does not exist in Pakistan even today.

1950 May 28

Mashriqi addresses the Khaksars (*Al-Islah* 1997, 8).

1950 June

Mashriqi's speech *Khitab-i-Lahore* is published (PT 1952 Apr. 29).

1950 September

An Islam League Conference is to be held in Karachi this month. The Government imposes a ban and the conference is rescheduled for October 1950 (PT 1952 Apr. 15; Zaman 1987, 381).
Editor's comments: In Pakistan, the development of political processes and liberties were crushed from the very beginning.

1950 October

An Islam League Conference is to be held in Karachi this month. The Government imposes a ban and the conference is rescheduled for November 1950 (PT 1952 Apr. 15).
Editor's comments: This conference could not be held because again the Government imposed a ban. Exact date is not available.

1950 October 03

Allama Mashraqi, along with his two sons, is arrested in Lahore. Police enter Mashraqi's house and search the premises in connection with a 32-page pamphlet entitled *Khitab-e-Lahore*. Police also search the houses of Mashraqi's followers (C&MG 1950 Oct. 04).

Editor's comments: Prime Minister Liaquat Ali Khan's Government pounced on the Khaksar organisation. The Khaksar premises were searched and hundreds of Khaksars were arrested. Mashraqi's office premises were sealed and *Khitab-e-Lahore* was confiscated. The publication of *Al-Islah* was also banned.

1950 October 04

Allama Mashraqi issues the following press statement after being released on bail:

"I have seen a statement in the Press regarding my arrest. Hundred lies put together cannot make one truth and there is no remedy of tyranny but resistance even to death. The pamphlet 'Khitab-e-Lahore' which was publicly uttered by me on May 28 last was never proscribed by Government. Ten thousand copies of it were sold in these four months and the pamphlet was publicly sold everywhere...

Any person could publish it, as all my public addresses are the property of the people. I or my colleagues, therefore, could not be held responsible for this publication.

The police, on entering, refused to show me any warrant of search. In fact one said that the warrant was for the search of office, the other said that it was for the house. The third, who was the filthiest in his talk, said that 'his word was law.' I told them that I had perhaps one copy in my possession and that I produced. They searched the office for two hours and no other copy was found. They said they wanted truck-loads of the pamphlet and began to enter my house.

I offered with my four sons in line that they could shoot all of us with the rifles and muskets they had brought with them and told them to desist as no warrant had been shown. I also added that if Government had permitted them to do all the tyrannies they had been doing for the last two hours that Government was a villain" (C&MG 1950 Oct. 05).

1950 October 07

The Civil & Military Gazette, Lahore reports that *Khitab-e-Lahore* was confiscated by the Government. The government's notification was published in the *Punjab Gazette* and is reproduced by *The Civil and Military Gazette* as follows:
"Whereas it appears to the provincial Government that a pamphlet entitled 'Khitab-i-Lahore,' published by Khadim Mohy-ud-Din, B.A., L.L.B., advocate, Secretary-General, Islam League, Ferozepore Road, Lahore, contains matter which tends to excite disaffection towards the Government established by law in Pakistan; now, therefore, in exercise of the powers conferred by Section 19 of the Indian Press (Emergency Powers) Act, XXIII of 1931, as adapted by the Pakistan (Adaption of Existing Pakistan Laws) Order, 1947, the Governor of the Punjab is pleased hereby to declare to be forfeited to the Government of Pakistan every copy wherever found of the said pamphlet or document and all other books, newspapers or documents containing all or any of the passages comprising the said Address or document." (C&MG 1950 Oct. 07).

1950 October 27

Mashraqi addresses the public in Gujranwala.

1950 October 29

Mashraqi arrives at Multan Railway Station, where a large crowd greets him (C&MG 1950 Nov. 02).

1950 October 29

The Islam League holds a large public meeting in Multan. Allama Mashriqi addresses the meeting. *The Civil & Military Gazette*, Lahore of November 01, 1950 would report:
"Allama Mashriqi, addressing a gathering of about 100,000 criticised the Pakistan Government for doing nothing for public welfare and said that the Muslim League was dying as it never raised voice against the increasing corruption, nepotism and favouritism prevalent in the country.
He further added various sorts of taxes were levied on poor people but the Ministers and their henchmen were enjoying luxurious life. He condmened the action of the Punjab Police in handcuffing him although he was on the right path...Concluding Allama Mashriqi said that Liaquat was busy in appeasing Nehru [Prime Minister of

India] but did not care for the safety of the helpless Indian Muslims numbering not less than 5 crores. He asked the people to vote in favour of candidates nominated by the Islam League so that revenge may be taken from agressor India" (C&MG 1950 Nov. 01).

Editor's comments: The lavish lifestyles of the uppermost leadership, their "couldn't care less" attitude towards the masses, ignoring of basic rights, and the power struggle within the Muslim League, beg the question, was Pakistan aquired for the Muslim cause or was it meant to benefit only a few?

1950 November

An Islam League Conference is to be held in Karachi. The Government again imposes a ban (PT 1952 Apr. 15).

Editor's comments: Again this conference could not be held because the Government imposed a ban. Under the circumstances the venue of the conference was changed to Lahore.

1950 November 01

The Civil & Military Gazette, Lahore reports, "Allama Mashraqi...had never traveled by train except in 3rd class compartment since he resigned from service, but for the first time after about 22 years he was forced to travel second class when he came to Multan..." (C&MG 1950 Nov. 01).

Editor's comments: Mashraqi was a man of conscience. He could not see himself traveling in luxury while his nation lived in poverty. Other leaders made statements on working for the masses, however they did nothing except for benefit from the resources of the new country. His contemporaries were leading the lives of their ex-masters and some were even crossing those standards; they acted not as public's servants but as their masters.

1950 November 19

Allama Mashraqi, founder of the Islam League, addresses a large public meeting outside Mochi Gate, Lahore. *The Civil & Military Gazette*, Lahore of November 20, 1950 would report:

"A large crowd outside Mochi Gate, Lahore, on Sunday afternoon heard Allama Mashriqi, chief of the Islam League, criticise the Muslim League organisation, says the A.P.P.

The Islam League leader believed that the formation of new parties was extremely detrimental to the interest of Pakistan. He saw a great reason for the Unity of Muslims, as the main task of strengthening Pakistan to preserve its independence was still to be accomplished. He advocated the unity of the people to change the mentality and ways of the leaders who dominated the Muslim League.

Severly criticising the Muslim League, he also called for a reorietation of its policy and programme.

The Islam League, he said, stood for service of the country and if any emergency arose, workers of the Islam League would shed the last drop of their blood to safeguard their sacred homeland.

Earlier, when he arrived at the meeting, he was heralded by the firing of 21 crackers" (C&MG 1950 Nov. 20).

1950 December 04

The Administrator of Karachi, Hashim Raza, issues the following press statement banning a Khaksar rally:

"My attention has been drawn to the proposed rally and meeting of Khaksars, also known as Razakars of the Islam League, fixed for the last week of December. The holding of a rally and meeting of Razakars, fully or partially armed, in the Capital is fraught with ugly possibilities and cannot be allowed in the present circumstances.

The Karachi Administration, therefore, propose to prevent the collection of people for such a purpose and to ban the rally and the meeting" (PT 1950 Dec. 05).

1950 December 19

The Civil & Military Gazette, Lahore reports that Allama Mashraqi, founder of the Islam League, accepted Hussain Shaheed Suhrawardy's invitation to meet at a joint conference of all five parties in opposition to the official Muslim League (C&MG 1950 Dec. 19).

1950 December 28-30

An Islam League conference is held in Lahore. On December 30, Mashraqi addresses over 100,000 people. He states that it was a mistake not to forcibly occupy Kashmir in 1947. According to Mashraqi, "Our rulers were coward, ease-loving and fearful of the Hindus, and therefore failed to take proper action in time." He further states that denying timely support to the Kashmiris was "a military as well as political blunder for which Pakistan is suffering today."

Mashraqi also warns that India could change the course of the rivers that flow from Kashmir:

"At the present moment, Hindu is in possession of entire water potential of the Ravi, the Chenab, and the Jhelum, and in a way also of the Indus. He is planning to build the mightiest dams on these rivers at a cost of Rs. 196 crores [Rs. 1,960,000,000] to divert water to East Punjab. The purpose is eventually to deny even a drop of water to West Punjab, or to flood it all of a sudden when water in reservoirs was not needed for East Punjab."

Mashraqi adds that Nehru took the issue of Kashmir to the U.N. Security Council at the end of 1947 as a political ploy to gain time and move his forces into Kashmir. The Muslim League failed to understand this (Hussain 1991, 240; Hussain 1994, 27-28; Zaman 1987, 372-373, 424; Mashraqi [1931] 1997, 31).

Editor's comments: C.I.D. police was present and took photos at this public meeting. This was revealed during the High Court proceedings regarding Mashraqi's unjust detention (PT 1952 Apr. 20). A few days after he made this speech, Mashraqi was arrested (on January 11, 1951) by Liaquat Ali Khan's Government.

1951

"A nation ceases to grow if the liberties of its people are crushed"

– Nasim Yousaf

1951

1951 January 10

A meeting of the Islam League is held in Lahore. Mashriqi attends the meeting. There is also a large audience present. Three parties, the Mazdoor Organization, Musawat-e-Islam, and Mujahadeen-e-Islam, announce that they will be joining the Islam League. C.I.D. police monitors the proceedings (PT 1952 Apr. 15).
Editor's comments: It is important to note that Mashriqi held no office in the Islam League and the party was completely independent to make decisions. Mashriqi, as founder of the Islam League, could have easily been the head of the party, but he chose not to use his popularity in this way.
  Furthermore, Mashraqi also declined Federal Ministries (offered at different times to stop him from talking against the government) within the Pakistan Government, because he felt that the policies of the Government did not help the people, and he being part of the same Government would be of no help to the masses.

1951 January 11

Around 5:00 am, a Magistrate and armed police raid Mashriqi's house in Ichhra, Lahore and conduct a thorough search. Police arrest Mashriqi and cordon his house. Mashriqi is arrested under the Punjab Public Safety Act. Police also raid other Khaksars' (members of Islam League) homes in various cities, including Lahore and Rawalpindi. Dr. Syed Abdul Wadood (Lahore), Ashraf Sandow (Haji Mohammed Ashraf) (Rawalpindi), Muhammad Akram (Rawalpindi) and many others are arrested. Rigorous precautionary measures are taken by the police to prevent a reaction from the public; armed police are posted in many parts of Lahore (PT 1951 Jan. 12; PT 1952 Apr. 15; C&MG 1951 Jan. 12).
Editor's comments: The Islam League's meeting of January 10 had continued into the night. The C.I.D. police kept a close eye on the proceedings and Mashriqi was arrested within hours of the meeting. It is important to note that the date for candidates to file nomination papers for the general elections was February 05, 1951. The elections were scheduled for the third week of March 1951 (PT 1952 Apr. 15).
  It is unfortunate that Mashraqi and his supporters were arrested prior to the elections for no reason and on the false pretext of the Public Safety Act. By putting Mashraqi and the Islam League candidates behind bars, the Muslim League had guaranteed

themselves victory. Thus, democracy in Pakistan was crushed from the very beginning and civil liberties continued to be crippled in the newly established country.

Hussain Shaheed Suhrawardy criticized the Punjab Public Safety Act under which Mashriqi was arrested. *The Pakistan Times*, Lahore reported on February 20, 1951, "Mr. Suhrawardy [in Lahore] described the amendement as a 'gross encroachment on whatever little liberty was left to the individual' and said it is now made impossible for an innocent person to escape. No defence of any kind is permitted.

He appealed to the people to observe March 2 as a Day of Protest against this iniquitous measure as well as a Day of Demands for the liberation of all persons who have been detained under the Public Safety Acts the Frontier Crimes Regulation and other repressive measures, for the repeal of all such measures, and for the recognition of civil liberties in general" (PT 1951 Feb. 20).

1951 January 12

Mashriqi's arrest sends shockwaves throughout the entire country. His imprisonment is strongly protested. In Lahore, a large public meeting is held under the auspices of the Islam League. At the meeting, furious speakers condemn the actions of the Punjab Government. The following resolution is passed:

"This meeting expresses its strong resentment against the arrest of Mr. Inayatulla Mashriqi, founder of the Islam League, and the candidates of the Islam League to the Provincial Assembly, and demands that they should be released immediately and unconditionally."
Another resolution states:

"This meeting regards the Public Safety Act as a great curse and demands its immediate repeal. The meeting feels that in the presence of the Safety Act it is not possible to work any democratic system whether of the Western type or of the Islamic pattern."

The Pakistan Times, Lahore of January 13, 1951 would also report, "The speakers...criticised the action of the Punjab Government in arresting Mr. Mashriqi at a time when the elections to the Punjab Assembly were at hand. They maintained that the arrest of Mr. Mashriqi was motivated by the anxiety of the Government to weaken the political opposition to the League in the Punjab. They strongly condemned the use of the Safety Act and held that it reduced to a mockery the Government's promise to give unfettered liberty to the Punjab voters to exercise their franchise" (PT 1951 Jan. 13).

Editor's comments: Even after the creation of Pakistan, Mashraqi was tremendously popular, and he had a large number of followers and supporters. The Government feared that the candidates of the Islam League would win the elections. Thus, to prevent them from participating in the elections, Mashraqi, many of his followers, and the election candidates were arrested.

1951 January 14

A public meeting is held in Lahore under the auspices of the Islam League. Leaders from various political parties attend the meeting and demand Mashraqi's release. They also demand the repeal of the Punjab Public Safety Act and the immediate release of the Islam League candidates contesting the forthcoming elections (C&MG 1951 Jan. 15).

Editor's comments: The Muslim League wanted to remain in power, and therefore, arrested Allama Mashraqi and the Islam League candidates under the pretext of the Public Safety Act.

While Mashraqi and the other Islam League candidates remained in jail, Liaquat Ali Khan (Prime Minister of Pakistan and President of the Muslim League) and the Muslim Leaguers campaigned for the elections, and thus, the Muslim League ultimately won the elections (C&MG 1951 Feb. 16; C&MG 1951 Mar. 21).

1951 January 18

Mashraqi writes a bitter letter to the Governor of the Punjab stating that it is un-Islamic to detain him without a trial. In his letter, he quotes the Holy Koran and also asks the Governor to postpone elections for as many days as he is kept in prison illegally (PT 1952 Apr. 15).

Editor's comments: Opposition was not tolerated, yet the Muslim Leaguers claimed to have created a Pakistan where everyone would be allowed to lead a free life and the basic rights of an individual would be fully protected. Mashraqi had sent a reminder of this to the Governor, but the Governor remained silent. Mashraqi remained in jail and the elections were not postponed. In reply to a question by the Advocate General in the High Court in Lahore on April 14, 1952, Mashraqi stated, "We could not put up any candidates because all important workers of the Islam League were arrested" (PT 1952 Apr. 15).

1951 February 13

The Punjab Public Safety (Amendment) Act, 1951 is announced. (C&MG 1951 Feb. 15).

1951 March 04

A big procession is taken out in Gujranwala (near Lahore). People demonstrate throughout the day with black flags. Slogans such as "Release Allama Mashraqi" and "Break down safety act or give up your Islamism. Safety Act makes Pakistan weak, not strong" are raised (C&MG 1951 Mar. 07).

1951 April 6

Agha Mansabdar Khan, another member of the Islam League, is arrested in Rawalpindi under the Punjab Safety Act (C&MG 1951 Apr. 09).

1951 May 30

Mashriqi begins writing *Hadees-ul-Quran* while in jail. The book would be published on November 25, 1952 (Mashraqi [1931] 1997, 9; Hussain 1988, 268)

1951 July 09

Mashraqi goes on a hunger strike in Mianwali Jail to protest the extension of his detention.

1951 July 20

Mashraqi sends a telegram to Prime Minister Liaquat Ali Khan regarding Nehru's tactics on the Kashmir issue (Mashraqi 1952, 276; Yousaf 2003, 61; Hussain 1994, 38; Hussain 1991, 246)
Editor's comments: Though under detention, Mashraqi did not forget the issues that plagued the nation. He continued to remind the government not to sit on the Kashmir issue and to take practical steps, otherwise Kashmir would never be liberated.

1951 August 04

A large number of Mashraqi's followers demonstrate in Lahore and demand Mashraqi's release. Furthermore, they express resentment against the gathering of Indian troops on Pakistani borders. A meeting is also held at night in the same connection (C&MG 1951 Aug. 05).

1951 August 06

Allama Mashraqi sends another telegram to Prime Minister Liaquat Ali Khan regarding Nehru's tactics on the Kashmir issue (Mashraqi 1952, 276; Yousaf 2003, 61; Hussain 1994, 38; Hussain 1991, 246).

1951 August 14

Daily newspaper, *Aafaaq* (Lahore), reports on Liaquat Ali Khan's Government's actions to suppress the Khaksar Tehrik. (Mashraqi [1931] 1997, 32).

1951 August 26

In Hasan Abdal, Mashraqi Day is observed (under the auspices of the Islam League) with great eagerness and enthusiasm. Islam League Razakars arrive from various cities for the occasion. A procession marches through the streets of the city and arrives at a location where a public meeting is held. A large number of people gather for the meeting and speeches are made on the life of Allama Mashraqi (PT 1951 Aug. 28).
Editor's comments: Mashraqi's health was quickly deteriorating at Mianwali Jail. The public highly resented Mashraqi's arrest and thus protested, demanding Mashraqi's immediate release.

1951 September 24

The Government announces that Mashraqi is gaining weight in Mianwali Jail.
Editor's comments: This was a completely absurd and false statement. Public pressure for the release of Mashraqi was increasing, and they were extremely concerned about his deteriorating health. In order to appease the public, the Government falsely announced that Mashraqi was gaining weight in jail. Mashraqi's family could not believe this fabrication by the Government.

1951 September 27

Maulana Fazal Hussain Dilawar (Nazim-i-Nashr-o-Isha'at/Publicity Secretary of the Punjab Islam League) issues a press statement in Lahore. He rejects the Government's claim that Mashraqi is in good health. He further demands that a deputation of the Islam League be allowed to meet with Mashraqi in jail "in order to find out the correct position regarding the health of Allama Mashriqi and to dispel the misunderstanding created by conflicting reports appearing in the Press about his health" (PT 1951 Sept. 28).

Editor's comments: Among Mashriqi's followers, supporters, and sympathizers, anxiety and unrest prevailed regarding his rapidly deteriorating health in jail. In order to quell their restlessness, the Government blatantly lied by stating that Mashraqi was in perfect health. The Government even went to the extent of saying that he was gaining weight and was provided excellent food as per his desire.

1951 September 28

Islam League Razakars from Gujranwala, Lahore, and other surrounding areas take out a procession in Gujranwala. A public meeting is held and speeches are delivered in support of Allama Mashraqi. Speakers demand Mashriqi's release and a resolution is passed demanding that Mashraqi be tried in an open law court (PT 1951 Sept. 30).

Editor's comments: The Government used baseless assumptions to try to implicate Mashraqi in anti-state activities in order to justify his detention and ease the pressure for his release. It was also feared that the Government was planning to harm Mashraqi and was making false allegations against him. Keeping the intentions of the Government in mind, there was no choice left for Mashriqi's supporters but to demand an open trial.

1951 September 29

The Punjab Government issues the following Press Note, providing a list of food Mashriqi was supplied in jail:

"...At his own request he [Mashriqi] is now being supplied with the following food every day: (1) Milk 1-1/2 seers; (2) Chicken soup as much as he may demand; (3) Tomatoes 1 lb.; (4) Grapes 4 chattaks; (5) Guava 2 chattaks; (6) Peaches 4 chattaks; (7) Sweet lemons (mitha) 4 chattaks; (8) Lemon 2 chattaks; (9) Sugar 1-1/2 chattaks; (10) Tea leaves 1/8 chattaks; (11) Bovril whenever he may demand; (12) Ovaltine whenever he may demand.

It has further been ascertained that the Allama's weight is at present 14 pounds more than the normal for his age and height" (PT 1951 Sept. 30; C&MG 1951 Sept. 30).

Editor's comments: There is no truth in this Press Note; it was issued purely to quell the concerns of the public. The Government tried to imply that Mashriqi was living in luxury and was being provided with excellent food, as per his demands. In fact, Mashraqi was not properly nourished and was kept in rugged conditions in jail; his family was extremely troubled by his deteriorating health due to these conditions. The Government, in issuing this Press Note, was behaving in the same manner as the imperialists, and using similar tactics to try to force Mashriqi to abandon politics.

1951 September 29

Representatives of the Islam League issue a signed Press Statement, stating:
"The contention of a Punjab Government's spokesman in a recent statement to the Press that Allama Inayatullah Khan Mashriqi is creating a private army where total loyalty may be pledged to his personal self is absolutely baseless in view of clear orders of Allama Mashriqi to dissolve the old Khaksar movement in July 1947...
...Allama Mashriqi has openly opposed the revival of that organisation [Khaksar Tehrik]...The Islam League is based on democratic principles...It is a false statement to say that Islam League or its Razakars section are anti-Pakistan organisations" (PT 1951 Sept. 30).

Editor's comments: As mentioned earlier, the Government used baseless assumptions to try to implicate Mashraqi in anti-state activities in order to justify his detention and ease the pressure for his release. People with vested interests wanted Mashriqi to leave politics so that they could use Pakistan's resources for their benefit and without any opposition.

1951 October 16

Liaquat Ali Khan, the Prime Minister of Pakistan, is assassinated in Rawalpindi (PT 1951 Oct. 17; C&MG 1951 Oct. 17).

Editor's comments: The Government's immediate reaction was to allege that the Khaksars were responsible for the murder. Many Khaksars were arrested on this pretense. However, C.W.E. U'ren's (British security expert) inquiry report (published in *Dawn*, Karachi on June 26, 1955) proved that the Khaksars had nothing to do with the assassination. It is clear that the Government pounced on the Khaksars and tried to implicate them for vested motives.

1951 October 21

The Civil & Military Gazette, Lahore reports that the Islam League set up an Election Board to select candidates for the forthcoming elections in NWFP. Potential candidates were invited to submit applications. According to the newspaper, the Election Board was headed by M.H. Qureshi (President, Islam League, NWFP) (C&MG 1951 Oct. 21).

1951 October 30

A public meeting is held in Lahore under the auspices of the Islam League. At the meeting, Mashraqi's immediate release is demanded and various resolutions are passed. One resolution offers unconditional cooperation to the Government. In another resolution, the Islam League sympathizes with the cause of Egypt against the British and calls upon the Government to support Egypt in its struggle. Deep shock and regret regarding Liaquat Ali Khan's murder on October 16, 1951 is also expressed at the meeting (PT 1951 Oct. 31).

1951 October 30

A public meeting is held in Lahore under the auspices of the Islam League. At the meeting, the immediate release of Allama Mashraqi is demanded. *The Civil & Military Gazette*, Lahore of October 31, 1951 would report, "In a resolution passed at the meeting the Pakistan Government was requested to accept the offer of 'unconditional co-operation' of the Islam League leader and utilize his services in the cause of the nation and Islam" (C&MG 1951 Oct. 31).

1951 November 09

The Islam League organizes "Egypt Day" to show support for Egypt in their struggle against the British. A public meeting is also held in Lahore under the presidentship of the Chief Organizer of the Islam League, Sheikh Fazal Ilahi. At the meeting, participants pass a resolution expressing support for Egypt and also demand the release of Allama Mashraqi. Similar meetings are held in other cities such as Gujranwala and Jalapur Jatan (C&MG 1951 Nov. 10).

1951 November 12

The Islam League announces the names of its candidates for the upcoming general elections in Peshawar District (NWFP). The candidates are Begum Nasiruddin Kamran, Ashiq Hussain (Advocate), and Qazi Sabahuddin (Advocate) (C&MG 1951 Nov. 13).

Editor's comments: Mashraqi was kept in jail so that he could not mobilize support in the NWFP.

1951 November 28

An Islam League deputation meets with Prime Minister Khawaja Nazimud Din in Rawalpindi to present the Islam League policy and demand Mashraqi's release. The deputation comprises of Dr. Abdul Wadood, Khawaja Afzal, S.A. Saeed, Qaiser Mustafa, and Khan Mohammed Niaz Khan (C&MG 1951 Nov. 30).

Editor's comments: The deputation discussed the policy of the Islam League with the Prime Minister, emphasizing the need to improve the lives of the masses. The Prime Minister promised to look into their proposals, but nothing came of this meeting.

1951 December 17

Maulana Fazal Hussain Dilawar (Publicity Secretary of the Punjab Islam League) issues a Press Statement condemning the highhandedness of the CID police against Mashraqi's Habeas Corpus Petition. He states:

"The [habeas corpus] papers were sent to Allama Sahib in jail for completion but the CID [Criminal Investigation Department] police did not allow the papers to reach him for completion and returned them as being incomplete

This action of the CID authorities is highly condemnable. They have, by this action, tried to deny the genuine rights of a detenu although the law of the country allows him such rights.

I appeal to all Democratic forces of the country to raise their voice against this high-handedness of the police and urge the Government to get the 'habeas corpus' petition papers completed by Allama Sahib" (PT 1951 Dec. 19).

1951 December 28

A large Islam League convention is held at Jalalpur Jatan (near Gujrat). The immediate release of Allama Mashraqi is demanded. *The Civil & Military Gazette*, Lahore of January 02, 1952 would report:

"The convention viewed with 'deep concern' the reports 'that the health of Allama Mashriqi is fast deteriorating in the jail.'

The convention also decided to intensify its campaign 'of educating the people to make Pakistan a strong, independent and prosperous country in the true sense.'

It further decided to start the annual general elections of the organisation on democratic basis shortly. The future policy and programme of the Islam League would then be chalked out after keeping in view the changed national and international situation.

The convention urged the Pakistan Government to 'allow the Islam League to function freely in the country and to release its workers who are still languishing in jails and thus to promote real democracy in Pakistan'" (C&MG 1952 Jan. 02).

Editor's comments: People from various parts of the country came to Jalalpur Jatan to attend this huge convention. The people showed their resentment towards the Government for the arrest of Allama Mashraqi and his followers. They also resented the Government's actions against the Islam League.

1952

"Leaders must be judged by deeds not statements"

– Nasim Yousaf

1952

1952 January 04

Prominent citizens of Karachi and Sind issue a press statement demanding Mashraqi's release. Among the citizens are Pir Elahi Buksh (Former Premier, Sindh Province), Syed Akbar Ali Shah (Member Legislative Assembly, Sind), G.M. Syed (well-known political leader from Sind), Ibraheem Jalees, Sheikh Abdul Majid, Hakim Muhammad Ahsan (Former Mayor of Karachi), Haji Maula Baksh, Hatim Alvi, and Mubarak Saghar (Secretary, Pakistan Socialist Party) (PT 1952 Jan. 05).

1952 January 06

The Pakistan Times, Lahore reports that the Punjab Government has extended Mashraqi's detention by six months. Mashriqi had been arrested on January 11, 1951 under Sec. 3 of the Punjab Public Safety Act (PT 1952 Jan. 06). Mashriqi is being kept in Mianwali Jail (C&MG 1952 Jan. 06).

1952 January 18

Mashriqi Day is observed throughout Punjab, the North-West Frontier Province (N.W.F.P.), and many other provinces. Public meetings are held under the auspices of The Islam League. At these extraordinary meetings, the Government is condemned and resolutions demanding Mashraqi's immediate release are passed. The Government is also reminded that Mashraqi's health is deteriorating quickly due to poor nourishment and miserable jail conditions (PT 1952 Jan. 20).
Editor's comments: Thus, the extension of Mashraqi's detention resulted in a great public outcry against the Government.

Another Mashraqi Day and public meeting are to be held in Mochi Gate in Lahore on January 20, 1952. The meeting is to be attended by various opposition parties, whose leaders are to address the public (PT 1952 Jan. 20).

1952 January 18

A joint public meeting is held in Multan under the auspices of the Islam League, the Jinnah-Awami League, and the Jamaat-e-Islami.

The public demands the immediate release of Mashraqi (C&MG 1952 Jan. 22).

1952 January 20

The Pakistan Times, Lahore reports that Islam League delegations have met with Prime Minister Khawaja Nazimuddin and Punjab Chief Minister Mian Mumtaz Mohammad Khan Daultana to demand Mashriqi's release (PT 1952 Jan. 20).

1952 January 30

The Pakistan Times, Lahore reports that at a recent meeting, the Islam League of Sialkot passed a resolution demanding Mashraqi's immediate release. The newspaper further reports that another resolution passed at the meeting expressed sympathy with the Muslims of Iran, Egypt, Tunisia, and Morocco and urged the Government of Pakistan to extend full support towards their fight against imperialism. According to the newspaper, Maulana Fazal Hussain Dilawar (Publicity Secretary of the Punjab Islam League) addressed the meeting and stated that the Government of Pakistan must revise its domestic and foreign policies "in view of the changed world situation." The Maulana also stated that the imperialists' atrocities in Tunisia and Egypt had disturbed the Middle Eastern countries (PT 1952 Jan. 30).

1952 February 03

At a convention in Lahore, Allama Mashraqi (who remains in jail) is among 32 people elected as Councillors to the Punjab Provincial Islam League. Islam League office bearers are also elected at the convention (PT 1952 Feb. 04).
Editor's comments: This election once again showed Allama Mashraqi's tremendous popularity among his followers. Mashriqi was in jail and yet was still elected.

1952 February 08

Dr. Syed Abdul Wadud issues a statement to the Press. *The Civil & Military Gazette*, Lahore of February 09, 1952 would report:
    "Dr. Syed Abdul Wadud, Member of the Executive Committee of the Islam League, has refuted the recent statement of the Punjab Government contained in a Press note that Allama Inayatullah Khan Mashriqi is in perfect health.

In a statement to the Press on Friday, he quoted several letters written by Allama Mashriqi from jail to his wife and said that according to those letters, Allama Mashriqi was suffering from indigestion, physical pains, blood in stools, constipation and uneasiness and that his general health was fast deteriorating.

Dr. Wadud also alleged that medical examination in the jail was not carried out satisfactorily and in support of his allegation he quoted his own case when he was in jail last year.

He alleged that the medical officers concerned did not take any interest to examine detenus and based their reports merely on the index of one's face.

He urged the Government to make a thorough inquiry into the state of health of Allama Mashriqi through some responsible persons and let the public know the facts" (C&MG 1952 Feb. 09).

1952 February 10

The General Secretary of the Islam League demands the immediate and unconditional release of Mashraqi. He reminds the Government of Mashraqi's poor health and states that Mashraqi is not being provided proper medical care in jail (PT 1952 Feb. 13).

Editor's comments: It is unfortunate that the Government turned a deaf ear to the public protests and provided no medical assistance for Mashriqi's recovery and continued to keep him in jail.

1952 February 17-18

The annual two-day convention of the Islam League is held in Lahore. At the convention, Mashriqi's immediate and unconditional release is demanded. A number of other resolutions are passed, including one condemning the British and French atrocities in Egypt and Tunisia. The convention further demands that the Pakistan Constituent Assembly speed up the making of the constitution. Also at the convention, elections for officer bearers as well as for a 28-man Executive Committee (representing the various units of Pakistan) are held (PT 1952 Feb. 19).

1952 February 18

Maulana Fazal Hussain Dilawar (Publicity Secretary of the Punjab Islam League) is arrested in Lahore under Section 3 of the Punjab Safety Act (PT 1952 Feb. 19).

1952 February 22

The Civil & Military Gazette, Lahore reports that the Islam League held a meeting at Jalal pur Jatan (near Gujrat). According to the newspaper, the release of Allama Mashraqi and Maulana Fazal Hussain Dilawar (Publicity Secretary of the Punjab Islam League) was demanded (C&MG 1952 Feb. 22).

1952 February 28

Police raid a number of places in Lahore. Ghazi Mohammed Ishaq (President of the Lahore District Islam League) and others are arrested (C&MG 1952 Feb. 29).

1952 March 17

The Lahore High Court grants bail to Islam League leader Qaiser Mustafa (C&MG 1952 Mar. 18).

The Government bans public meetings and parades in Lahore. The order of the Government states:
"[For a period of one week beginning March 17, 1952,] no person, party or organisation shall arrange a gathering of five or more persons in a public place, practice or take part in or be concerned in any parade, exercise, movement, evolution or drill which is either of a military nature or involves the use or preparation for the use of weapons of offence or defence or in particular arrange or take part in any sham fight or give or take a guard of honour within the limits of the Lahore Corporation" (C&MG 1952 Mar. 18).
The Civil & Military Gazette of March 18, 1952 would further report:
"This order shall not effect parades, demonstrations or sham fights or taking or giving a guard of honour by legally constituted organisations and gatherings of a religious nature, including marriage and funeral processions.
Giving reasons for the step, a Press note says that 'reliable information has been received that preparations are being made by certain political and other organisations to hold public gatherings of five persons or more parades and exercises of military nature or to arrange guards of honour or sham fights' and that 'there are sufficient grounds to believe that such public gatherings, parades, exercises, guards of honour and sham fights are likely to cause disturbance of the public tranquility and danger to human life'" (C&MG 1952 Mar. 18).

Editor's comments: This ban was imposed to prevent Khaksars from observing a day of remembrance for the martyrs of March 19, 1940. Furthermore, the ban was also meant to prevent any demonstrations for Allama Mashraqi's release.

1952 March 20

A habeas corpus petition is filed in the Lahore High Court for Mashraqi's detention (C&MG 1952 Mar. 22).

1952 March 21

Mohammed Munir, Chief Justice of the Lahore High Court, issues a writ for Allama Mashraqi's appearance in court on March 31, 1952 (C&MG 1952 Mar. 22).

1952 March 31

The hearing for Mashraqi's Habeas Corpus petition begins in the Lahore High Court. Hussain Shaheed Suhrawardy (who later became Prime Minister), Mian Mehmood Ali Kasuri (who later became Law Minister), and Khawaja Abdul Rahim represent Mashraqi. The courtroom and surrounding premises are packed with people.

Abdul Aziz, the Punjab Advocate General, presents three orders; the first is from January 1951, while the two subsequent orders extended Mashraqi's detention by six months. The Chief Justice questions, "Assuming that on the basis of evidence laid before me I find that the Allama was detained with a view to preventing him from taking part in the elections what will be the legal effect." The Advocate General replies, "On this hypothetical question the detenue will be entitled to release." Furthermore, the Advocate General denies that Mashraqi was detained because of the election and states that Allama Mashraqi was arrested during the Governor's rule in Punjab. He states that the Governor is above party politics. The Chief Justice responds, "It is not necessary that a Governor is above party politics." The Advocate General: "On principal a Governor is to be considered above party politics and the Governor who ordered the petitioner's arrest was above party politics."

After hearing the Government's version, the Chief Justice orders that Mashraqi should be present at the next hearing on April 14, 1952 to be examined in camera (C&MG 1952 Apr. 01).

Editor's comments: The Advocate General's replies do not make sense. In Pakistan, people in high positions have always been involved in party politics. Even the Prime Minister and President are involved in party politics.

1952 April 14

Mashraqi's Habeas Corpus petition hearing is resumed in the Lahore High Court. Hussain Shaheed Suhrawardy assisted by Mian Mehmood Ali Kasuri and Khawaja Abdul Rahim, represents Mashraqi. The Home Secretary (Punjab) and Advocate General (Punjab) are also present. Admission to the courtroom is restricted. Mashraqi states in court that he formed the Indo-Pakistan Islam League upon requests from the people. He further says that the Islam League is totally different from the Khaksar Movement. One of the Islam League's purposes is to acquire lawfully and constitutionally those Indian territories that are culturally Muslim. Mashraqi also answers questions during his Habeas Corpus Petition hearing. *The Pakistan Times*, Lahore of April 15, 1952 would report these proceedings:

"Mr. Suhrawardy: 'Have you ever disobeyed the orders of the Government?'
Mashriqi: 'Absolutely not. I always respected the Government orders.'

Respecting the Islam League Conference which was proposed to be held at Karachi in September 1950, Mr. Mashriqi said that after the Government had placed a ban on the holding of the proposed conference in September he had advised the Islam League to hold it in October. The Government imposed another ban and he advised them to hold it in November. But the Government again imposed a ban where upon he met the Administrator of Karachi and advised him to lift the ban since the Islam League was a constitutional organisation. The venue of the conference was then transferred to Lahore.

Suhrawardy: 'Have you a private army?'
Mashriqi: 'No. I have been discouraging the idea. There is no need of a private army now since there is an Islamic Government.'
Suhrawardy: 'Do you agree with the Muslim League in its present form?'
Mashriqi: 'No, not only as regards its form but as regards its doings also.'
Suhrawardy: 'Is it your claim that though the Muslim League claims to be a national organisation, it is not?'

Mashriqi: 'Yes. They consider everything said against the Muslim League as disruption though it is correction and not disruption.'
Suhrawardy: 'Is there any feature of the Islam League to which Pakistan Government took objection on the ground that it may be objected to by India?'
Mashriqi: 'I do not consider the protection of the Indian Muslims which is one of the objectives of the Islam League as an objectionable thing.'
Suhrawardy: 'Were you ever asked by the Government to desist from sending literature to Muslims in India and your plan to conquer Indian territory?'
Mashriqi: 'No such thing was asked by the Government...'
Suhrawardy: 'Do you remember that the date for the filing of the nomination papers by the candidates in general elections was February 5, 1951, and elections were to begin in the third week of March?'
Mashriqi: 'Yes.'
Suhrawardy: 'Do you remember that the then Prime Minister of Pakistan claimed that he was Prime Minister of the Muslim League and pledged to advance the cause of the Muslim League and that he was not the Prime Minister of the Constituent Assembly?'
Mashriqi: 'Yes.'
Suhrawardy: 'Do you remember that the position he took was that all Muslims should unite under the Muslim League and that Opposition to the Muslim League was disruption?'
Mashriqi: 'Yes, this was his attitude.'
Suhrawardy: 'Do you remember that the then Governor of the Punjab spoke in the same strain and that he accompanied the Prime Minister during his tour?'
Mashriqi: 'Yes.'
Suhrawardy: 'Did the Islam League propose to set up its candidates to contest each and every seat against the Leaguers?'
Mashriqi: 'Yes.'

Mr. Mashriqi replying to another question deposed that he held no office in the Islam League and that everything done by the Islam League was done independently. He said: 'They only respect my advice which I did give on certain occasions.'

Suhrawardy: 'Did you make an attempt to bring round all the Opposition leaders in order to forge a united front against the Muslim League?'

Mashriqi: 'Yes, that was our constant effort. I made special efforts in this connetion to bring round Pir of Manki Sharif, Mian Iftikhar-ud-Din, Maulana Maudoodi, Mr. Suhrawardy and the Khan of Mamdot.'
Suhrawardy: 'Do you remember that on Janurary 9, 1951 Khwaja Shahab-ud-Din spoke against the Opposition and said that there was no scope of Opposition and further that the safety laws were not to be repealed?'
Mashriqi: 'Yes.'

Answering a question regarding a meeting of the Islam League on the night of January 10 [1951], Mr. Mashriqi deposed that the meeting was held at the residence of Dr. Abdul Wadood. There was a large audience. The same night three parties, namely the Musawat-i-Islam and Mujahadeen-i-Islam and a large Mazdoor Organisation proclaimed that they would join the Islam League. 'I proposed that I will be giving a sum of Rs. 10,000 for the elections. I was arrested at 4 a.m. on January 11. Dr. Abdul Wadood had told me that a large number of C.I.D. people were present downstairs when the meeting was going on.' The most prominent leaders of the Islam League were arrested among whom were Haji Mohammad Ashraf, Malik Akram, Safdar Saleemi and Dr. Wadood.

Suhrawardy: 'Was there a demand for your release?'
Mashriqi: 'Yes a demand for my release was made by almost all the parties including the Muslim League.'
Suhrawardy: 'Do you remember that in September 1951, a Government spokesman got released through the A.P.P. grounds justifying the Government's action in arresting you?'
Mashriqi: 'Yes, I remember.'

BITTER LETTER

In reply to another question Mr. Mashriqi said that seven days after his arrest he wrote a most bitter letter to the Punjab Governor quoting Quranic authority that he could not detain him without putting him on trial. He had also asked the Governor to postpone the elections by as many days as they were kept in jail. Many days had passed but the elections were not postponed nor did he receive any reply to his letter. He sent a reminder but still there was no reply. He thought that it was the duty of the Governor to clear his position to a leader of the Opposition but the Governor did not do so.

Suhrawardy: 'Do you remember that Mr. Yusaf Khattak, on January 4, 1951, suggested that you should be put behind the bars and that on

January 13, Khwaja Shahab-ud-Din made a statement to the effect that there was 100 per cent chance of the Muslim League in the Punjab coming out successful in the elections?'

Mashriqi: 'Yes. I remember. The statement of Khwaja Shahab-ud-Din after the meetings outside Mochi Gate, University Grounds and at Sialkot sounded to me very strange. I felt that the chief obstruction in their way had been removed by my arrest.'

Chief Justice: 'What were your plans to make Muslims the sole possessors of India?'

Mashriqi: 'My sole hope was that Mr. Jinnah and I should amalgamate ourselves—he politically and I militarily. After my clash [1939] with the Congress Government of U.P., Mr. Jinnah offered himself as a mediator. He sent a message through Dr. Ziauddin to accept his mediation. I accepted the offer and thereafter we became good friends. After sometime, however, differences arose between Mr. Jinnah and myself. I had written the pamphlet "Majority of blood." Mr. Jinnah disagreed with me on the question of partition of India and we were never able to reconcile on this issue.'

Chief Justice: 'But what was your plan.'

Mashriqi: 'My only hope was that Mr. Jinnah and I should join hands.'

Chief Justice: 'What concrete steps did you intend to take to protect the Muslims in India?'

Mashriqi: 'I wanted help from the Pakistan Government as much as Mr. Nehru extended to the Mahasabha. I also desired that we should be allowed to raise our voice against the Hindus.'

Chief Justice: 'What form of Government you wanted to establish in Pakistan?'

Mashriqi: 'A Government that looked to the happiness of the largest number. I do not believe in religious or secular Government. My idea of Islam is scientific idea. I believe that it stands for the happiness of the greatest number. I am against mullaism.'

Chief Justice: 'What was your plan to acquire more territory from India for Pakistan?'

Mashriqi: 'I wanted to achieve that by creating world opinion in favour of our demand. It could be done by telling them that the Pakistan given to the Muslims was insufficient for their population.'

Chief Justice: 'What was the cause of your arrest?'

Mashriqi: 'The cause of my arrest was that I was an obstacle in the way of their (Muslim League) success in the election.'

CROSS EXAMINATION

Mr. Abdul Aziz Khan, Advocate General, starting his cross-examination showed a letter to Mr. Mashriqi and asked him if the letter had been written by him to the leaders of the Opposition parties. Mr. Mashriqi replied that the said letter was issued by the Islam League to the various leaders.

Advocate-General: 'In what capacity did you advise the Islam League?'
Mashriqi: 'As a founder of that organisation.'
Advocate-General: 'Was a conference at Karachi convened by the Islam League?'
Mashriqi: 'Yes.'
Advocate-General: 'Did you intend to address it?'
Mashriqi: 'Yes'
Advocate-General: 'Has the Islam League an organisation of Razakars?'
Mashriqi: 'Yes.'

The Advocate General then produced a pamphlet issued by the Islam League in connection with the conference to be held at Karachi.
Advocate-General: 'Was it intended that a body of 10,000 Razakars armed with firearms, bows and arrows, sticks, axes and *belchas* should attend the conference to make it successful?'
Mashriqi: 'Yes. I know it was intended and the Islam League had made an announcement in this connection.'
Advocate-General: 'Is the code of the Razakars of the Islam League the same as that of Khaksars?'
Mashriqi: 'No.'
Advocate-General: 'Did you see the pamphlet directing the Razakars to attend the conference?'
Mashriqi: 'I did not actually see but I remember that some pamphlet was issued by the Islam League to the Razakars.'
Advocate-General: 'Did you intend to raise an army of your own?'
Mashriqi: 'No, If I had wished that I would have continued the Khaksar organisation.'
Advocate-General: 'Are you aware that during December 1950 there was a ban on carrying of arms and on military parades within the limits of the Lahore Corporation?'
Mashriqi: 'I am not aware of it.'
Advocate-General: 'Did you address the Lahore conference on three occasions?"
Mashriqi: 'Yes.'

...

Advocate-General: 'Before the conference at Lahore did you go to Rawalpindi and address a public meeting there?'
Mashriqi: 'Yes I did.'
Advocate-General: 'Is it a fact that the Islam League held public meetings during the months of October, November and December 1950 where the Razakars defied the ban on the carrying of arms?'
Mashriqi: 'No ban was defied. At least not to my knowledge.'
Advocate-General: 'Did the Punjab Government proscribe about 10 pamphlets issued by the Islam League including "Khitab-i-Lahore" on the ground that they were likely to harm the Muslim in India?'
Mashriqi: 'Not a single pamphlet was banned or proscribed by the Government.'
Advocate-General: 'Was "Akhri Umeed" [Last Hope] proscribed by the Government?'
Mashriqi: 'It never went into printing. I still do not know whether this pamphlet was proscribed or not.'
Advocate-General: 'Was any order proscribing these pamphlets served on you?"
Mashriqi: 'No.'

The Advocate-General amplifying his question further said that an order was served on certain Islam League workers by the Government under Section 4 of the Punjab Public Safety Act prohibiting them from publishing certain pamphlets. Mr. Mashriqi professed ignorance about the order.

Advocate-General: 'How many members of the Islam League are there in the Punjab Assembly?'
Mashriqi: 'Through the kindness of the Muslim League not even one.'
Advocate-General: 'How many candidates did the Islam League put up for the election?'
Mashriqi: 'We could not put up any candidate because all important workers of the Islam League were arrested?'
Advocate-General: 'I put it to you that you were arrested neither for your Indo-Pakistan plans nor for your election activities, but because you were preaching defiance of law in Punjab. Do you deny it?'
Mashriqi: 'Yes. Tell me one line where I have done so.'

GHIASUDDIN

After the cross-examination of Mr. Mashriqi by the Advocate-General, Mr. Ghiasuddin Ahmad [Home Secretary] was called in the witness-box. In reply to the question put to him by the Advocate-General, Mr. Ghiasuddin Ahmad deposed that in January 1951, he was Secretary to the Punjab Governor and that all files that came from the Secretariat were sent to the Governor through him.

Advocate-General: 'May I know who passed the order of detention of Allama Mashriqi.'
Mr. Ghiasuddin: 'The order was passed by the Governor himself.'
Advocate-General: 'Did you sign any order extending the detention of Allama Mashriqi on behalf of the Punjab Governor?'
Ghiasuddin: 'Yes. The order was issued under the direction of the Punjab Government. The case was put up by me before the Minister Incharge, who ordered the extension. The former order was drafted by me.'
Chief Justice: 'What was the object of extending the detention of Allama Mashriqi?'
Ghiasuddin: 'To prevent him from resorting to activities in which he was engaged before his detention.'
Chief Justice: 'Was the order extending Allama Mashriqi's detention passed with a view to preventing him from fighting the elections in the Punjab?'
Ghiasuddin: 'No.'
Advocate-General: 'Was he arrested for his anti-India activities?'
Ghiasuddin: 'No. Nor was his arrest ordered because of his activities regarding the Muslims of India.'

Replying to questions relating to a White Paper issued by the Government, Mr. Ghiasuddin said that he did not draft the White Paper but if it was desired he could give his opinion about it. He further stated that an order under Section 4 of the Punjab Public Safety Act was served on some workers of the Islam League prohibiting them from publishing certain pamphlets.

During the course of cross-examination by Mr. Suhrawardy, Mr. Ghiasuddin was asked to state the activities for which Mr. Mashriqi was arrested. He said that he could not disclose those facts without the permission of the Government.

Suhrawardy: 'Are you referring to any activities of Allama Mashriqi apart from his speeches and writings?'
Ghiasuddin: 'I have already stated that I cannot disclose without the permission of the Government.'
Suhrawardy: 'Can you point to any speech considered by the Government objectionable?'

Ghiasuddin: '"Khitab-i-Lahore" for instance.'
Suhrawardy: 'Is there any writing of Allama Mashriqi in which he himself defied the law or called upon others to defy the law?'
Ghiasuddin: 'I did come across some writings of that sort by Allama Mashriqi.'
Suhrawardy: 'Can you point out any passage in "Khitab-i-Lahore" which constitute a challenge to the lawfully constituted authority?'
Ghiasuddin: 'I have not gone through that pamphlet.'

When asked whether the pamphlet "Khitab-i-Lahore" had anything to with the order extending Allama Mashriqi's detention, Mr. Ghiasuddin replied that the order proscribing this pamphlet was passed on a separate file." (PT 1952 Apr. 15; C&MG 1952 Apr. 15)

1952 April 18

Mashraqi's Habeas Corpus petition hearing resumes in the Lahore High Court. During the proceedings, Hussain Shaheed Suhrawardy (defence counsel) questions Mashriqi's detention. The Home Secretary (Punjab) is cross-examined and states that he is not prepared to disclose the reasons for Mashraqi's arrest. Mashraqi is also present in court. *The Civil and Military Gazette* of April 19, 1952 would report:

"Hearing of the Habeas Corpus petition of Allama Mashriqi, founder of the Islam League, was resumed on Friday in the court of Mr. Justice Muhammad Munir, Chief Justice of the Lahore High Court. After cross-examining Mr. Ghias-Ud-Din Ahmad, Home Secretary Punjab, for about two hours, Mr. H.S. Suhrawardy, counsel for the petitioner [Allama Mashraqi] began his arguments in the case.

He submitted that the burden on the detenu to make out the want of bonafides on the part of the Government was not so heavy as the burden on the Government to prove its bonafides in case there was sufficient material to shift that onus on the Government.

The Government, Mr. Suhrawardy submitted, would not admit nor would it disclose the reasons of the Allama's arrest, but there were certain surrounding circumstances which showed bad faith of the Government. He also submitted that detention was only legitimate when it was with reference to activities which were proximate to the orders and which may give rise to apprehension on the part of the Government that the man should be prevented from acting in that manner. Therefore the satisfaction of the Government after six months for further extension should only be relating to the activities of the detenu for the detention period.

The cross-examination of Mr. Ghias-ud-Din Ahmad was resumed by Mr. Suhrawardy when hearing began at 9 a.m. on Friday.

During the course of cross-examination by Mr. Suhrawardy, Mr. Ghias-ud-Din Ahmad, deposed that Allama Mashriqi had only ostensibly disbanded the Khaksar movement. When asked whether he knew about the Allama's speech at Quetta, where he spoke in disparaging terms about the Khaksar organisation, he professed ignorance.

Suhrawardy: 'Have you gone through the 'Khitab-i-Lahore,' since the last hearing?'
Ghias-Ud-Din Ahmad: 'No.'
Suhrawardy: 'Is there anything in it which is incitement to break the law?'
Ghias-Ud-Din Ahmad: 'It was considered objectionable by legal officers of the Government. So far as I know, the pamphlet contained passages which brought the Government into contempt.'
Suhrawardy: 'Is there any speech other than the 'Khitab-i-Lahore' which has been proscribed by the Government?'
Ghias-Ud-Din Ahmad: 'As far as I know, there are two other such pamphlets: the 'Akhri Umeed' and 'Izhar-i-Haqiqat.' Whether they produce the Allama's speech verbatim or they were comments on the speeches made by him I cannot say.'
Suhrawardy: 'Can you tell about any writings of the Allama in which he has called upon the people to defy the law or break it, or made any such speech.'
Ghias-Ud-Din Ahmad: 'The only speeches which I know are the 'Khitab-i-Lahore,' 'Akhri Umeed' and 'Izhar-i-Haqiqat.'

He said in a reply to a question that these articles were not exactly on the file on which the Allama's detention was ordered. They only furnished the background. He said that he was not prepared to disclose the matter about the reasons of the Allama's arrest.

Suhrawardy: 'Are you aware of the objectives of the Islam League?'
Ghias-Ud-Din: 'Yes.'
Suhrawardy: 'Is there anything in this calling upon people to public disorder?'
Ghias-Ud-Din: 'There is. They invite the people to attend meetings and ask them to come armed.'
Suhrawardy: 'Was that objectionable?'
Ghias-Ud-Din: 'Yes in particular instance in those days of December, 1951, when Islam League Conference was held in Lahore, there was a ban on the carrying of arms of any nature and against the holding of

parades and they disregarded it. The Allama took the salute and participated in this. They were parading with arms and in uniform.'

Suhrawardy: 'To what document are you referring when you say that the Islam League calls upon the people to come armed at their meetings?'

Ghias-Ud-Din: 'I definitely saw a public poster stating that the public should come armed to the conference. Then there was another poster which said they would stage a mock battle for members of the Islam League. The idea of this mock battle was abandoned after a deputation of the Islam League had seen the Deputy Commissioner of Lahore.'

Suhrawardy: 'I put it to you that at no time has the Allama called upon the Razakars to come armed at the Lahore conference.'

Ghias-Ud-Din: 'I do not know what the Allama's directions on the occasion of the Lahore meeting were. At a Rawalpindi meeting, people came even armed with rifles. There was no ban in Rawalpindi against the carrying of arms but the situation was so menacing that the Deputy Commission of Rawalpindi had to draw the attention of the Government to this.'

Replying to another question he said that there was no actual violence or disturbance at the Rawalpindi meeting.

When asked whether he knew that the Allama had no office in the Islam League, Mr. Ghias-Ud-Din said that he had definite information that the Allama was the real force behind the movement. He deposed that he knew that the Islam League had a president, secretary and other office bearers but was not aware who held those offices.

Suhrawardy: 'Do you agree with me that office bearers of the Islam League may take any action or produce any documents with which the Allama may have nothing to do?'

Ghias-Ud-Din: 'I do not know the internal working. For anything that they do they obtain the blessing and approval of Allama Mashriqi or follow the general policy of the organisation.'

Suhrawardy: 'Are you aware that the Executive Committee of the Islam League is comprised of high intellectuals?'

Ghias-Ud-Din: 'Their high command is called the Majlis-e-Nafiza. But I do not know the intellectual capacity of the office bearers.'

Mr. Ghias-Ud-Din further said that he had instructions to say that the Government would release the Allama immediately when the reasons for which he was arrested did not exist or would not exist if he were released.

Mr. Ghias-Ud-Din further deposed that the Prime Minister of Pakistan, late Mr. Liaquat Ali Khan, visited the Punjab several times to strengthen the Muslim League and that he appealed to the

people to flock round this organisation, which he called the sole national organisation. He replied to a question that the Prime Minister used strong language against the Opposition parties at times.
Suhrawardy: 'Are you aware that there is a feeling in Muslim League circles that a Khaksar attacked the Qaid-e-Azam in Bombay in 1943 as a result of the Allama's preachings?'
Ghias-Ud-Din 'In 1943, I was neither in Bombay nor in the Punjab.'
Suhrawardy: 'Are you aware of the existence of such feelings in Government circles?'
Ghias-Ud-Din: 'I am not aware of feelings but of the facts on which the Allama was arrested, thought I cannot disclose. I know what the Khaksars have been doing or intend to do and what the present body is doing or intends to do.'
Suhrawardy: 'Are you aware if the Allama committed any prejudicial act while in jail?'
Ghias-Ud-Din: 'He has been very unhelpful to the administration, but has not done anything prejudicial to the Government.'
Suhrawardy: 'Can you say whether there is a feeling in Government circles that the Allama sabotaged national demands of Pakistan?'
Ghias-Ud-Din: 'We have definite information that the Allama was opposed to the idea of Pakistan as conceived by Qaid-e-Azam.'

Stating his case, Mr. Suhrawardy submitted that the tendency of the court should always be in favour of the liberty of the subject.
Chief Justice: 'It has always been so.'
Suhrawardy: 'My Lord, without any invidious reference to any honourable court. I would submit that in this country, there is a tendency on the part of some courts to feel bound by the orders of the Government. In India, courts have in many recent decisions shown a firm tendency in favour of the liberty of the citizen that where in a case the Government refuses to disclose the grounds of detention, the surrounding circumstances should be taken into consideration while construing the *bonafides* of the order of detention.'
Chief Justice: 'The law there is different from the law here.'
  Mr. Suhrawardy then referred to two decisions of the Indian courts, namely, 1949 Bombay and 1950 Rajhasthan.
  Continuing, Mr. Suhrawardy submitted that courts in this country were apt to take a narrow view of the law. Courts ought to interpret the statue keeping in view the surrounding circumstance. He then referred to the views of British courts on the interpretation of the statues.
Chief Justice: 'What principle do you want to impress upon the court?'

Suhrawardy: 'That Your Lordship will interpret the statue with liberality of view in relation to the surrounding circumstances and not with a closed mind.'

Chief Justice: 'There is no question of interpreting this law.'

Suhrawardy: 'My Lord, I submit there is. Safety Act cases are governed by section 194 of the Criminal Procedure Code. But there are innumerable decisions holding that interpretation of the law is open to courts.'

Chief Justice: 'You tell me the precise principal for interpreting the Safety Act.'

Suhrawardy: 'My Lord, here in this case, the Government has refused to disclose the grounds of detention. But there are surrounding circumstances that show that there was a bad faith on the part of the Government. The Government was actuated by ulterior motives which fall outside the scope of the Safety Act.'

Mr. Suhrawardy then stated two propositions of law for the attention of His Lordship. He submitted: (a) that in a habeas corpus petition, the proof has not to be as meticulous as in a civil suit; (b) that the burden on the detenu to make out the want of bonafides on the part of the Government is not so heavy as the burden on the Government to prove its bonafides in case there is sufficient material to shift the onus on the Government.

Mr. Suhrawardy then submitted that it was within the jurisdiction of courts to trace the origin of law and direct the Government whereever necessary. He said: 'My Lord, the legislation of restrictive nature is an emergency measure. It should not be continued indefinitely. An emergency cannot exist for all times. In normal times, there may be a Central Safety Act dealing with external emergency, but the provincial Government should not have safety acts dealing with internal emergency. When public acts exist for maintenance of law and order, courts should trace the origin of law and direct the Government on their view.'

Chief Justice: 'It is not in the dignity of the court to make recommendations to the Government.'

Suhrawardy: 'Not recommendations, My Lord, but you can trace the origin of the law and direct the authorities.'

Chief Justice: 'My duty is to interpret the law.'

Mr. Suhrawardy then submitted that detention was legitimate only when it was proximate in reference to the prejudicial activities. The extension of detention, he submitted, could only be with reference to the acts after the original detention.

Elaborating his point, he submitted that where there was restrictive power to extend the detention, it must depend on further satisfaction.

Extension of the detention of a detenu who had been in jail for six months could not be said to have been based on the fact that the extending authority was satisfied, for he did not commit any prejudicial act during his detention. In this particular case, Mr. Suhrawardy submitted, there was sufficient material to show that the Government had been actuated by motives outside its scope. Mr. Suhrawardy was still urging when the Court rose for the day. Hearing will be resumed at 1 p.m. on Saturday (today). The detenu Allama Mashriqi was also produced in the court" (C&MG 1952 Apr. 19).

Editor's comments: From this, the reader can understand that there was no justification for keeping Mashraqi under detention. It is unfortunate that civil liberties and the development of the political system in Pakistan have been crushed from the very beginning. This must end or the growth of the nation will continue to suffer.

1952 April 19

Mashraqi's Habeas Corpus petition hearing continues in the Lahore High Court. An official of the Criminal Investigation Department (C.I.D.) is examined about a film he had recorded at an Islam League meeting on December 30, 1950. Hussain Shaheed Suhrawardy, Mashraqi's Counsel, continues his arguments. Suhrawardy discusses the pamphlets proscribed by the Government in August 1948 and 1950. *The Civil & Military Gazette*, Lahore of April 20, 1952 would report:

"Mr. Suhrawardy said that it had been clearly established that the Allama was creating an Opposition to the Muslim League, that he was calling upon the people not to vote for the Muslim League during the elections, that he was holding election meetings in Rawalpindi, Multan and Lahore, that the Government was afraid of his influence and of the fact that he would be able to create a body of volunteers who would be a formidable force against the Muslim League and would be instrumental in making the Opposition successful. It was ridiculous to call this body a private army. At this rate, even volunteers of the Muslim League could well be called a private army.

He [Mashraqi] had also addressed the leaders of various parties for the creation of a united front and was on the point of succeeding. A meeting had been held on the 10th evening where organisations had promised to join the united front. There were a number of C.I.D. officials at the place and the Allama was arrested in the early morning of the 11th [January 11, 1951]" (C&MG 1952 Apr. 20).

1952 April 22

A bill designed to replace the Pakistan Public Safety Ordinance is discussed in Parliament (C&MG 1952 Apr. 23).

1952 April 28

Mashraqi's Habeas Corpus petition hearing resumes. Hussain Shaheed Suhrawardy concludes his arguments. He states that according to the Advocate General, one of the reasons for Mashraqi's arrest was the proscription of *Khitab-e-Lahore*. Suhrahwardy argues that this clearly showed that at least one of the reasons for the arrest was outside the provincial sphere. Suhrawardy also states that the election activities started in Punjab in June and that *Khitab-e-Lahore* (published in the same month) was Mashraqi's first election speech. He further argues that Mashraqi was endeavouring to organize the oppostion parties, including Jamaat-i-Islami, Jinnah-Awami League, and others for the elections. *The Civil & Military Gazette*, Lahore of April 29, 1952 would report, "If he [Mashraqi] was indulging in the activities prejudicial to the law of the land long before the elections then why was he arrested just on the eve of Punjab elections, he [Suhrawardy] stated." Suhrawardy rejects the argument that Mashraqi violated Section 144 in Karachi. He states that Mashraqi had moved the venue of the party conference after the restriction had been imposed. Suhrawardy also presents proof from speeches by Muslim League leaders that Mashraqi was arrested to prevent him from participating in the forthcoming elections (C&MG 1952 Apr. 29).
Editor's comments: Section 144 was imposed in Karachi to prevent Mashraqi and his followers from taking part in political activities.

1952 May 12

Mashraqi's Habeas Corpus petition hearing resumes in the Lahore High Court. The Advocate General states that after the partition of India, the Islam League sent literature to the Indian Muslims. The Government of India resented this action. As a result, the Punjab Government, under Section 4 of the Public Safety Act of 1947, proscribed pamphlets by the Islam League and prohibited Allama Mashraqi and other members of the Islam League from publishing such materials. The Advocate General presents some of the pamphlets in court and reads excerpts from them.

The Advocate General further argues that authorities can extend the detension of a detenue if they believe that the detenue will commit prejudicial acts. He argues that Mashraqi was arrested because his activities were prejudicial to public safety.

The Civil & Military Gazette, Lahore of May 13, 1952 would report that the Advocate General "submitted that reference in Pakistan Government's White paper of 1951 about drastic action against the Islam League related to the seizure and proscription of these pamphlets."

Mian Mehmood Ali Kasuri, counsel for the defence, states that the Home Secretary refused to disclose the reasons for Mashraqi's arrest. In response to a question by the Chief Justice, Kasuri states that the writings of Allama Mashraqi that were quoted by the Advocate General do not preach violence at all. He further states that Mashraqi postponed the Karachi conference three times, again proving that Mashraqi did not believe in violating the law. Kasuri further informs the court that the Government has taken two positions on Mashraqi's arrest and it is unjustified that the reasons for his arrest as stated in court are different from what the world has been told (C&MG 1952 May 13).

Editor's comments: The Government arrested Mashraqi so that the Islam League could not win the upcoming elections.

Regarding the Muslims of India, Mashraqi tried to do whatever he could to protect their rights. Meanwhile, the Government of Pakistan had completely abandoned them soon after the creation of Pakistan. The Government had forgotten that the partition was supposed to protect the Muslims of the entire India. If all the Muslims were not to be protected, then the purpose of creating a separate homeland fails. In the Khaksar circles, the partition was seen as a means of benefiting the upper class of the Muslim League and not actually helping the Muslims of the entire India. The prevailing circumstances in Pakistan since its creation, with the masses living in poverty, lead one to believe that the Khaksar theory was correct.

1952 May 19

Arguments are concluded in Mashraqi's Habeas Corpus petition hearing. Mahmood Ali Kasuri (Mashraqi's counsel) cross-examines Syed Nur Ahmed (Director of Public Relations, Punjab). Syed Nur Ahmed informs the court that he did not issue the news that appeared in *The Civil & Military Gazette*, Lahore and *The Pakistan Times*, Lahore on September 28, 1951 under the authority of the Punjab Government. Hussain Shaheed Suhrawardy also asks Syed Nur Ahmed about the news item. The Advocate General responds to Hussain Shaheed Suhrawardy's arguments.

Syed Nur Ahmed further informs the court that Allama Mahraqi was prohibited from producing and posting Khaksar literature to the Muslims of India.

At the conclusion of arguments, Chief Justice Muhammad Munir reserves judgement (*Dawn* 1952 May 20; *Dawn* 1952 May 21).

1952 May 30

Mohammad Munir, the Chief Justice of the Lahore High Court, rejects Mashraqi's Habeas Corpus Petition, despite criticism of the Government for not disclosing the grounds for Mashriqi's detention (PT 1952 May 31).
Editor's comments: It is unfortunate that the judiciary was not an independent body and the Government could control its decision.

1952 June 22

Abdul Rasheed of Sialkot (Former Salar-e-Suba, Islam League) states that Allama Mashraqi's release on July 11, 1952 is being anxiously awaited. He also announces that a peaceful demonstration and a protest day would be observed if Mashraqi is not released.
Editor's comments: Although Mashraqi's habeas corpus petition was rejected, people were still hoping for his release, as his detention period was to expire. Indeed, the Government, under public pressure, could no longer extend his detention and was forced to release him on July 9, 1952.

1952 June 26

The Civil & Military Gazette, Lahore reports that Mashraqi's confinement is not likely to be extended and that he would be released on July 10, 1952, at the expiry of his detention period (C&MG 1952 Jun. 26).
Editor's comments: Mashraqi was actually released on July 9, 1952.

1952 June 27

The Civil & Military Gazette, Lahore reports on press statement by Dr. Syed Abdul Wadud (Secretary General of the Islam League) (C&MG 1952 Jun. 27).

1952 June 28

Dawn, Karachi reports that Mashraqi is to be released on July 11, 1952 (*Dawn* 1952 Jun. 28).
Editor's comments: Mashraqi was actually released on July 09, 1952.

1952 July 09

Allama Mashriqi is released after one and a half years of detention. His period of detention had been extended twice (PT 1952 Jul. 10; C&MG 1952 Jul. 10).
Editor's comments: It is so unfortunate that opposition was not tolerated in Pakistan. The Muslim League considered Pakistan its personal property and anything said against it was considered unacceptable and almost treason against the state.

With Mashraqi's release, the Government had conveniently forgotten all of the fabricated reasons for Mashraqi's arrest. Furthermore, keeping in mind that the Chief Justice of the Lahore High court had rejected Mashriqi's Habeus Corpus petition less than two months earlier, it seems that the Government authorities had now sent a signal to the court to release Mashraqi. This clearly shows that the judiciary has never been independent and that Government authorities have been dictating its decisions from the very initial years of Pakistan's creation.

It seems that although Pakistan was supposed to be created so that justice would be granted to every citizen, this was not the reality. Basic human rights continue to be crushed in Pakistan even today.

1952 July 11

Allama Mashraqi delivers a speech in Lahore after Jumma (Friday) prayers. *The Pakistan Times*, Lahore of July 12, 1952 would report:

"Allama Mashriqi in a brief post Jumma prayer speech in Lahore declared that the only panacea for the present-day ills and sufferings of the people was a Government by the downtrodden, who formed the bulk of the population in the country.

'This type of Government which will be by the majority of the people will be in perfect accord with the tenets of Islam,' he added.

Talking with emotion, the Allama said that although he was weak in health after this long-incarceration, nevertheless his faith in the ultimate victory of the underdog was 'unshakable.'

He assured the congregation that he would continue his fight to bring about the desired change in the present-day political set-up of the country through peaceful and constitutional means" (PT 1952 Jul. 12).

1952 July 11

The Civil & Military Gazette, Lahore reports:
"Allama Inayat Ullah Khan Mashriqi, leader of the Islam League, who was released on Wednesday night [July 09, 1952] after 18 months detention under the Punjab Public Safety Act, has expressed concern over India's plans to divert the course of rivers flowing from Kashmir.

Allama Mashriqi said during the course of a Press interview that he had informed the Pakistan authorities about this in 1950, and added that he honestly believed that if Dr. Graham prolonged his parleys, thereby potponing accession of Kashmir to Pakistan, Pakistan would after a few years face tremendous difficulties, as several lakh acres [several hundred-thousand acres] of land would be turned barren with the change in the course of rivers.

Allama Mashriqi, said that there had been tremendous political and economic changes in Pakistan during the last 18 months, which demanded a change in the policy of Pakistan Government. He maintained that India's plans regarding Kashmir rivers flowing through, and feeding West Pakistan, increasing unemployment, shortage of food, general administrative deterioration etc., were problems about which he could not say anything at present. He would consult Islam League workers and then make public his impressions and opinions about them" (C&MG 1952 Jul. 11).

1952 July 13

The Civil & Military Gazette, Lahore reports that Allama Mashraqi has applied for a passport to go to Jeddah (Saudi Arabia) for Haj (Pilgrimage). The newspaper also states, "The Allama, it was further learned, was refused passport by the Government in 1948, when he intended to visit Paris to raise the question of Muslim massacre in India and other allied subjects before the [United Nations] Security Council" (C&MG 1952 Jul. 13).

1952 July 23

Mashraqi suggests the formation of a coalition Government in Pakistan "for a general cure of the ills from which the country is suffering at present." He further states, "we must show to India and other foreign countries that there is no opposition to the Government in Pakistan." Mashraqi also states:

"I still have a conviction that all the ills of Pakistan can be cured if best men from all parties are wholeheartedly invited by the present Government to co-operate and form a permanent coalition Government. If this step is not taken immediately, I have grave fears that Pakistan may not be able to retain its entity for long in view of the grave deterioration in administration that has occurred during the past five years. I give this as a food for thought to all and make this public appeal to men at the top" (C&MG 1952 Jul. 24).

The Civil & Military Gazette, Lahore of July 24, 1952 would report, "he [Mashraqi] added, he felt that not only parties but even the general public wished a stable and all-representative Government in the country. He refused to accept the view that Islam permitted the present form of democracy which meant Government on the party system and which was only a legacy of the British. There was no party in Islam and it constantly reminded its followers that they were all equal, he emphasised."

In reference to the Islam League, Mashraqi states that he founded it "to protect five crores [50 million] of Indian Muslims from the Hindu tyranny and to unite the two wings of Pakistan by constitutional means...Under the present circumstances, when the present Muslim League Government could not save one Pakistani national from the clutches of the Hindu, the idea of saving five crores of Indian Muslims by a private organisation like the Islam League looks like a joke. When this conception was envisaged by me as early as 1947, I had an extremely favourable notion of the strength of Pakistan as an Islamic State. I pictured then that within a few years, Pakistan could, through the force of Islam alone, become one of the most powerful countries in the world economically, militarily, as well as in civil manpower." He also adds that he wants the main purpose of the Islam League to remain the protection of Indian Muslims.

Regarding the state of affairs in Pakistan, Mashraqi states, "The situation after five years is that Pakistan's very existence is in most serious danger owing to the sources of our rivers being in the hands of the enemy. The Hindus have surrounded us with enemies. Pakistan's natural military strength is already far above that of the Hindu, but the improvement claimed by the present Government looks to me very doubtful.

The position of Pakistan in international politics is that of a camp follower of the Commonwealth or U.N. Its proposal to unite the Muslim world under its own tutelage may even be harmful to the Muslim world. Pakistan's economy is deteriorating alarmingly through the Hindus' enmity, extremely insufficient administration, want of knowledge, proper planning, and experience. Better men, as well as public confidence in the Muslim League, is fast disappearing and the little momentum bequeathed by the British in their waning days is losing its strength in every field of national and administrative activity."

Mashraqi thanks the Press and different Muslim organizations for demanding his release. However, he expresses regret that the Press has become divided "at a time when it should have united with all strength in order to tide over a critical period full of external as well as internal difficulties." He states that he had devoted his entire life to strengthening the Muslims against the British and thus it is unthinkable that "I would do anything anti-national or prejudicial to an Islamic State." He further adds that he has no militant intentions and that he is against taking the law into one's own hands in an Islamic State (C&MG 1952 Jul. 24).

The Pakistan Times, Lahore of July 24, 1952 would also report Mashraqi's plea for a coalition government:
"In these circumstances individual power must become more unbridled as it goes on and it may do worse things under the guise of 'law and order'...

I disbanded the Khaksar organisation in 1947 for the sake of Pakistan. To say that I have now militant intentions is, therefore, meaningless. I declined the offer of the late Quaid-i-Azam in 1942 to join him and become his successor because I disagreed with him sharply on the demand of two portions of Pakistan...

Law in Pakistan is not so much for the good of the people as it is for the security of the seats of the few at the top. I vehemently reject the Government charge that I have done or will do anything against law. I am not in favour of taking law in my own hands in an Islamic State...

As regards Islam League, which I founded in 1947 for the protection of five crores of Indian Muslims from the Hindu tyranny and the uniting of the two Pakistans by constitutional means, I can only say that under the present circumstances when the present Muslim League Government cannot save one Pakistani National from the clutches of the Hindu, the idea of saving five crores of Indian Muslims by a private organisation like the Islam League sounds like a joke. I am nevertheless in favour of keeping this as the main object of the Islam League especially when the Muslim Government of Pakistan have washed their hands off those helpless people" (PT 1952 Jul. 24; C&MG 1952 Jul. 24).

1952 July 25

The Civil & Military Gazette, Lahore's publishes an editorial regarding Mashraqi's statement of July 23, 1952:
"At a Press conference in Lahore, Allama Inayatullah Khan Mashriqi, the Islam League Chief has expressed the fear that Pakistan may go down on account of deterioration in administration and has suggested the formation of a coalition Government composed of the 'best men' drawn from all parties. He has based his suggestion on the assumption that Islam does not recognise the kind of Opposition which is indispensable for the working of modern democratic machinery. As regards his diagnosis, few will disagree that there has been an unparalleled decay in moral standards which alone make a nation truly strong and independent and the State must come to great harm if the drift is not arrested. It will also be readily agreed that all deterioration starts at the top and unless we have the 'best men,' there, mere sermonising on moral virtues will not mend matters. ...Allama Mashriqi's main point that something must be done to arrest the present drift deserves the earnest consideration of every patriotic Pakistani. Equally sound is his suggestion that the reins of Government must be in the hands of the best men. ...By their superior intellectual and moral stature they should be able to capture the national organisation and purge it from within. ...Allama Mashriqi's reading that at the present juncture Pakistan must show to the world that the whole nation stands solidly behind the Government is perfectly correct. Solidarity of front is the only guarantee of Pakistan's stability and future. This can only be achieved by a strong Government, commanding the respect and confidence of the people. ...Strengthening of the Muslim League organisation by incorporating the best elements of society is the only practicable constitutional method to achieve the kind of strong Government which Allama Mashriqi has in view. ...True, of late, forces of disruption, corruption and lawlessness have flared up to unusual dimensions and that is perhaps what is making the Allama, like every patriotic Pakistani, apprehensive. The remedy lies, as rightly emphasized by the Islam League leader, in a strong Government deriving strength as much from popular backing as from the integrity of its purpose and purity of its methods." (C&MG 1952 Jul. 25).

1952 August 01

The Civil & Military Gazette, Lahore publishes Mashraqi's statement:
"I have not yet received my passport but I have been given to understand that permission is being granted to me to proceed for Haj (Pilgrimage).

I intended to proceed to European and Islamic countries as well for holiday visits and I had to deliver scientific lectures before the Royal Society of Arts in England. These were not matters which should have delayed the granting of the passport.

I am a citizen of a supposedly free nation and it is most sad that such ordinary matters may be delayed and people may not be allowed to proceed to foreign countries for academic or holiday purposes.

I once again request the Government to grant me full passport so that I may make preprations for Haj and for other countries mentioned in the passport. I was never without a passport even under the British Government" (C&MG 1952 Aug. 01).

Editor's comments: Mashraqi's statement shows his frustration at the Government's delays in granting him a passport. These delays provide yet another example of the denial of civil liberties in Pakistan from the moment the country was created. Going through the newspapers of the time, it seems that there was chaos in the nation and that Safety Acts were introduced to crush individual liberties. Pakistan was supposedly created so that every Muslim, rich or poor, powerful or powerless, could enjoy freedom. Unfortunately, those in power have denied real freedom to the people since the country's independence.

1952 August 17

Maulana Fazal Hussain Dilawar (Publicity Secretary of the Punjab Islam League) is released from Lahore Central Jail. He was arrested on February 28, 1952 under the Punjab Public Safety Act (C&MG 1952 Aug. 18).

1952 August 19

Mashraqi sends a telegram to the Home Secretary (Central Government of Pakistan) regarding the Government's delay in issuing him a passport (C&MG 1952 Aug. 20).

1952 August 19

An Islam League spokesman informs the Press that Allama Mashraqi has not been issued a passport thus far for travel to some European and Muslim countries, despite repeated telephonic and telegraphic reminders to the provincial and Central Governments (C&MG 1952 Aug. 20).

1952 August 24

Mashraqi arrives in Karachi en route to Saudi Arabia (to perfom Haj). Pir Ilahi Baksh (Former Minister) is among those present at the airport to receive Mashraqi (C&MG 1952 Aug. 26).
Editor's comments: The Government had delayed issuing a passport to Mashraqi for reasons known only to them. This again shows the Government's complete disregard for civil liberties. Mashraqi was eventually issued a passport, but it restricted his travel to Saudi Arabia only. He could not go to Europe due to this reason.

1952 August 28

Mashriqi leaves for Saudia Arabia for pilgrimage (Haj). Mashraqi is given a warm send-off at the time of departure for Haj (Hussain 1991, 243).

1952 September 05

The Pakistan Times, Lahore reports that a meeting of the Islam League is to be held on September 12, 1952. The meeting is to discuss the Kashmir situation and other issues (PT 1952 Sept. 05).

1952 September 14

Prior to his return to Pakistan from Haj, Mashriqi sends the following letter to King Abdul Aziz Ibn-us-Saud of Saudi Arabia:
"Your Majesty,
...Public service never ends anywhere for those who take it up as their duty. It is in that spirit that I suggest to Your Majesty the following small proposals carrying great consequences for your immediate consideration. They involve the general good of the Musalmans throughout the world and are as follows:
Much physical pain of the Hujjaj [Pilgrims] will be relieved at the time of Hajj if everything is done in an organized way, which is comparatively easy thing for a government and can be done with the

beneficent help of the police at a very small expense. In the Holy Quran these are the following well-known words which I translate as follows: *And verily God has built up the Firmament (with millions of stars moving in it) and has established a 'balance' there so that you may not get astray in (your own) 'balance'; also so that you may establish your own balance with (perfect) uprightness and do not put the balance to loss.*

All Western nations have got on to the highest pitch of progress by sticking to these commandments of the Quran, but Muslims have not done. I, therefore, propose:

(a) During *Saee* between *Safa* and *Marwa*, also *Tawaf-i-Kaaba* and *Rami-ul-Hijjara*, also during the Hajj days, all people going one way should be kept separate from people going the other way by the police, and women should also go in separate rows.

(b) Diseased people with dirty clothes (cough, cholera typhoid) should not be allowed to enter Harmain Sharifain.

(c) People who make the surroundings of Harmain Sharifain dirty with *najasat* should be severely punished.

(d) At least 200 urinals should be made round about Harmain where there should be ample water.

It is a disgrace to Islam that in the centre of the Muslim world (viz Saudi Arabia) every article connected with social life be of Europe or American manufacture; everything in Mecca, Medina and Jeddah, from a pin or needle to motor car, and every article of food, viz fish, butter, cheese, milk, biscuits, clothes, etc. etc. be of European manufacture or American made. These articles make most vigorous propaganda among Muslims of the world that Islam is weak and Europeans are strong. The religion of God i.e., Islam, will become strong only if the Muslims and the whole world come to know that Muslims are not behind Europeans in the knowledge of Nature and industries. It is, therefore, necessary that Your Majesty introduce various industries and manufactures in Saudi Arabia very soon and train up Arabs in factories. Muslims should be sent to Europe, America, Japan, Germany to get training in the start of manufactures quickly so that in the next 25 years we get at least some articles made in Arabia.

I entreat Your Majesty to give earnest consideration to the above two proposals which will surely bring high prestige to Saudia Arabia throughout the Muslim World. In the end I send Your Majesty the first volume of my book *Tazkirah* again for your perusal so that you may think over the viewpoint of Islam as understood by me. I also send my address to the Motamar-ul-Islami in Cairo in 1926…

Your Brother,
Inayatullah"
(Hussain 1991, 249-251).

1952 September 16

The Civil & Military Gazette, Lahore reports:
"Allama Mashriqi is expected to arrive in Lahore on Friday [September 19, 1952], when an address of welcome will be presented to him at a public meeting by the Islam League, says Dr. Abdul Wadud, General Secretary Pakistan Islam League. According to a telegraphic message received by the Markazi [Central] Islam League, Lahore from Karachi, the Allama was to land in Karachi on Monday [September 15, 1952] night.

Public meetings and receptions are also being arranged in Karachi" (C&MG 1952 Sept. 16).

Editor's comments: According to Syed Shabbir Hussain's *Al-Mashriqi: The Disowned Genius*, Mashriqi returned to Pakistan on September 17, 1952 (Hussain 1991, 243).

1952 September 17

Mashraqi returns from Saudi Arabia after perfoming Haj. (Hussain 1991, 243).

1952 September 18

Mashraqi meets with Fatima Jinnah (Quaid-i-Azam Mohammad Ali Jinnah's sister), Din Mohammad (Governor of Sind), and Hadwin (Canadian High Commissioner) in Karachi (C&MG 1952 Sept. 19).

The Civil & Military Gazette, Lahore reports, "Allama Mashriqi, founder of the Islam League, who will arrive at Walton Airport [Lahore] from Karachi at 10 a.m. on Saturday [September 20, 1952], will address a public meeting outside Mochi Gate, Lahore, at 7-30 p.m. the same day" (C&MG 1952 Sept. 18).

1952 September 19

The Civil & Military Gazette, Lahore reports, "Allama Inayatullah Khan Mashriqi, founder of the Islam League will not be able to arrive in Lahore on Saturday [September 20, 1952], as reported earlier, says the APP. He will now arrive on Monday [September 22, 1952] morning by air" (C&MG 1952 Sept. 19).

1952 September 21

The Civil & Military Gazette, Lahore reports that Mashraqi "is returning to Lahore on the morning of September 22 [1952].
He is expected to address a public meeting in Lahore the same evening" (C&MG 1952 Sept. 21).

1952 September 22

Allama Mashraqi is given a rousing welcome upon his arrival in Lahore after performing Haj (Pilgrimage). He later addresses a massive public meeting. *The Civil & Military Gazette*, Lahore of September 23, 1952 would report:

"Allama Mashriqi, founder of the Islam League, on Monday [September 22, 1952] fervently appealed to all political parties to eschew differences and strengthen the hands of the Government, as the country was passing through a critical juncture.

The Allama, who was addressing a largely-attended public meeting sponsored by the Central Islam League and presided over by Dr. Syed Abdul Wadud, Islam League General Secretary, in Lahore, also called upon the people to stand united and co-operate with the Government in solving the Kashmir issue and economic problems of the country. The Allama said: 'It is an hour of emergency. The Pakistan Government is beset with many difficulties and our country is surrounded by enemies. We should not create difficulties for the Government but, rather, extend our full co-operation to it in solving the Kashmir problem and other issues confronting the country.'

He said that he was sure that if the public extended a helping hand with a solemn faith, all the difficulties and problems confronting the country could be solved within a few months.

The Allama criticized the Muslim League Government for committing a number of blunders and said that it had failed to industrialize the country, which offered the only solution for economic development of Pakistan, which consisted of provinces considered to be defecit areas.

Referring to the Kashmir problem, Allama Mashriqui said that the Pakistan people should depend upon their own inherent strength to solve it. He deplored that every effort to solve the issue amicably had failed and the Government had incurred a huge expenditure without any fruitful results. 'We should no longer remain silent, but try to find an early solution of the Kashmir question,' he added.

The Allama said that the food problem was also directly connected with the Kashmir dispute, for the Indian Government was responsible for the inadequate supply of canal water in Pakistan. 'If we succeed in getting Kashmir, our crops will find enough water to flourish and the food shortage will automatically disappear,' he added.

The Allama declared that he proposed to convene an All-Party meeting to consider the political and economic situation in the country.

Allama Mashriqi, who had recently returned to Pakistan after performing Haj, apprised the public of the social, economic, political and moral conditions of Saudi Arabia and said that the Saudi Government had provided many facilities to Haj pilgrims.

Mr. Qaisar Mustafa, General Secretary of the Punjab Islam League, and Mr. Safdar Saleemi also addressed the meeting.

Later, a procession, led by Maulana Fazal Husain Dilawar and Mr. Zia Ambalvi, paraded the Chamberlain Road and terminated at the headquarters of the Islam League.

Earlier, Allama Mashriqi was given a rousing reception at the Lahore Civil Aerodrome when he arrived in Lahore on Monday morning" (C&MG 1952 Sept. 23).

1952 September 24

The Civil & Military Gazette, Lahore publishes an editorial regarding Allama Mashraqi's statement in Lahore on September 22, 1952. According to the editorial:
"Allama Mashriqi, Islam League Chief, gave a very sound lead to the country in his Lahore public address in calling upon the nation to eschew the path of differences and strengthen the Government's hands in this hour of emergency when so many vital problems were confronting Pakistan. No one knows better than founder of the former Khaksar movement of which *ita'at-i-amir* (obedience to constituted authority) was the corner-stone that Islam conceives of Muslim bodypolitic as a well-knit and well disciplined organism, functioning with complete unity of purpose under a single high-command known as Imam, Amir, Khalifa or, in modern political parlance, the Prime Minister who is supposed to be the executive head of the State. Be it said to the credit of the Khaksar movement that for a while it restored that cohesion to the scattered ranks of Islam in this country and Muslims of all schools and shades of political and religious thought rubbed shoulders in a common endeavour to reconstruct and uplift the nation through discipline and social service. Allama Mashriqi's advice to the people to close up their ranks and rally around the Government in this difficult hour is quite in keeping with the Islamic philosophy of *ul-ul-Amr*. Time and again we have stressed in these

columns that mere unity and solidarity of front will mean half the battle against our problems won. Disruption and disintegration, even though fomented in the name of religion, are the negation of Islam. The Prophet had even a mosque pulled down because it tended to show dissensions in Muslims' ranks. The Quran specifically mentions this mosque and condemns it unsparing terms. We believe those who split up the ranks of Islam into 'sects' were guilty of the same offence as the founders of the Divinely condemned Zarrar Mosque. Islam aims at the unification of the whole of the human race. Like air, water, sunshine, Islam caters to the basic needs of human nature and is of universal application. Its only weapon to convert others is to appeal to their innate light of reason and conscience. It is a tragedy that this great cementing force has been converted by our Ulema, well versed in the letter of the law but foreign to its spirit, into a cult of force, coercion, hatred, disruption and disintegration. For the last five years, they have been quarreling over what an Islamic Constitution should be like – not because it is not a very simple affair, but because they want something to quarrel about. Allama Mashriqi is a thinker and scholar of repute. He can make a great contribution towards the conservation of the inner spirit of Islam among Muslims, which alone, not the observances and rituals, can make Pakistan strong and great. His call to the nation to stand united, to strengthen the Government's hands and to shun disruptive tendencies truly reflect the essence of the Islamic message" (C&MG 1952 Sept. 24).

1952 October 10

Mashraqi addresses a huge gathering in Gujranwala. *Dawn*, Karachi of October 14, 1952 would report:
"The leader of the Pakistan Islam League, Allama Inayatullah Khan Mashriqi, accused the Nehru Government of constructing stupendous dams in Kashmir to dry up the Pakistan rivers.
Addressing a mammoth gathering here on Friday night, Allama Mashriqi revealed that the dam projects would cost the Bharati [Indian] exchequer Rs. 1,960,000,000 and would be completed in 1956.
'This conspiracy has been hatched up to spread death and starvation in Pakistan and thus force us to seek re-union with Bharat [India],' he added.
He said that the best way to counter these intrigues was to forge a united front of all the political parties in the country and then to make a 'supreme' effort to liberate Kashmir.

Allama Mashriqi accused Muslim League Ministeries for the present 'crisis.' He declared that he did not want to say anything which would simply add to the present difficulties of the Pakistan Government" (*Dawn* 1952 Oct. 14).

1952 October 11

Allama Mashriqi, who is Convener of an All-Party Conference, sends a telegram to Khawaja Nazimud Din (Prime Minister of Pakistan) regarding the Muslim League session in Dacca:
"On behalf of the Islam League, Jinnah Awami Muslim League and other prominent political parties and persons about to represent to the Pakistan Government jointly for amalgamation of all parties, including the Muslim League, and for the constitution of a strongest possible Government sucessfully to face the grave aggression of Pandit Nehru on Kashmir, I request the Pakistan Premier to compel the Dacca Muslim League session to consider most seriously the practical method of possession of Kashmir, disregarding altogether the penmethod so far adopted.

With respectful emphasis, I warn you again against the calamity which must befall Pakistanis if Kashmir is finally lost through U.N. Only before such an unfortunate thing happens can Pakistan take an effective step. I can assure the Premier that matters can still be amended by courage and determination.

I request the Premier not to disregard our serious request at this grave juncture and give general satisfaction to the public of Pakistan by giving me an assuring reply."
Mashraqi also sends copies of the telegram to Mr. Hashim Gazdar (M.C.A.), Sardar Abdur Rab Nishtar, Mr. Muhammad Ayyub Khuhro, Mr. Altaf Hussain (Editor, *Dawn*), and others (C&MG 1952 Oct. 13).

1952 October 24

Kashmir Day is observed throughout Pakistan. Mashraqi addresses a huge crowd at a public meeting in Rawalpindi. *The Pakistan Times*, Lahore of October 25, 1952 would report:
"The Islam League leader Allama Mashriqi said in Rawalpindi on Friday that the Kashmir issue and the fast deteriorating economic situation were the two 'most serious' problems now facing Pakistan. He said that in this 'extreme situation' the party in power should no longer adopt an isolationist attitude and should win the confidence of the people and the Opposition to 'avert a major crisis'...

Allama Mashriqi was speaking at the Kashmir Day celebrations in the Liaquat Bagh. Dr. Syed Abdul Wadud presided.

The Islam League chief warned the Pakistan Government that the United Nations had definite plans to shelve the Kashmir issue indefinitely to please India. He said that the Western Powers, together with India, were under the impression that there was disruption in Pakistan and the people were no longer behind the Government. It was therefore, imperative that we should unite as one in the battle of Kashmir and tell the entire world that on this issue the people were at the back of their Government. He declared, 'Meanwhile India is busy in her plans to turn Pakistan into a desert by diverting the course of rivers now irrigating West Pakistan'" (PT 1952 Oct. 25; Hussain 1994, 39; Zaman 1987, 386; Mashraqi [1931] 1997, 33).

1952 October 27

Mashraqi's book, *Hareem-e-Ghaib*, is published (Mashraqi [1931] 1997, 9, 261).

1952 November 10

Mashriqi's book, *Deh al' baab*, is published (Mashraqi [1931] 1997, 9, 261).

1952 November 18

The Civil & Military Gazette, Lahore's delegate interviews Mashraqi. Mashraqi warns the leaders and the nation of the designs of the powerful nations regarding Kashmir issue.

"'Various devices are being adopted by big Powers to overawe the Pakistan Goverment in regard to the dangerous consequences of starting a war with India so that Pakistan may become a perfect nonentity in the ensuing world struggle and one of these devilish devices has already come forth in the form of a peace move from Russia,' declared the 64-year old chief of the Pakistan Islam League and the founder of the former Khaksar organisation, Allama Inayatuallah Khan Mashriqi, in an exclusive interview with the *Civil and Military Gazette* representative, in Lahore on Tuesday, when asked to give his reaction to the recent Communist-sponsored peace rallies in the Punjab just after the return to Pakistan of the delegates to the Asian peace Conference held in the capital of Communist China.

The Allama who has been known for his anti-imperialistic proclivities, added that 'meaningless people, who cannot see politics beyond their noses have been stage-managed...have been shown only what was intended to be shown, and have come forward with new trumpets of Russia's so-called peace move.'

The Islam League leader, who had earlier accused the Anglo-American bloc of sidetracking the Kashmir issue and dodging its solution, further said that Russia, too, intended 'to make Pakistan perfectly impotent in the matter of Kashmir, to make India perfectly satisfied and safe from Pakistan and to prepare India for Russian domination in the next world war.'

The 'great' Azad Pakistan Party, the Allama regretted, whose members were now granted passports for every imaginable trifling occasion in the world, was 'performing a double service in this respect, and its tenacity to let the Kashmir matter be shelved looks most ominous.'

Allama Inayatullah Khan Mashriqi, who is the author of a foremost book on the scientific aspect Islam, 'Tazkara', and is known for his opposition to mullaism, with a grim look on his face and a glow in his eyes, emphatically declared: 'For a Musalman, Jehad is the sole line of his life and nothing but downright jehad has saved him these 1400 years. We are already suffering the terrible consequences of 100 years of harangues by our politicians against jehad and the result is the poor pittance, along with enormous sufferings, that we have got as our share in the form of Pakistan.'

'If even this Pakistan is not going to remain with us without a struggle and after the empty threats of Hindus concerning Kashmir, then Lord alone save Pakistan and the 100 million Muslims of the Indo-Pakistan sub-continent,' he added.

Profusely quoting from the Quran, the Allama said: 'The Quran unequivocally says that a *momin* is only he who takes active part in *jehad*.'

The best part of the foreign game, the Islam League leader said was perhaps, the verdict of 'our own religious men,' who had suddenly switched themselves on to the Communist Russian way of thinking with Quran on their lips.

In the course of the one and a half hour interview, the Allama further said that his Rawalpindi speech in October this year was sufficiently forceful to rouse the imagination of Pakistani Musalmans as to what was going to happen with regard to Kashmir in the United Nations.

'I laid emphasis on the point that Kashmir issue will be virtually shelved by the UNO and both parties will be asked to 'settle' the matter among themselves. This has, indeed happened since then and the rest I said in this connection will follow.'

Allama Inayatullah Khan Mashriqi said that at this critical moment of Pakistan's life 'I make an appeal to the young men, specially the student community and women of Pakistan to stand again upon their legs and teach their elders and so called superiors to realise the terrible situation they are in and prepare every possible individual for the coming struggle.'

'I feel sure that only these two disinterested communities can see Islam in its original form and not those who have got vested interests and blurred imagination out of fear and wrong training,' he added.

The Islam League leader further said: 'What has actually come from the American side was forecast by me in a warning I gave in Rawalpindi that an unusually large number of American stooges were coming into Pakistan. In various innocent garbs to prepare the way for a complete showdown in Kashmir affair'" (C&MG 1952 Nov. 19).

1952 November 20

The Civil & Military Gazette, Lahore publishes an editorial entitled "Mashriqi's Warning." The editorial states:

"The Moscow-inspired 'peace' drive in this country...was described by Allama Mashriqi, in a Press Interview, as a deliberate move to cripple this country's war potential vis-à-vis the Kashmir liberation struggle in which Russia's strategy, according to him, was as pro-Indian as that of the Anglo American bloc. He uttered a grim warning against any attempt to weaken the 'Jihad' spirit which was the only guarantee of the survival of Pakistan as an independent State. An attempt has been made in some quarters to show that the 'peace' movement is inspired by nothing but humanitarian motives, that it has nothing to do with Russia or Communism and that it is an all-human issue. This claim is belied by the fact that while speeches and resolutions at these 'peace' conferences condemn hostilities and bloodshed in Malaya and Indo-China where the Western Powers are involved, there is not a whisper about the USSR's part in undermining world peace. The sum-total effect of the campaign is that while the Anglo-Americans are war mongers, Communists who foment discontent and class hatred the world over, thereby breeding the germs of war, are just innocent lambs. Those engaged in this campaign cannot, therefore, honestly disown responsibility for acting as Communist agents, even though unwittingly in some cases, as well as for the disastrous consequences of such activities to the security of Pakistan. This State was founded to work out the Islamic ideology. Any attempt to weaken faith in that ideology or divert attention to a rival ideology is decidedly an anti-State activity. Allama Mashriqi rightly described these activities applauding the so-called 'wonderful achievements' of Communism as 'trumpet blowing.' They have little foundation in reality, because foreign visitors are shown, as the Allama put it, 'Only what is intended to be shown.' One of these delegates to the Peking Conference, Mr. Mahmud Ali Qasuri, who spent only fourteen days in China – a period too brief to fully know even one's own home town – gave the Lahore rotarians a rosy picture of the wonderful all-round progress in every sphere of life by a huge country like China. Obviously he was only passing on the information he had gathered during his two weeks' stay in Peking from official sources. This kind of trumpet-blowing only throws dust in the people's eyes and undermines the ideological solidarity of this State. Nothing is more dangerous to this young State than to sow seeds of intellectual disintegration by trying to divide the people's loyalties between Islam and Communism. This State was founded on the Islamic ideology and by that ideology it must stand or fall. Muslims will simply refuse to look at any other ideology in the presence of an inspiration like the Quran – the fountain-head of all light and life. A strong Pakistan, capable of defending her territorial integrity with the hot blood of her youth, is the only guarantee of a free Pakistan. By her very geographical and historical situation, she has either to become a first rate military power or perish" (C&MG 1952 Nov. 20).

1952 November 23

The Civil & Military Gazette, Lahore reports, "Mashriqi refuses to compromise basic principles." According to the newspaper:

"Allama Inayatullah Khan Mashriqi, founder of the Islam League and chief of the former Khaksar movement took a very firm stand against an overwhelming majority of hostile 'opportunist' members of the Islam League Executive Committee who accused the Allama of 'saying a right thing at the wrong moment' in an interview with the *Civil and Military Gazette* representative in which he had condemned the communist-sponsored Peace movement and those propagating it in Pakistan, when the Committee met in Lahore on Friday night under the chairmanship of Sheikh Qamar-ud-Din.

The Allama declared: 'I cannot compromise principles and the ideology for which I have stood all my life.'

The accusers of Allama Mashriqi pointed out that no doubt he had given a truthful statement against the peace movement but it was not 'diplomatic' to do so in view of the fact that efforts were being made for an all-party convention.

The founder of the organisation further said: 'The Committee had full right to amend the policy and programme of the organisation but in major national and Islamic issues, no check could be put on him.'

The founder of the Islam League further said: 'I do not hold any office in the Islam League, nor am I a member of the organisation, I would also not like to interfere with the decisions of the organisation. As the founder of the Islam League, too, I need not to be connected to the organisation. Whatever I speak or write is concerned with Islam and the nation rather with the Islam League.

The Allama declared in unequivocal terms that being the founder of the Islam League he was free from and unconcerned with every policy and programme of the organisation. Whatever he was doing for the country and the nation was not as the leader of a political party but as a person who feels and translates national demands.

The Allama, who is 64, having to his credit more than 30 years of political struggle went to the extent of saying: 'If in the interest of the country and the nation, at any stage, the need be to dissolve the Islam League then he would irrespective of any counsel and expediency, dissolve it.'

Some prominent workers of the Islam League declared his reply to their criticism as undemocratic and called upon him to clarify his position with respect to the Executive Committee as well as his own rights and powers.

Allama Mashriqi, in reply to the criticism, said: 'Pakistan and the Islamic world at the moment, was confronted with gigantic problems and the question of life and death. The need for national unity in Pakistan and the unity of the Islamic world were so urgent and internationally important that it would not be fair for him to be a mere party man.

The Committee also took some other decision regarding the organisational work of the Islam League" (C&MG 1952 Nov. 23).

Editor's comments: Mashraqi was never above criticism and was not a dictator, as has been implied in some published works. The above example shows that he was open to criticism from others. His words also illustrate that he always kept the larger public interest in mind. There are countless such examples that support all of this.

1952 November 23

Mashriqi's book, *Armughan-e-Hakeem*, is published (Mashraqi [1931] 1997, 9, 261).

1952 November 25

The Pakistan Times, Lahore reports that the executive committee of the Islam League held a meeting in Lahore. Mashraqi was invited to attend the meeting as an observer. Certain members objected to Mashraqi's statement, which was published in *The Civil & Military Gazette*, Lahore on November 19, 1952. *The Pakistan Times*, Lahore states, "The Allama, replying to the objection declared that he was not even a 2-anna member of the Islam League. His statements and views, therefore, could not be interpreted as the deliberations of the Islam League" (PT 1952 Nov. 25).

1952 November 25

Mashriqi's book, *Hadees-ul-Quran*, is published (Mashraqi [1931] 1997, 9, 262).

1952 November 29

The Civil & Military Gazette, Lahore publishes, Mashraqi's Press Statement.
Allama Mashriqi, the founder of Islam League has issued the following statement to the Press:

"Our Governor-General has very astutely put forward in his Bahawalpur speech the plea that the Opposition of Pakistan must be based on sound footing. This looks a very sound piece of advice for those who would leave exploration of that sound footing to the Opposition, as this may never come about to the entire satisfaction of the party in power. As, however, the Government appears to me to be slowly and steadily realizing the disadvantages of its isolation at this critical juncture. I put forward a definite proposal to the Muslim League in the light of what the Governor-General has said.

'I feel that sound footing for all times in the striving for the material strength of Pakistan disregarding all the particular ideologies which any party, including the Muslim League, holds. If this basis is accepted, no party in the land can come exclusively to power and this is exactly what the Prophet means by saying: 'Opposition in my ummat is a blessing."

TWO ISSUES

'At this particular moment, two things have been laid before the Opposition parties at the several meetings held lately—the question of possession of Kashmir and rectification of economic deterioration. Both require a supreme effort by the whole ummat to solve them.'

'I have appealed to all the parties to let their particular ideologies not interfere with this scheme of the strengthening of Pakistan. I have every hope that Opposition parties will all agree on this highest common factor of Islamic politics. It is time now for the Governor-General of Pakistan and his Government to come forward and without fearing an Opposition staring in the face, welcome the help they ought to give as Muslims, so that the Opposition might become a blessing in fact.'" (C&MG 1952 Nov. 29).

Editor's comments: Mashraqi attempted to cooperate with the government on various occassions in order to put Pakistan on the right track. Yet, the government remained unresponsive for vested interests.

1952 December 01

The Communist Peace Committee invites the President of the Punjab Islam League, Qamar ud Din, to attend a Peace Congress in Vienna on December 12, 1952. Qamar ud Din declines the offer.

Editor's comments: According to the *The Civil & Military Gazette* newspaper, Mashraqi, despite his poor health, had no objection to attending the conference in order to get first hand information as to what the Communists Peace Committee was doing behind closed doors. He conveyed his message to the Committee through Mian Mehmood Ali Qasuri. (C&MG 1952 Dec. 05).

1953-54

"Blessed is the nation which selects the best leaders"

– Nasim Yousaf

1953

1953 January 27

Mashraqi meets with the Prime Minister of Pakistan, Khawaja Nazimuddin, in Karachi. The meeting lasts for two hours (C&MG 1953 Feb. 25).

1953 February 08

The Islam League holds a meeting in Lahore. At the meeting, it is decided that elections for the City Islam League will be held on February 15, 1953 (PT 1953 Feb. 09).

1953 February 14

In Lahore, Mashraqi addresses a symposium held under the auspices of the Punjab University Journalists Association. *The Civil & Military Gazette* of February 15, 1953 would report:

"Allama Inayatullah Khan al-Mashriqi, founder of the Islam League, declared in Lahore on Saturday that Islam was the greatest upholder of the freedom of writing and pointed out that this freedom was restricted in the Islamic State of Pakistan.

He was speaking at a symposium on the functions and problems of 'our Press' and 'our political parties' held under the auspices of the Punjab University Journalists Association in the Talim-ul-Islam College Hall. Allama Alauddin Siddiqi, Head of the Department of Islamiat, Punjab University presided.

Allama Mashriqi also appealed to political parties and the Press to join hands together to face the grave threat to the solidarity of Pakistan. He said that all must rise above party politics and without giving up their ideologies agree on certain matters to work unitedly for the good of the nation and State...

Allama Mashriqi said that since the inception of Pakistan, there had been a steady of deterioration in the morale of the Press, so much so that at present, no journalist pursued his professional duties according to the dictates of his own conscience. The main cause of it was that, to maintain itself in power, the Government had devised peculiar methods. He said that, on the other hand it was very essential that the Press should have enjoyed greater freedom in an Islamic State.

'We are confronted with many serious problems, which should have been solved four years ago. It is as a result of our disunity and non-cooperation among ourselves that Pakistan to-day finds itself confronted with a very serious situation,' he said.

The Allama made a strong appeal for unity of thought among an independent and freedom-loving nation.

He said that it was high time that politicians and journalists get together further to strengthen the solidarity of the nation and State." (C&MG 1953 Feb.15).

1953 February 20

Mashraqi leaves Lahore for Sind to attend Islam League meetings in various cities, including Sukkur, Mirpurkhas, and Nawabshah. He is accompanied by Dr. Abdul Wadood (Secretary General of the Islam League) and other members of the party (C&MG 1953 Feb. 21).

1953 February 21

Mashraqi speaks to an audience in Hyderabad. *The Civil & Military Gazette* of February 23, 1953 would report:

"The Islam League leader, Allama Inayatullah Khan Mashriqi, appealed on Saturday to the people of Pakistan to intensify their efforts to liberate their Kashmiri brethren from the clutches of Dogra-cum-Indian tyrants.

He asked them to volunteer themselves in large numbers for 'jehad' in Kashmir...

Allama Mashriqi told his audience that India had decided to starve West Pakistan by diverting the canal waters from flowing into these areas. The Pakistan Government, he added, were fully aware of the danger. But they were continuing a policy of appeasement towards India.

He urged upon the people of Pakistan to force a united front for consolidating Pakistan and saving it from the evil designs of its enemies.

Allama Mashriqi advised the people not to launch any agitation against the Government at this stage lest it should help Pakistan's enemies.

Earlier, Allama Mashriqi, on his arrival at Hyderabad railway station was given a rousing reception by the citizens and members of the Islam League and was taken in a procession through the main thoroughfares of the city" (C&MG 1953 Feb. 23).

1953 February 22

At a public meeting in Hyderabad (Sind), Maulana Fazal Hussain Dilawar (an Islam League leader) announces that he will fast unto death. *The Civil & Military Gazette*, Lahore of February 24, 1953 would report:

"Maulana Fazal Hussain Dilawar, an Islam League leader, declared at a public meeting here last night that he would start a fast unto death with effect from March 15 on the Indo-Pakistan border at Wagah if Pandit Nehru's Government did not stop its plan to starve the people of West Pakistan by diverting the flow of canal waters into Pakistan territory.

Maulana Fazal Hussain Dilawar appealed to Pandit Nehru to give up that inhuman plan. The aim of his fast, he explained, would also be to force the Pakistan Government to take some concrete and effective steps to save the people of Pakistan from starvation that would follow in the wake of closure of the canals.

The Islam League leader appealed to all lovers of humanity, irrespective of caste, creted [creed], colour or religion to support the cause for which, he said, he had decided to lay down his life" (C&MG 1953 Feb. 24).

1953 February 25

The Civil & Military Gazette, Lahore publishes a letter sent to the newspaper by an individual from Lahore. The letter states:

"Sir,- Allama Mashriqi's statement to the Press regarding his two-hour talk with the Prime Minister [Khawaja Nazimuddin] on 27th January at Karachi, has created the hope that conditions in Pakistan will improve. Khwaja Nazimuddin is to be congratulated for saying that he is ready to hear Mashriqi in all matters of grave importance. The Kashmir question and the canal water problem are matters of grave importance to Pakistan. Such disputes cannot be solved through negotiations. But according to Mashriqi they can be solved without resort to war. By this he means that the Government should militarise the whole nation. He believes that the Hindu has never been a fighter and that he can be demoralised and dissuaded from his bad intentions, if the whole of our nation is organised properly on military lines. In my opnion, such a difficult task can be accomplished by none other than Allama himself. If supported by the Government he can make us a soldier nation in short while. The Hindus have always been afraid of him. When in November 1947 he gave a call to the nation to come to Kashmir, some Hindu papers wrote: 'Mashriqi in command of

Muslims in Kashmir' and 'he is soon going to attack East Punjab.' The result was that several Hindus began to evacuate East Punjab.
The organising capacity of the Allama should be utilized by the Government. I would request all political parties to join hands with him and form a united front in this national emergency.
-'Emergency'" (C&MG 1953 Feb. 25).

1953 March

Mashriqi addresses people at Jacobabad (Mashraqi [1931] 1997, 33).

1953 July

Mashraqi invites Nehru for a meeting to solve the Kashmir and canal water issues during Nehru's upcoming visit to Pakistan (PT 1953 Jul. 20).
Editor's comments: Mashriqi's telegram to Nehru was sent prior to July 25, 1953, but the exact date of the telegram was not traceable.

1953 July 19

The Civil and Military Gazette, Lahore publishes Mashriqi's statement warning the Government to settle the Kashmir and river water issues during Nehru's forthcoming visit (C&MG 1953 Jul. 19; Zaman 1987, 393-394).

1954

1954

Mashriqi delivers an address in Peshawar (Mashraqi [1931] 1997, 40).
Editor's comments: The exact date of his address could not be traced.

1954

An American woman visits Mashriqi and offers him funds. Mashraqi declines (Zaman 1988, 68-69).
Editor's comments: The source does not list the exact date of her visit. Further details on the incident can be found in Sher Zaman's book *Khaksar Tehrik Ki Jiddo Johad Volume III*, pages 68-69.

1954 June 09

The Civil and Military Gazette, Lahore publishes a statement by Allama Mashraqi (Zaman 1987, 395).

1954 October 08

Dawn, Karachi publishes an exclusive interview with Allama Mashraqi (Zaman 1987, 397).

1954 November 05

Mashriqi delivers a speech at Shahi Mosque, Lahore (Mashraqi [1931] 1997, 29).

1954 December 31

Dawn, Karachi publishes a proposal by Allama Mashraqi. In the proposal, Mashraqi provides an election procedure in which the poor masses could also have representation in the Government (Zaman 1987, 398).

1955

"The first step to defoliation of a nation: wrong selection of leaders"

– Nasim Yousaf

1955

1955

Mashriqi writes the *Human Problem: A Message to the Knowers of Nature* (Mashraqi [1931] 1997, 9).
Editor's comments: The exact date of publication was not listed in the source used.

Dr. Mahmood Hassan (Vice Chancellor, University of Dhaka) writes to Mashriqi:
"Not only in Pakistan but in the Middle East countries of which I have personal knowledge and experience I have had many discussions with (educated) and so called Westernised Muslims, European and Christian Orientalists like Zwemer, Margoliouth, Gibb, Gillaume, Tritton, Ceon, Hitti, Costi, Zurayk etc., and have read almost all the books which have been written in English and French during the last 20 years. I had the privilege of knowing Allama Iqbal intimately and had to seek his guidance. I came to the conclusion that we need badly a violent jolt, and if it comes from you it will be most effective, for there is hardly anyone today who has your knowledge and scholarship and who has thought so deeply about the fundamentals of Islam" (Hussain 1988, 272).
Editor's comments: The exact date of Dr. Mahmood Hassan's letter was not listed in the source used.

1955 June 25

The inquiry report into the assassination of Prime Minister Liaquat Ali Khan states that the Khaksars were not involved in his murder and that there was no conspiracy. C.W. U'ren, a British security expert, had been appointed by the Government of Pakistan to conduct this inquiry into the circumstances surrounding the murder of the Prime Minister (PT 1955 Jun. 26; PT 1955 Jun. 28).
Editor's comments: From the very creation of Pakistan, the Government did not miss any opportunity to blame and arrest Mashraqi's followers to prevent them from taking part in political activities. This was again the case when Liaquat Ali Khan was murdered and anti-Mashraqi elements tried to implicate the Khaksars/Razakars. As usual, the Khaksars were not involved and therefore were cleared of any wrongdoing.

1955 June 26

Dawn, Karachi publishes C.W.E. U'ren's report regarding Prime Minister Liaquat Ali Khan's murder. C.W.E. U'ren, a British Security expert, had been appointed by the Government of Pakistan to investigate the circumstances surrounding Liaquat Ali Khan's assassination. According to his report:

"Whatever political differences may have existed amongst Pakistan's leading men, there is no evidence whatsoever to suggest that anyone of them was in the remotest way interested in the murder of their Prime Minister...

The first reaction of the Rawalpindi authorities to the murder was that a Khaksar or Khaksars were responsible for it and leading Khaksars were rounded up with a view to taking them into protective custody and interrogating them.

Their leader, Allama Mashriqi was under detention at the time and it was reasonable to assume that this action of the Government might have incensed the members of the Organisation to such an extent that they plotted to take the life of the Prime Minister, under whose orders the Allama was said to have been detained...

After full consideration I think that any suggestion that the Khaksars were concerned in a conspiracy to murder the Prime Minister or to inspire Said Akbar to do so can be definitely discounted" (*Dawn* 1955 Jun. 26).

Editor's comments: Anti-Khaksar elements had tried to put the blame on the Khaksars for the murder of Prime Minister Liaquat Ali Khan. The Government's first reaction always seemed to be to blame the Khaksars. However, the Khaksars were once again exonerated of any wrongdoing.

1955 September 21

In a public address in Karachi, Mashraqi suggests the establishment of a scientific institute in Karachi. He appeals to wealthy businessmen and the affluent to come forward and contribute towards this cause, as Pakistan's development in the field of science is extremely important. He states that scientific supremacy over India is necessary to obtain Kashmir (Hussain 1994, 78-79).

Editor's comments: Mashraqi was the first prominent leader who valued the importance of educating the entire nation and developing Pakistan in the field of science. He regretted that the Government of Pakistan was not placing emphasis on education and scientific development, which should be the highest priority for any nation. He stressed that the development of scientific minds would help the nation to achieve supremacy in the world.

1955 September 23 - 25

An Islam League Convention is held at Jehangir Park, Karachi. The Convention is attended by Fazlul Haq (Minister of the Interior), Sardar Abdul Hameed Dasti, Col. Abid Hussain (Minister for Kashmir Affairs), and Sardar Abdul Qayyum (President All-Jammu and Kashmir Conference). On September 23, 1955, Allama Mashraqi addresses 200,000 people at the Convention (Zaman 1987, 400). *The Civil and Military Gazette* would report:

"Allama Inayatullah Khan Mashriqi, the Islam League President, yesterday [September 23, 1955] made an impassioned appeal to his countrymen to put a stop to day-dreaming and face the hard facts of life, courageously and boldly.

He was addressing a public meeting held here last night in connection with the All-Pakistan Islam League Convention which commenced yesterday. The Convention will continue till Sunday [September 25, 1955].

Allama Mashriqi underlined the need for strengthening the moral fiber [of the nation]. He exhorted his audience to inculcate in them the spirit of true Islam, i.e., the spirit of self-sacrifice, ceaseless work and bold attempt to conquer the nature.

The urge to live and conquer nature he said, was the first requisite of a living and progressive nation.

'If this urge dies,' he added 'the nation's lease of life on this planet ends.'

He said for the last eight years 'we Pakistanis have been living on hopes – pious and false hopes – now the time has come when we should break this glorious cobweb and face the hard facts of life in all their nakedness.

If you develop this concept of life and create this spirit in you Kashmir will be yours for the asking' he declared.

Allama Mashriqi averted 'you will have nothing to fear and your creative energies will swell you on to the top of the creation'" (C&MG 1955 Sept. 25).

Allama Mashraqi also addresses the people at the conclusion of the Convention on September 25, 1955. *Dawn*, Karachi of September 26, 1955 would report:

"Allama Inayatullah Khan Mashriqi, the Islam League leader, yesterday advised the people to forget their petty and personal differences for a common cause in the larger interest of the country.

He was speaking at the third and concluding session of the Islam League Convention at the Jehangir Park last night.

Allama Mashriqi said that it was the constant struggle, the faith in the principles of Islam and the teachings of the Holy Quran which established Pakistan. The same struggle, he added could now lead Pakistan towards strength and prosperity.

Allama Mashriqi announced that he had received several letters from the people of every walk of life pledging that they would sacrifice their lives and belongings for the great cause of the liberation of Kashmir.

The Minister for Kashmir Affairs, Syed Abid Husain, who presided over the session said that the all-party convention which was scheduled to be held shortly would provide an occasion for the thorough consideration of the matter.

On the appeal of Allama Mashriqi, Syed Abid Husain pledged that his private and public life would be free from falsehood" (*Dawn* 1955 Sept. 26).

Yusuf Haroon (MCA) also makes a statement at this meeting (*Dawn* 1955 Sept. 26; Hussain 1994, 50).

Editor's comments: Thousands of Khaksars/Razakars from all over Pakistan attended this convention.

1955 September 25

The Civil & Military Gazette, Lahore publishes an editorial entitled "Sound Diagnosis." In the editorial, the newspaper writes:

"Allama Mashriqi, addressing the Islam League convention last Friday [September 23, 1955] dismissed the idea of regaining the lost paradise of Kashmir through satyagraha as pure moonshine. Few will disagree with his diagnosis of the nation's 'guts' and stamina when he, with almost brutal frankness, reminded that the 'Kashmir chalo' movement might attract a train-load of volunteers at Karachi but by the time they reached the Kashmir border, very few of them would be left to face the ordeal. Unless the nation built up its delapidated character, he emphasised, it could not wrest even a small hut from the hands of India, to say nothing of Kashmir. With truly 'Islamic character' to stand up and suffer for a cause, Kashmir, he assured, would like a ripe apple, fall in our lap. This old Khaksar Founder-leader, it must be admitted was cent per cent right in his diagnosis. We are at the moment fast becoming a nation of slogan mongers. It is time we called a halt to this cheap view of life's struggle. That is not the path to national survival. In strength of national character lies the only key to Kashmir, as indeed, to all national problems" (C&MG 1955 Sept. 25).

1955 October 27

Mashriqi is invited to attend a Kashmir conference in Karachi starting on November 26, 1955. Invitations to attend the conference are issued on behalf of Ch. Mohammad Ali (Prime Minister of Pakistan) to leaders of all political parties in the country (East and West Pakistan) (C&MG 1955 Oct. 28).

1955 November 07

Allama Mashriqi addresses a large public meeting in Lyallpur (now Faisalabad) at an open session of a two day conference of the district Islam League. *The Civil & Military Gazette* of November 09, 1955 would report:

"Allama Inayatullah Khan Mashriqi founder of the Islam League declared here last night that the solution of Kashmir problem had passed the stage of a negotiated settlement and thought satyagraha of Razakars and army personnel as the only alternative. Allama Mashriqi was addressing a public meeting at the open session of the two-day conference of the district Islam League.

Addressing a gathering of over 20,000 people he said the Islam League at its recent Karachi convention raised the demand of securing Kashmir for Pakistan. He made two proposals for winning Kashmir for Pakistan.

Firstly, he said that the eight crores [80 million] of Pakistanis should unite solidly for the purpose. They should also raise their moral standards, he added. The officials should also become honest in discharging their duties. This he said, would instill a spirit of patriotism and sacrifice in the people.

Secondly, he offered the services, if need be, of 10,000 volunteers or even of a 100,000 for satyagraha. He said these volunteers would gladly accept the bullets of Nehru in Kashmir. But he said, that army personnel should also take part...

He added, if these measures were adopted Kashmir could be won within six months from now.

He also said that the failure of the Government to hold an all-parties convention for solving the Kashmir problem at an early date was killing the enthusiasm of the people for liberation of Kashmir.

Winding up his speech he moved a resolution which stated that now Kashmir could not be secured through negotiations. The only way left open was an armed struggle. For this purpose the resolution expected that all political, religious and social organisations will join hands for making the satyagraha a great success. The resolution was passed by the audience.

All the other speakers who addressed the gathering favored the idea of strong action on the part of the Government and the people.

Other problems like rehabilitation of the flood-affected people and raising the standard of people were also discussed by the speakers.

The speakers appealed to the people to contribute liberally to the relief funds. For more equitable distribution of wealth it was proposed that the lowest paid employee should not get less than Rs. 100 and the highest paid not more than Rs. 1000 (C&MG 1955 Nov. 09).

1955 November 09

The Pakistan Times, Lahore reports that Prime Minister Ch. Mohammed Ali has invited Allama Mashriqi and other top leaders to attend the All-Parties Talks on Kashmir (All-Parties Leaders' Conference on Kashmir), to be held on November 26, 1955 (PT 1955 Nov. 09).

1955 November 10

The Civil & Military Gazette, Lahore reports that Governors and Federal Ministers will also attend the All-Parties Kashmir Conference to be held in Karachi on November 26 - 27, 1955 (C&MG 1955 Nov. 10).

1955 November 16

The Civil & Military Gazette, Lahore reports that the agenda is being finalised for the All-Parties Kashmir Conference to be held in Karachi on November 26-28, 1955 (C&MG 1955 Nov. 16).

1955 November 22

The Civil & Military Gazette, Lahore publishes a list of more invitees to the All-Parties Kashmir Conference to be held in Karachi on November 26 - 27, 1955 (C&MG 1955 Nov. 22).

1955 November 25

In Jehanghir Park, Karachi, Allama Mashraqi addresses a largely attended public meeting on the Kashmir issue. The meeting is held under the joint auspices of the Jammu and Kashmir Muslim Conference and the Kashmir Committee. *The Pakistan Times*, Lahore of November 26, 1955 would report:

"Jehangir Park - the venue of the meeting - echoed with spirited slogans like 'United Nations se rishta tor do,' [withdraw from the U.N.] 'Bharat se sifarti taluqaat tor do,' [break diplomatic relations with India] and 'Azadi-i-Kashmir ke lye jang karo' [fight for the freedom of Kashmir] when the speakers asked the huge audience to offer sacrifices for the cause of Kashmir.

They pledged to fight for the cause of Kashmir...It was announced at the meeting that a big procession would be taken out from the Mere Weather Tower at 1p.m. tomorrow. It would parade the main streets of the city, go to the Govenor-General's House and terminate at the gates of the Sind Assembly building - the venue of the All-Parties Conference on Kashmir called by the Prime Minister, Mr. Mohamad Ali tomorrow.

There will also be a complete hartal [strike] in the city tomorrow...

Allama Mashriqi said the Kashmir problem was already well known to the people of Pakistan. The All-Parties Conference on the question was being held tomorrow. In his opinion, it was not proper to say anything on the question before the Conference was over. However, he said, he would oppose from every stage and also in the Conference any idea that might delay the solution of the problem.

He declared that if the Conference tried to 'hoodwink' the people on this issue 'as the Government of Pakistan has been doing for the last eight years,' he would 'expose' it before the people and disassociate himself from it. But if it took any decision for expediting justice to the people of Kashmir, he would offer every sacrifice required for implementing the decision of the Conference" (PT 1955 Nov. 26).

Dawn, Karachi of November 26, 1955 would also report:

"The large assemblage unanimously adopted a three-point resolution for implementation by the All-Parties Conference on Kashmir [to be held on November 26-28, 1955], demanding (1) Pakistan's withdrawl from the United Nations (2) break of Diplomatic ties with Bharat [India], and (3) resort to fighting to free Kashmir...

Allama Inayatullah Khan Mashriqi, the Islam League leader, while referring to the All-Parties Conference said that he would support everything in the Conference if he felt that the leaders were really sincere to liberate Kashmir" (*Dawn* 1955 Nov. 26; C&MG 1955 Nov. 26).

Editor's comments: Sardar Ibraheem, Chaudhry Hamidullah (former Minister of the Azad Kashmir Government), and other Kashmiri leaders also addressed this public meeting. The meeting and the public procession were arranged to show solidarity and to arouse world opinion on the Kashmir issue. This public meeting (held on the evening of November 25, 1955) was separate from the All-Parties Kashmir Conference convened by Prime Minister Ch. Mohammed Ali on November 26, 1955 at the Sind Assembly building in Karachi (PT 1955 Nov. 26; *Dawn* 1955 Nov. 26; C&MG 1955 Nov. 26).

1955 November 26

As requested at the public meeting at Jehanghir Park on November 25, 1955, a huge procession starts from Mere Weather Tower. A complete *hartal* (strike) is also observed in Karachi to show solidarity with Kashmiris and to draw the world's attention toward the Kashmir cause. The Prime Minister emerges from the Sind Assembly building and addresses the participants of the procession. Schools and colleges remain closed (PT 1955 Nov. 27).

1955 November 26

The Civil & Military Gazette, Lahore reports that nearly 100 leaders of various political parties of Pakistan and Azad Kashmir have arrived in Karachi to attend the All-Parties Kashmir Conference on November 26-28, 1955 (C&MG 1955 Nov. 26).

1955 November 26

The All-Parties Kashmir Conference opens at the Sind Assembly building in Karachi. Prime Minister Ch. Mohammed Ali addresses the conference. Allama Mashriqi also makes a speech (PT 1955 Nov. 21; PT 1955 Nov. 27).

Editor's comments: Besides Allama Mashriqi, others who spoke at the conference included Hussain Shaheed Suhrawardy, Sardar Mohammed Ibraheem, Begum Shahnawaz, and Ch. Ghulam Abbas. The entire proceedings were held in camera, except the Prime Minister's speech (PT 1955 Nov. 27; *Dawn* 1955 Nov. 27).

1955 November 26

The Civil & Military Gazette, Lahore publishes an editorial regarding the All-Parties Kashmir Conference (C&MG 1955 Nov. 26).

1955 November 26

Allama Mashraqi attends a reception hosted by Prime Minister Ch. Muhammad Ali. Others at the reception include Iskandar Mirza (Governor General of Pakistan), cabinet ministers, heads of diplomatic missions, and other political leaders (*Dawn* 1955 Nov. 27).

1955 November 27

Dawn, Karachi publishes a list of the invitees who attended the All-Parties Kashmir Conference convened in Karachi by Ch. Muhammad Ali (Prime Minister of Pakistan). The list includes leading political leaders from West Pakistan, East Pakistan (now Bangladesh), Azad Kashmir, Cabinet Ministers, and leaders from the business community. Among the invitees are Allama Mashraqi, Hussain Shaheed Suhrawardy, Maulana Maududi, Abdul Hamid Khan Bhashani, Sardar Abdul Qayyum, Mujibur Rahman (who later founded Bangladesh), Iftikhar Hussain Khan (of Mamdot), Dr. Khan Sahib (Chief Minister of West Pakistan), M.A. Khuhro, Nawab of Dir, Mian Mumtaz Mohammad Khan Daultana, Mushtaq Ahmad Gurmani (Governor of West Pakistan), Begum Shah Nawaz, Chaudhry Khaliquzzaman, and Abdul Ghaffar Khan (*Dawn* 1955 Nov. 27).

1955 November 28

In Karachi, the All-Parties Talks on Kashmir conclude at 11 p.m. A resolution adopted unanimously deplores "the weak policy adopted by the Security Council in acquiescing in India's evasive tactics." The conference deliberations lasted three days (PT 1955 Nov. 29; C&MG 1955 Nov. 29; *Dawn* 1955 Nov. 28).
Editor's comments: At the conference, India was highly condemned for its deceitful policy. The Pakistan Times of November 29, 1955 reported that "The Conference declared that the Kashmir question was a truly national one, to which all consideration should be subordinated and the nation 'would consider no sacrifice too great for it.'" The Government of India expressed displeasure with the All-Parties Talks on Kashmir and questions were raised in the Indian

Parliament on December 22, 1955 (PT 1955 Nov. 29; PT 1955 Dec. 23).

1955 November 30

Allama Mashraqi announces the start of a large-scale nationwide campaign to implement the decisions taken at the All-Parties Kashmir Conference, which concluded on November 28, 1955. Mashraqi makes this announcement while speaking at another large public meeting convened by the Islam League at Jehanghir Park. Mashraqi states that the original plan of the Islam League to enlist Razakars for satyagarha shall be reorganized on a very large scale. He appeals to the people to volunteer as Razakars and he calls upon all the political parties to unite selflessly to liberate Kashmir. Mashraqi also criticizes the attitude of the Indian Government on the issue of Kashmir (*Dawn* 1955 Dec. 01).

1956

"Allama Mashraqi's life — a beacon for humanity"

– Nasim Yousaf

1956

The name of the Islam League is changed to the (Khaksar) Muslim League. (PT 1958 Jun. 11)
Editor's comments: Exact date of change of name could not be traced.
At the time, the Muslim League was disintegrating fast and there were many political differences within the party. India was ridiculing the country for not being able to maintain solidarity and some feared that Pakistan might disintegrate. Therefore, in order to provide a united front to the outside world, Mashraqi changed the name of the Islam League to the Khaksar Muslim League.

1956 February 11

A three-day Islam League Conference starts in Hyderabad (Sind). Delegates arrive from various locations and a large number of people gather for the conference. At the opening of the conference, various speakers and delegates make forceful speeches. People are told that merely making speeches and passing resolutions will not liberate Kashmir. If people are desirious of liberating Kashmir, then firm action is needed. Some of the speakers earnestly urge people to take up arms if they desire to liberate Kashmir (*Dawn* 1956 Feb.12).
Editor's comments: According to the news, Allama Mashraqi could not attend the conference, as he was ill.

June 1956

Mashraqi's Prediction That Came True

Mashraqi, while addressing the Khaksars, predicts the separation of East Pakistan:
"Ye Muslims! Today from this platform I sound you a warning. Listen carefully and ponder. Sometime in the future, probably in 1970, you will be confronted with a perilous situation. In 1970 - I see it clearly - the nation will be stormed from all sides. The internal situation would have deteriorated gravely. A panic of widespread bloodshed will sweep the nation. The frenzy of racial and provincial prejudices will grip the whole country. *Zindabad* and *murdabad* will defean your ears. Plans will be initiated to dismember the country. Take it from me that in 1970, Pakistan will be plagued with a grave threat to its sovereignty. You might actually lose it if the

reigns of the country were not in the hands of courageous and unrelenting leadership.

India will, in that grave situation, try to take advantage of your internal turmoil and devour you. Or, the governance of the country will fall in the hands of spineless self-seekers or self-centred opportunists who might on their own accord push you into the Indian lap. I warn you about 1970. I warn you to prepare from now to face the situation which will emerge in that year. In 1947, you had a refuge to protect yourself but in the coming days of 1970 - I can clearly visualise – you will have river Attock on one side and the Chinese border on the other, and you will have no place to go. Nations which deviate from God's path are eliminated through their own misdeeds" (Hussain 1991, 256-257; Zaman 1987, 423, 425-427; Hussain 1994, 85; *Al-Islah* 1997, 66; Yousaf 2003, 65).

Editor's comments: Mashraqi's prediction came true when East Pakistan became Bangladesh in 1971.

1956 June 12

The Islam League Executive Committee decides to amalgamate the organization with the Muslim League. Nasir Ahmed Shaikh and Aminuddin Sehrai are authorized to discuss the merger with Prime Minister Ch. Muhammad Ali and Sardar Abdur Rab Nishtar (Muslim League Chief). *Dawn*, Karachi of June 14, 1956 would report:

"The following nine conditions have been telegraphically communicated by the Islam League chief Allama Mashraqi, to [Pakistan] President Iskander Mirza; the President of the Muslim League, Sardar Nishtar [Sardar Abdur Rab Nishtar], and the Prime Minister, Mr. Mohamad Ali:

"(1) The Muslim League will be renamed as the Bharat-Pakistan Muslim League affiliating its branches all over Bharat. (2) The acquisition of Kashmir at all costs and with all sacrifices will remain the dominant aim of the Muslim League with immediate practical steps. (3) Fifty-one members of the Islam League Executive will be taken on the Central Working Committee on bloc. (4) Presidents and Secretaries of all Islam League branches in East and West Pakistan will be taken as councillors of the Muslim League. (5) Ordinary additional members of the Islam League throughout Pakistan will be accepted as Muslim League members without payment of additional subscriptions. (6) Islam League razakars throughout Pakistan will be merged with the Muslim League National Guards and renamed as Muslim League Razakars. (7) Messrs Aminuddin Sehrai, Mian Inayatullah, Kunwar Saadatullah, Nasir Ahmad Sheikh, Malik Akram Khan, Ahmed Khan Langa, Manzur

Elahi and Dr. K. N. Islam of East Pakistan will be taken as ordinary Vice-presidents of the Central and Provincial Muslim Leagues. (8) Allama Mashriqi will be an ordinary member without any office, but his advice on any internal or external matter will be accepted by the Muslim League President and Prime Minister. (9) Vigorous joint tours will be undertaken for intensive mass contact in both wings.

Allama Mashriqi told 'Dawn' that his offer to join the Muslim League was motivated by his desire to save the organisation and the country. He said he believed that the end of the Muslim League will mean the end of Pakistan" (*Dawn* 1956 Jun. 14).

Editor's comments: Mashraqi did not agree with the way the Muslim League had been working. He thought they were never sincere in uplifting the masses and had no solid agenda to put the nation on the right track. So the terms and conditions of amalgamation had to be made in a manner so that the Muslim League leadership could not hoodwink the people of Pakistan and also ensure protection of the Muslims of India who were left alone after the division of India.

1956 June 13

An Islam League meeting is held in Chiniot, near Lyallpur (now Faisalabad) (C&MG 1958 Jun. 21).

1956 June 21

Al-Islah publishes *Tehrik-e-Pakistan aur Kayyam-e-Pakistan* by Allama Mashraqi (*Al-Islah* 1997, 60).

1956 July 23

Mashraqi issues a Press statement:
"We are determined to keep the present Prime Minister firmly seated in the Centre at all costs till the present wave of hooliganism over Pakistan passes away resulting in permanent peace.

The regrettable intrigue has been going on even in the absence of the Prime Minister who is on an important mission abroad, and it looks that some of our unscrupulous political leaders are at their wits end in making Pakistan a laughing stock of the world by making the position of the Prime Minister shaky at a moment when utmost unity and harmony is required to back him whole-heartedly.

Dragging a strenuous and honest worker like Mr. Mohamad Ali into the dirty quagmire of dishonest politics is to my mind perfidy to Pakistan of the highest order, and from whichever side this perfidy comes, I feel sure, is not going to pay.

The Muslim League has already gone to the winds and the new Republican Party has yet nothing to show except empty words. It has no background and has no pedestal to stand. Its making is ridiculously defective, as vigorous and live organisations are never made with dead and rejected material.

Dr. Khan Sahib's previous record as Chief Minister of the former Frontier Province is also not particularly glowing, rather it has bad scars of narrow mindedness, tyranny and favouritism" (*Dawn* 1956 Jul. 25; C&MG 1956 Jul. 25).

1956 September 01

Abdul Jabbar Dehlvi, a former Khaksar leader, is arrested in Delhi. He is later released on bail (C&MG 1958 Jan. 22).

Dawn, Karachi reports:
"Allama Mashraqi has advised the Prime Minister, Mr. Mohamad Ali to stick to the Muslim League and not to join the Republican Party. In a message, sent both to Mr. Mohamad Ali and President Iskandar Mirza, Allama Mashriqi stressed the need of strengthening the Muslim League " (*Dawn* 1956 Sept. 01).

1956 September 12

Mashraqi calls upon the Muslim League to accept the conditions laid down by the Islam League for the amalgamation of the two parties for the betterment of the people of Pakistan. *Dawn*, Karachi of September 13, 1956 would report:

"He said it was the constitution of the Muslim League which had brought the organisation to its deathbed and if the Muslim League wanted to become a living organisation once again it shall have to face facts boldly.

He argued that the aim of the Muslim League was to survive and its constitution was only a means to that end, but if the means prove to be an obstruction in the realisation of the end it should be readily done away with.

'Let the Muslim League read the dreadful writing on the wall,' he added.

Allama Mashriqi said the Islam League could not indefinitely prolong the offer to amalgamate with the Muslim League and added that his organisation would start alone to save the country with the help of God, who helps those who help themselves" (*Dawn* 1956 Sept. 13).

Editor's comments: Again the Muslim League ignored his offer for its vested reasons. Mashraqi meant business whereas the League seemed to be insincere. They were more interested in personal gains so why would they join hands with a party that wished to lift the masses?

1956 September 23

Dawn, Karachi reports Mohammad Hussain's (a representative of Allama Mashraqi) statement. According to Hussain:

"Never has the necessity of amalgamation and absorption of the two political parties like the Muslim League and the Islam League been more marked than at the present juncture, when dissentions at home and bluffs from abroad are threatening the very existence of our State. The offer is being made by the Head of the Islam League to bring about a much-needed merger of the two parties: one has what the other has not; one completes the other and is completed by the other.

I, as the representative of Allama Inayat-ullah Khan Al-Mashriqi, make a sincere and fervent appeal to the Press and public to help expedite this merger, which is calculated to administer a quietus to the treacherous misgiving born out of frustrations, created by agents provocateurs than the actual conditions in the country. Let us all pray together that Allah give us wisdom enough to close up our ranks and combat the sinister forces of disruption that have been smuggled into our country" (*Dawn* 1956 Sept. 23).

1956 November 11

An Islam League meeting is held at Mochi Gate, Lahore (C&MG 1958 Jun. 22).

1956 November 23-25

The Islam League holds meetings at Minto Park, Lahore (C&MG 1958 Jun. 21; *Dawn* 1958 Aug. 12).

1956 November 27

Mashraqi addresses workers of his Muslim League in Lahore. *The Civil & Military Gazette*, Lahore of November 29, 1956 would report:

"Allama Inayat Ullah Khan Mashriqi…addressing the workers of his [Khaksar] Muslim League in Lahore on Tuesday [November 27, 1956] exhorted them to devote themselves to the service of people

He said the aim of his party was to establish a representative government in the country and promote a democratic system of life.

Allama Mashriqi said that he had chalked out a plan for establishing a 'people's government' [in] Pakistan, and according to the plan, the poor and the rich would be divided into different constituencies. If he succeeded in implementing his plans, no rich person would be allowed to contest any seat from the constituency of the poor and vice versa" (C&MG 1956 Nov. 29).

1956 December 24

Allama Mashriqi's address at Lahore.

1957

"Deeds that benefit a nation represent true leadership"

– Nasim Yousaf

1957

1957 January 01

Mashraqi addresses a public meeting in connection with the 100th anniversary of the 1857 Revolution at Minto Park, Lahore (Hussain 1994, 89; *Dawn* 1957 Jan. 02).

1957 January 01

The Khaksar Muslim League holds public meetings in various cities. In Peshawar, the meeting is held in the city as well as in Cantonment. The Khaksar Muslim League unfurls its flag at Chowk Yadgar. Speeches are made and tributes are paid to the heroes of the first war of independence. A special message from Allama Mashraqi is read out predicting a glorious future for the Muslims (*Dawn* 1957 Jan. 02).

1957 January 10

Mashriqi addresses the Razakars in Lahore. *The Pakistan Times*, Lahore of January 12, 1957 would report:

"Allama Inayatullah Khan Mashriqi…said in Lahore on Thursday that the cloak of secularism, worn by the Indian National Congress with a view to carrying on the genocide of the Muslims in India, was a perpetual threat to peace between the two countries.

Addressing a rally of his soldierly 'Razakars,' the Allama urged them strictly to follow his organisation's principles before Muslims of Pakistan took some concrete action.

He asked his volunteers to assemble in Lahore on January 20 to get a 'set programe' for the future" (PT 1957 Jan. 12; *Dawn* 1957 Jan. 12).

1957 January

Mashraqi and 51 Razakars are arrested (PT 1957 Sept. 20; PT 1957 Oct. 03).
Editor's comments: The date of their arrest and release was not specified in the source used.

1957 January 22

Former Khaksar leader Abdul Jabbar Dehlvi is again detained in Delhi (C&MG 1958 Jan. 22).

1957 January 29

Mashriqi writes to Nehru stating that handing over Kashmir to Pakistan would relieve both countries of the financial losses resulting from the confrontation over Kashmir. These losses, when retrieved, could be used for the welfare of the people of both countries. Mashraqi further writes:
"The people of Pakistan, being no more able to bear hardships, are now constrained to put this proposal to you in the interest of the people's welfare and desire to present it to you and the people of India in person. They will await your favourable reply from February 1 till March 30" (Hussain 1994, 146, 177).
Editor's comments: A news item appeared in the newspaper (supporting the government view) that stated that Mashraqi's one million march plan was based on superstition. This was an attempt to mislead and dissuade the public from joining the march. Anti-Mashraqi parties tried to prove that the march was not possible, ignoring the fact that Mashraqi was a great organizer, had a large number of supporters, and would ensure that it took place. His plan was in place and would work without a doubt, and that is the reason why governments (Pakistan and India) on both sides were nervous. As a result, the Government of Pakistan left no stone unturned to stop this march.

1957 February 01

Mashraqi's speech/address is read to hundreds of thousands of people in the entire Pakistan (Hussain 1994, 115, 139, 147).

1957 February 07

The Pakistan Times, Lahore reports on the registration of the Khaksar Muslim League (PT 1957 Feb. 07).
Editor's comments:
Mohammed Khursheed Khalid (President of the Khaksar Muslim League) informed the court on June 10, 1958 that the name of the Islam League was changed to the (Khaksar) Muslim League at a meeting in Minto Park in 1956 (PT 1958 Jun. 11; PT 1958 Jun. 12; PT 1958 Oct. 15). According to the statement in the newspaper (C&MG 1958 Jun. 11), the Khaksar Muslim League was named in 1956 instead of 1957.

Differences within the Muslim League, as well as their extremely poor handling of affairs in Pakistan, led people to believe that Pakistan would disintegrate. Mashraqi rebutted India and those who thought that Pakistan would fall apart by renaming the Islam League to the Khaksar Muslim League.

1957 February 24

The Dawn reports that Mashraqi asks Fakir of Ipi to preside over Razakar Camp to be held on the first of March. According to the newspaper, the President of the Khaksar Muslim League (Peshawar) has left for Waziristan tribal areas to deliver Mashraqi's message to Fakir of Ipi. *The Dawn* reports " ...according to a Lahore report circulated by a news agency the Fakir of Ipi offered his 'Lashkar' to participate in the Jehad for the liberation of Kashmir"(*Dawn* 1957 Feb. 24).

1957 February 29

Mashriqi delivers a speech (Hussain 1994, 170).

1957 March 01

Mashraqi addresses a public meeting at Minto Park, Lahore. He vows that the people of Pakistan will not rest until their four million Kashmiri brethren are liberated from India (Hussain 1994, 151, 164; C&MG 1957 Mar. 02).
Editor's comments: Mashraqi's speech/address was again read to hundreds of thousands of people in the entire Pakistan (Hussain 1994, 164). Razakrars were asked to assemble in by March 31, 1957. (Hussain 1994, 169).

1957 March 04

Dawn reports "An impassioned appeal for the formation of a United Front of all parties to expedite the liberation of Kashmir by direct action was made by top leaders of Allama Mashriqi's [Khaksar] Muslim League at a meeting held here [Rawalpindi] on Friday night [March 01,1957] (*Dawn* 1957 Mar. 04).

Announcing their programme of a peaceful march on Kashmir on March 31, Allama Mashriqi's followers called upon all political parties to unite and pool up their resources for a major offensive again Bharat [India] on Kashmir. They welcomed the Pakistan Government's Kashmir policy but urged it to bow to the people's will and 'act soon' instead of falling a prey to the dilatory tactics of Bharat and her allies to delay settlement of Kashmir issue. They said the people were just fed up with negotiations either directly with Bharat or indirectly through intermediaries. 'Before there is a real explosion in Kashmir, we want to march peacefully to New Delhi and warn the Indians against the unwise policies of their leaders. Our intentions vis-à-vis India are very peaceful. We shall march to Delhi, unarmed. We shall impress upon Nehru that he is playing with fire. Our rivers have their sources in Kashmir and India is trying to deprive us of our waters in order to mother our economy. We desire to live as India's peaceful neighbours but that opportunity is being destroyed by India's leadership which refuses to let the people of Kashmir join their brothers-in-faith in Pakistan.'

Allama Mashriqi's followers also said that Pakistanis should beware of Bharat's hostile intentions. 'India is building up strength to destroy Pakistan. Against whom will all these armed forces be used? Obviously the target is Pakistan. The Government of Pakistan must see the writing on the wall and realize the seriousness of the Indian threat'.

The meeting also passed resolutions condemning the Soviet veto on the four-Power Kashmir resolution, urging the Government of Pakistan to break off diplomatic and trade relations with Bharat liquidate the cease-fire agreement with Bharat over Kashmir and expressing full confidence in the leadership of Allama Mashriqi.

Allama Mashriqi's League leaders supported Prime Minister Suhrawardy and his foreign policy and condemned the 'ill-advised section of people' which unwisely opposed his foreign policy.

A memorandum presented by leaders of Alama Mashriqi's [Khaksar] Muslim League to the United Nations Kashmir truce observers on Friday after demonstrations and processions favouring plebiscite in Kashmir expressed grave concern over the Bharati troop concentrations in Kashmir. The memorandum asked the UN truce observers to take immediate action to get the Bharati threat removed... The memorandum violently condemned the Bharati-framed constitution for Occupied Kashmir as a hoax on the world" (*Dawn* 1957 Mar. 04).

1957 March 31

Razakars begin assembling in various places in preparation for a Million-Man March to India to seek freedom for Kashmir.

1957 April 01

The Secretary General of the Islam League (Rawalpindi) receives the following letter from the United Nations:

"In as much as your letter pertains to a matter of which Security Council is seized, it will be included in a list of communication circulated to the representatives on that organ and will be kept at the disposal of all the members of the United Nations."

The Pakistan Times, Lahore of April 03, 1957 would report that this letter was in response to a memorandum submitted by the Razakars of the Islam League to the Security Council. The newspaper would further report that the letter was handed over to the United Nations headquarters in Rawalpindi after a huge demonstration on Kashmir day. According to the newspaper, Ashraf Khan stated that volunteers of the party were watching for the outcome of Security Council deliberations before marching into Kashmir (PT 1957 Apr. 03).

1957 April 02

The Islam League (Khaksar Muslim League) receives a reply from the United Nations regarding a memorandum on settling the Kashmir issue. The Islam League had submitted the memorandum to the United Nations headquarters in Rawalpindi following a huge demonstration in Rawalpindi on Kashmir Day. The United Nations' reply states:

"Inasmuch as your letter pertains to a matter of which the Security Council is seized, it will be included in a list of communications circulated to the representatives on that organ and will be kept at the disposal of all the member States of the United Nations."

Ashraf Khan, a Khaksar Muslim League leader, states in Rawalpindi that the Razakars are watching the result of the delibrations of the Security Council before "they start marching into Kashmir" (C&MG 1957 Apr. 03).

1957 April 03

The Civil & Military Gazette, Lahore reports that the Razakars of the Khaksar Muslim League have establishd a camp at Liaquat Garden, Rawalpindi. Razakar volunteers parade and do exercises in front of thousands of spectators. The newspaper writes:

"Covering almost the whole ground of the Liaquat Garden, this camp is supposed to be the biggest and most organised in this region where well-disciplined volunteers are seen at parade and doing different exercises throughout the day.

Thousands of people daily flock to the Liaquat Gardens to witness the parade of the 'razakars.'

The camp will continue until April 5" (C&MG 1957 Apr. 03).

1957 April 20

A Criminal Investigation Department (C.I.D.) police officer and two constables lodge a complaint alleging that Razakars at Wahgah Border (near Pakistan-India border near Amritsar) detained and harassed them and stole Rs. 19/- from their pockets.
Editor's comments: This was a false charge against the Razakars. The authorities made these allegations for vested reasons.

1957 April 21

Mashraqi along with a large number of Razakars are arrested at Wahgah border (near Pakistan-India border near Amritsar). (PT 1957 Apr. 23; PT 1958 Oct. 11; C&MG 1957 Apr. 23).
Editor's comments: The newpaper reported that Mashraqi was later released on bail. Mashriqi had planned a peaceful march into India with one million volunteers and supporters in order to bring the Kashmir issue to the world's attention and force Nehru, who claimed to be a great humanitarian, to settle the problem. Thus, Mashriqi ordered the Khaksars to set up camps along the Pakistan-India borders, and "he led 3,00,000 [300,000] followers to the border of Pakistan and India . . ." (*Hindu* 1963 Aug. 29; Yousaf 2003, 66)

Mashraqi was visting the Razakar camp at Wahgah Border in Lahore. This camp had been established as part of the effort to organize a million-man march to India.

On April 20, 1957, a C.I.D. police officer and two constables lodged a false complaint with local police that the Razakars had detained and harrassed them at Wahgah Border. Mashraqi was arrested on April 21, 1957 on this flimsy and false charge while he was visiting the Wahgah Border volunteer camp. In actuality, these arrests were made because police had been instructed by the Government of Pakistan to ensure that the million-man march did not materialize.

1957 April 22

Mashriqi's arrest is resented and a protest procession is taken out in Lahore (PT 1957 Apr. 23).

1957 May 11

The centenary of the 1857 War of Independence is celebrated in Rawalpindi. National flags are hoisted on the roofs of shops and houses. A procession (brought out jointly by all the political parties) parades through the city and ends at Liaquat Gardens, where a public meeting is held. Representatives of the Khaksar Muslim League and other parties address the meeting (C&MG 1957 May 12).

1957 May 21

Jawaharlal Nehru, Prime Minister of India, addresses the Indian parliament and criticizes Mashraqi (Zaman 1987, 345; Hussain 1994, 179).
Editor's comments: In the first source used (Zaman), the date of Nehru's address is listed as May 31, 1957. However, this appears to be incorrect because Allama Mashraqi rebuffed Nehru's statement on May 22, 1957. Mashraqi's statement was published in *The Pakistan Times*, Lahore on May 24, 1957.

1957 May 22

Mashriqi makes a statement regarding Nehru's hostile comments (Hussain 1994, 179; Bhatti n.d., 52-53).

1957 May 24

The Pakistan Times, Lahore reports Mashriqi's rebuffs to Jawaharlal Nehru, Prime Minister of India:
"In a rejoinder to Pandit Nehru in which he described Allama Mashriqi as a self-style Allama, the latter said, 'I am called Allama on my own merits, and not on the merits of my father.'
He said he fully knew Pandit Nehru as his contemporary at Cambridge [University, U.K.] where he was rated as a mere mediocre of no merit. But calling him (Mashriqi) mad, 'the Pandit has only further frightened the Indians,' he added" (PT 1957 May 24; Hussain 1994, 179).

1957 May 25

Mashriqi delivers a speech (*Dawn* 1958 Aug. 12).
Editor's comments: The source does not specify where Mashraqi delivered his speech.

1957 September 20

Charges are framed against Allama Mashriqi and ten other prominent Razakar leaders. Mashriqi and the others are charged with detaining and beating policemen at the Razakar camps at Wahgah border in Lahore. 40 Razakars (out of 51 who were arrested in January 1957) are acquitted in Lahore (PT 1957 Sept. 20).

1957 October 02

The hearing of the case against Allama Mashraqi and the Razakars (for allegedly detaining and beating policemen at Wahgah Razakar camp) resumes in Lahore (PT 1957 Oct. 03).
Editor's comments: The date of October 02, 1957 is approximate. The exact date of the hearing could not be traced.

1957 October 11

Border police arrest Razakars from a camp at a village in Shah Gharib Police Station (PT 1958 Jun. 11).
Editor's comments: According to Mohammed Khurshid Khalid's statement in court on June 10, 1958, people from Gujrat and Sialkot established the camp at a village in Shah Gharib Police Station. Khurshid Khalid further informed the court that the case against those arrested was still pending in the court of the Resident Magistrate, Shahgarh (PT 1958 Jun. 11).

1957 October 19

Mashraqi is arrested. Mashriqi informs the Lahore court that he plans to march towards India on October 21, 1957. Mashraqi and the Razakars are sent to judicial lock-up by a Lahore Magistrate and the announcement of his decision is postponed to October 22, 1957. A large number of Razakars are present at the premises of the District Court to hear the Magistrate's judgment. Slogans such as "Allama Mashriqi Zindabad," "Punjab Police Murdabad" are constantly heard (PT 1957 Oct. 20; C&MG 1957 Oct. 20).
Editor's comments: The judgement was to be announced on this date, but was delayed. People were highly distressed and emotionally charged when Mashriqi and the Razakars were taken to judicial lock-up.

1957 October 20

The West Pakistan Government issues an order to the Deputy Commissioners of the border districts. *The Pakistan Times*, Lahore of October 21, 1957 would report:

"The West Pakistan Government has instructed the Deputy Commissioners of the border districts not to allow the Khaksars to set up their camps for crossing over to the Indian territory.

The Khaksars, it may be mentioned, had announced their intention to march to India on Monday [October 21, 1957] and the Government has taken this measure to frustrate the plans of the followers of Mr. Inayat Ullah Khan Mashriqi, if any.

The decision to send instructions to the District Officers was taken at a meeting of the officers of the Home Department and the Police convened by the Chief Minister, Sardar Abdur Rashid, at his residence on Sunday.

The Deputy Commissioner, Lahore, it is learnt, has already moved in the matter and some of the camps set up by the Khaksars near Wahgah were removed" (PT 1957 Oct. 21).

Editor's comments: Many Razakars were arrested and harassed by the Pakistan Government to prevent them from organizing a million-man march to seek freedom for Kashmiris.

1957 October 20

The Lahore District Magistrate issues a Press Note. In the Note, he prohibits (under Section 144 Cr. P.C.) the establishment of camps, holding of parades, gatherings, mock battles, and any processions by the Razakars in the entire district of Lahore for a period of two months (PT 1957 Oct. 21).

1957 October 21

On this day, the million-man march (also known as "Delhi Chalo") to seek freedom for Kashmir is to take place (Hussain 1994, 180-181).

Editor's comments: There was a lot of resentment among the public due to Mashraqi's detention. However, Mashraqi was released on October 21, 1957. A very large number of police, including the Deputy Commissioner and other high-ranking officers, were present to prevent Mashriqi from taking out a procession of Razakars/Khaksars from Nila Gumbad (Anarkali). The entire area was cordoned off; all vehicular and pedestrian traffic was banned and people in the area were directed to disperse. The government managed to prevent the march.

1957 October 22

Mashriqi is again arrested (Hussain 1994, 182). Allama Mashraqi is sentenced to an aggregate term of two years of rigorous imprisonment and fined Rs. 1,200 (C&MG 1958 Jan. 11; PT 1958 Jan. 11). Ten of Mashraqi's followers are also sentenced.

Mashraqi, who had been released on bail on October 21, 1957, is again imprisoned. He would remain in jail until January 1958 (Hussain 1994, 182).

Editor's comments: The arrest of Mashraqi on October 22, 1957 was the last nail in the coffin by the Government to prevent Mashraqi from taking out one million men on a march towards India.

1957 October 22

The Civil & Military Gazette, Lahore reports that Mohammad Sadiq, a Khaksar leader, appealed to the Razakars and the Khaksars "to keep the peace in the country and not try to break the law of the Government" (C&MG 1957 Oct. 22).

1957 October 24

The Civil & Military Gazette, Lahore reports that Mashraqi and his followers have filed an appeal against their sentence of imprisonment, which was handed down by a Lahore First Class Magistrate on October 22, 1957. The appeal was filed in the court of the District and Sessions Judge, Lahore. The newspaper further reports that Mashraqi and his followers have applied for bail until a decision is made regarding their appeal (C&MG 1957 Oct. 24).

1957 October 25

The District Magistrate of Khairpur bans (under Section 144) all camps, meetings, processions and any movement towards the border or parading in formation by Razakars/Khaksars for a period of two months (PT 1957 Oct. 26).

1957 October 25

Many Razakars of the Khaksar Muslim League are arrested in Sialkot. Security measures are tightened all along the border to prevent the peaceful march into India by Mashriqi's followers. The purpose of the march was to compel the world and the Indian Government to resolve the Kashmir issue (PT 1957 Oct. 26).

1957 October 28

Mashraqi released and arrested again.
Editor's comments: Mashraqi and nine followers are granted interim bail by the District and Sessions Judge in Lahore. *The Pakistan Times*, Lahore of October 29, 1957 would report that Mashriqi and his followers have filed an appeal challenging their conviction of October 22, 1957 (PT 1957 Oct. 29).

Just as Mashriqi is being released from Bahawalpur jail (in accordance with the orders of October 28, 1957 of the Sessions Judge, Lahore), he is re-arrested under the Public Safety Act (PT 1958 Jan. 11).

1957 October 30

The Pakistan Times, Lahore publishes details of the Magistrate judgement in Mashriqi's conviction of October 22, 1957 (PT 1957 Oct. 30; Zaman 1987, 346).

1957 November 03

Inayatullah Hassan, General Secretary of the Pakistan Awami League, condemns Mashraqi's arrest (under the Public Safety Act) and demands his immediate release (PT 1957 Nov. 04).

1957 November 14

The West Pakistan High Court rejects Mashriqi's bail application (PT 1958 Jan. 11).

1957 December

Mashriqi begins writing *Takmillah* in Mianwali jail (Mashraqi [1931] 1997, 263).
Editor's comments: The source used did not list the exact date that Mashraqi began writing *Takmillah*.

1957 December 24

Police raid the Shah Alam Office of the Khaksar Muslim League and at least a dozen homes of Khaksar leaders in Lahore. The first raid is conducted at Khaksar Manzil, the house of Captain Rashid Kamal (Allama Mashraqi's Press Secretary). Other places raided are the homes of Pir Alhan Shah (Khaksar Volunteer Organizer, Shah Alam

Market), Shaikh Fazal-e-Elahi (Treasurer of the Khaksar Muslim League, Shah Alam Market), Mushtaq Ahmed Qureshi (President of the Khaksar Muslim League, Lahore), Chaudhary Muhammad Rafi (Salar of the Khaksar Volunteers, Bhatti Gate, Lahore), and Miraj Din (Salar). Raids are also conducted at Mochi Gate and other locations. Police confiscate Khaksar documents, but fail to find any explosives, bombs, or ammunition (C&MG 1957 Dec. 25; PT 1957 Dec. 25).

1958

"Those nations fail that are incapable of distinguishing between the leader and the exploiter"

– Nasim Yousaf

1958

1958 January

Mohammad Khursheed Khalid is elected President of the Khaksar Muslim League (PT 1958 Nov. 19).
Editor's comments: Anti-Mashraqi elements have claimed that Mashraqi was a dictator. On the contrary, Mashraqi was highly democratic and a supporter of the masses. The election of Muhammad Khurshid Khalid proves that Mashraqi supported empowering the masses, instead of taking the position himself or nominating another rich person to be the leader. The exact date of Khursheed Khalid's election as President could not be traced.

1958 January 10

A Division Bench of the West Pakistan High Court, comprising of Chief Justice Dr. S.A. Rehman and Justice Yaqub Ali, rejects Mashriqi's bail application (C&MG 1958 Jan. 11). The Division Bench observes, "Petitioner can approach the Supreme Court, if he is so advised. So far as this Court is concerned, it is committed to the view taken in recent Full Bench decision. Dismissed." Thus, Mashriqi remains in Rawalpindi Central Jail, where he was imprisoned under the West Punjab Public Safety Act of 1949 (PT 1958 Jan. 11).
Editor's comments: It was highly deplorable that the West Pakistan High Court ignored everything in its decision, including Mashraqi's deteriorating health. Health concerns had been one of the reasons for filing the petition, which stated, "Allama Inayat Ullah Khan Mashriqi is an aged person and is unwell" (PT 1958 Jan. 11).

1958 January 14

A writ petition challenging the detention of Allama Mashraqi comes up for hearing before the West Pakistan High Court. The Additional Advocate-General, S.A. Mahmud, states that the provincial Government is considering releasing Allama Mashraqi on January 30, 1958. *The Civil & Military Gazette,* Lahore of January 15, 1958 would report:

"Earlier Khawaja Abdur Rahim contended that most of the grounds in the detention order were vague and the petitioner Allama Mashriqi, was deprived of the right to effectively represent against his detention. 'This is a denial of a constitutuional right,' he argued" (C&MG 1958 Jan. 15).

1958 January 21

Abdul Jabbar Dehlvi, a former Khaksar leader, is released in New Delhi. *The Civil & Military Gazette*, Lahore would report on January 22, 1958:

"Mr. Abdul Jabbar Dehlvi, a former Khaksar leader of Delhi, was released this morning from jail after a year's detention.
He was arrested on September 1, 1956, in connection with the Delhi bomb case. Later he was bailed out but was detained on January 22 last year.

One of the grounds supplied to him explaining his detention was that he had written against the Indian occupation of Kashmir by the army in 'Naya Payam' a weekly of Delhi.

The weekly, however, had ceased publication six months prior to his detention.

The Supreme Court of India had also held the detention of Mr. Jabbar as valid.

Five other exiled leaders of Kashmir were also arrested in the Delhi bomb case but were later detained for a year each because Delhi police could not find any evidence against them" (C&MG 1958 Jan. 22).

1958 January 30

Mashraqi is released from jail in January 30, 1958. During the time of Mashraqi's detention, restrictions on his party had remained in place (Hussain 1994, 182).
Editor's comments: The source used did not specify the exact date of Mashraqi's release. January 30, 1958 is taken from the statement of The Additional Advocate-General, S.A. Mahmud on January 14, 1958 (C&MG 1958 Jan. 15).

1958 April 28

Khan Abdul Qayyum Khan, President of the Pakistan Muslim League and former Chief Minister of the NWFP, meets with Mashraqi in Ichhra, Lahore. Mohammed Khursheed Khalid, President of the Khaksar Muslim League, is also present (PT 1958 May 16; PT 1958 Jun. 11).
Editor's comments: This meeting was held to discuss the amalgamation of the Khaksar Muslim League with the Muslim League.

1958 May 05

Alhaj Alla Dad Khan, Alnaj Muhammad Ashraf, Sardar Amir Azam, and Khan Jalal Baba meet with Qizilbash (Chief Minister of West Pakistan) to persuade him to withdraw various criminal cases pending against Allama Mashraqi and Muhammad Khursheed Khalid (*Dawn* 1958 Jul. 11).

1958 May 09

Dr. Khan Sahib (former Chief Minister of NWFP and former Chief Minister of West Pakistan) is assassinated in Lahore by Atta Mohammed (PT 1958 May 10; PT 1958 July 06; C&MG 1958 May 10; *Dawn* 1958 May 10).

A post mortem examination is conducted on Dr. Khan Sahib's body. Later in the day, the same doctor also examines Ata Mohammed (the accused) (PT 1958 Jun. 23).

1958 May 10

Mashraqi is arrested at 3:45 a.m from his residence in Ichhra, Lahore. Others arrested include Mashriqi's son and four followers: Hassan Mohammed, Ali Mohammed, Rehan Shah, and Samin Khan. They are kept in custody at Lahore Fort. Mashraqi's house is thorougly searched and documents and papers are confiscated (C&MG 1958 May 11). *The Civil & Military Gazette*, Lahore of May 11, 1958 would report, "After a four-hour search the house [Mashraqi's house] looked as though it had been throughly ransacked by burglars." A large police force, headed by Malik Habibullah Khan (Assistant Inspector General), cordon off the area in Ichhra, Lahore. Malik Habibullah Khan has been appointed by A.B.A Awan (Inpector General of Police for West Pakistan) to investigate Dr. Khan Sahib's murder. The raiding party also includes the Superintendent of Police (S.S.P., Lahore) and other officers of the Lahore District and Crimes Branch. Police also arrest others in Lahore (PT 1958 May 11; PT 1958 Jul. 06; PT 1958 Nov. 19).

Editor's comments: Mashraqi was 70 years old and was ill and suffering from high fever, but the Government of Pakistan ignored this. His illness was also reported in *The Civil & Military Gazette*, Lahore of May 12, 1958.

The police wanted Ata Mohammad (the accused) to implicate Mashraqi in the murder of Dr. Khan Sahib, despite the fact that Ata had never actually met Mashraqi. Thus, they brought Ata with them at the time of Mashraqi's arrest. In public, police stated that Ata had accompanied them in order to identify Mashraqi. However, in reality, they had brought Ata along so that he could familiarize himself with Mashraqi and his house. The police then tortured Ata to state in court that Mashraqi was behind the murder. Ata Mohammed did just this initially, but later revealed the truth, and Mashraqi was honorably acquitted on November 17, 1958.

Regarding the four Khaksars arrested at Mashraqi house, they were facing trial for supporting Mashraqi in the million-man march for the liberation of Kashmir in 1957. They were from far off places, but were staying at Mashraqi's house to attend the court proceedings against them (*Dawn* 1958 May 11).

Ata Mohammed is produced before a Lahore Magistrate. He is remanded to police custody for ten days (PT 1958 May 11) and his home is searched (C&MG 1958 May 11).

Three more of Mashraqi's followers, Muhammad Khursheed Khalid (President of the Khaksar Muslim League), Mohammad Asghar, and Zafar Haider (Vice President of the Khaksar Muslim League), are arrested in connection with Dr. Khan's murder (PT 1958 May 12; PT 1958 Nov. 19). Muhammad Khursheed Khalid is imprisoned in Lahore Fort at night (C&MG 1958 Jun. 15; C&MG 1958 Sept. 25). Many other people are detained and questioned by the police in Lahore (C&MG 1958 May 12).

Editor's comments: Muhammed Khursheed Khalid was brought to Lahore at 2 a.m. on the night of May 10 (early morning of May 11) (PT 1958 Nov. 19).

Police raid the office of Fazal Elahi (Secretary of the Khaksar Muslim League, Shah Alam Market) in Lahore. They search the premises and confiscate documents. Fazal Elahi is also taken into custody for questioning (C&MG 1958 May 11).

Police raid many places in Lahore in search of Mashriqi's followers (PT 1958 May 11).

1958 May 11

Malik Habibullah (Assistant Inspector General) records the statements of Qazi Khail (Dr. Khan Sahib's driver), Khuda Baksh (Dr. Khan Sahib's Gardener), Mir Afzal (Dr. Khan Sahib's bearer), and Baptist Perara (Dr. Khan Sahib's servant) (PT 1958 May 12).

Mashraqi and four of his followers are produced before a Lahore Magistrate. They are remanded to police custody for ten days (PT 1958 May 12).

Three of Mashriqi's followers (arrested in Sialkot on May 10, 1958) are produced before a Magistrate in Sialkot. They are remanded to police custody for ten days. Two of them are brought to Lahore for interrogation (PT 1958 May 12; PT 1958 Sept. 24).

Rashid Kamal, Chief Publicity Secretary of the Khaksar Muslim League, vehemently denies that Ata Mohammed has any connection with the organization. He states in a press statement:
"Atta Mohammad has never been a Khaksar so the question of his participation in the *jehad* camps established by our party on the Indo-Pakistan borders does not arise" (PT 1958 May 12; *Dawn* 1958 May 13).

1958 May 12

Mian Mohammad (President of the Khaksar Muslim League, Peshawar) regrets Mashraqi's arrest and issues a press statement. *The Civil & Military Gazette*, Lahore of May 14, 1958 would report:
"The President of the Khaksar Muslim League, Peshawar, Mian Muhammad, expressed great astonishment at the arrest of Allama Mashriqi in connection with Dr. Khan's assassination.
In a statement issued to the Press on Monday Mian Muhammad regretted that 'whenever any mischief is created from any quarter the Government imputes it to the Khaksar Muslim League.' He added that even Mr. Liaquat Ali Khan's assassination was at first imputed to Khaksars. Later the charge proved to be false.
He appealed to the Government to show consideration to the age and reputation of Allama Mashraqi who he said could never take part in treachery and conspiracy" (C&MG 1958 May 14).

1958 May 14

Dawn, Karachi reports that police from the North-West Frontier and Sind provinces have been requisitioned in the investigation of Dr. Khan Sahib's murder (*Dawn* 1958 May 14).

Khan Abdul Qayyum Khan, President of the Pakistan Muslim League (also former Minister of the NWFP), is interrogated by Malik Habibullah (Assistant Inspector General) regarding Dr. Khan Sahib's murder. Khan Abdul Qaiyum Khan is questioned about his relations

with Dr. Khan Sahib and his meeting with Allama Mashraqi on April 28, 1958 (*Dawn* 1958 May 15; PT 1958 May 15; C&MG 1958 May 15).
Editor's comments: The meeting between Mashraqi and Khan Abdul Qayyum on April 28, 1958 was held to discuss the amalgamation of the Khaksar Muslim League and the Pakistan Muslim League. Police interrogated Khan Abdul Qayyum Khan in an attempt to gather some information regarding Dr. Khan Sahib's murder.

Khaksar leader Ch. Rehmat Ullah is arrested in Lahore (PT 1958 May 15).

Atta Mohammed, the accused in Dr. Khan Sahib's murder, is produced before Lahore Magistrate Shaukat Tarar. Mohammed is sent to judicial lock-up (PT 1958 May 16; PT 1958 Jul. 06; PT 1958 Oct. 22; *Dawn* 1958 Jun. 18).

1958 May 15

Ibrahim, the driver of Abdul Hameed Khan of Ferozsons, is examined in Lahore Fort (C&MG 1958 May 17).
Editor's comments: Ibrahim had driven Khan Abdul Qayyum Khan to Allama Mashraqi's house for their meeting on April 28, 1958.

The police take Muhammad Khursheed Khalid to Wazirabad (C&MG 1958 Sept. 26).
Editor's comments: On September 25, 1958, Muhammad Khursheed Khalid informed the court that on May 15, 1958 the police took him to Wazirabad. While he was in the police car, many people were brought by the police to see him. According to Muhammad Khursheed Khalid satement, his face was shown "So as to become witnesses against me" (C&MG 1958 Sept. 26).

The Lahore Additional District Magistrate deputes Magistrate Mohammed Shaukat Tarar to visit Mashraqi and others in Lahore Fort to record their statement as to whether they accept Khwaja Wali Mohammed as their counsel. (PT 1958 May 16; C&MG 1958 May 16).

Muhammad Akram (Deputy Suprintendent of Police) interrogates Mirza Shamsul Haq (Former Health Minister of the Frontier Province and Khan Abdul Qayyum Khan's Private Secretary) in Lahore Fort in connection with Dr. Khan Sahib's murder. Muhammad Akram was especially summoned from Peshawar to assist in the investigation of the murder (*Dawn* 1958 May 16). According to his statement to the Press, he is mainly questioned about Khan Qayyum's meetings with Mashraqi. He informs the court that Khan Qayyum had met Mashraqi at Mashraqi's house in 1954, 1956, and on April 28, 1958 (PT 1958 May 16; C&MG 1958 May 16).

Editor's comments: Khan Qayyum Khan's secretary informed the court that he was present at the time that Khan Qayyum met with Mashraqi on April 28, 1958. The secretary was asked if during the meeting at Mahriqi's house, he was introduced to Atta Mohammed (Dr. Khan Sahib's assailant). He informed the interrogating officer that he did not see Ata Mohammed there. It is clear that the police were trying to establish that Mashraqi and Khan Qayyum had collaborated in Dr. Khan Sahib's murder, or at least that Mashraqi had been behind the murder.

1958 May 16

Syed Hasnat Ahmed, Additional District Magistrate, grants permission to Khawaja Wali Mohammad to interview Mashraqi in Lahore Fort (*Dawn* 1958 May 17). Khawaja Wali Mohammad interviews Mashraqi the same day. *The Civil & Military Gazette*, Lahore of May 17, 1958 would report:

"Khwaja Wali Muhammad interviewed Allama Mashraqi in the [Lahore] Fort for about 75 minutes. Khwaja Muhammad later said that Allama Mashraqi was not satisfied with the conditions in which he was being kept in the Fort. He said Allama Mashraqi had been running temperature since his arrest and the room in which he had been lodged was unhygenic. No facilities according to his status were being provided to him, Khwaja Wali Muhammad added: Allama Mashraqi, he said, had mental worries and his health was not good and he was being given medicines daily.

Allama Mashraqi told Khwaja Wali Muhammad that he was quite innocent and was being unneccessarily harassed.

Allama Mashraqi said he was arrested because he and his party had decided to contest the forthcoming elections" (C&MG 1958 May 17).

Editor's comments: It was wrongly reported in the newspaper that Khwaja Wali Muhammad was granted permission to interview Mashraqi on the same day. In fact, while arguing for Mashraqi, Barrister Ijaz Hussain Batalvi informed the Session Judge that the permission to Khawaja Wali Mohammed to interview Mashraqi was withheld for three days. Khawaja Wali Mohammed had applied to the Additional District Magistrate (A.D.M.Lahore) for an interview with

Mashraqi on May 13, 1958. However, Khawaja only succeeded in meeting Mashriqi on May 16, 1958 (PT 1958 Oct. 29).

Barrister Ijaz Hussain Batalvi was appointed by Manzoor Qadir to fight the case, however input from Mashraqi's son, Inamullah Khan Akram, was also important in the matter. Mashraqi's son met Manzoor Qadir (who later became Chief Justice of High Court and Foreign Minister of Pakistan in President Ayub Khan's cabinet). Manzoor Qadir (who personally would not appear in lower courts being a senior lawyer) designated Barrister Ijaz Hussain Batalvi (who was then junior advocate of Manzoor Qadir). However, Manzoor Qadir discussed the case with Mashraqi's son before each hearing. Here I must give credit to Manzoor Qadir for not charging any fee (this was disclosed by Mashraqi's son, Inamullah Khan Akram) for preparing the case. Barrister Ijaz Hussain Batalvi prepared the case as per guidance from Manzoor Qadir. However, full fee to Barrister Ijaz Hussain Batalvi was paid. Barrister Ijaz Hussain Batalvi also deserves appreciation for fighting the case that resulted in Mashraqi's acquittal, otherwise anti-Mashraqi forces had planned to hang him.

The Chief Minister of West Pakistan addresses a Press Conference in Lahore and responds to questions. He states that the investigation officer (in Dr. Khan's murder investigation) was not appointed by him but by the Inspector General of Police (I.G. Police). The Chief Minister also disagrees with the suggestions made by the Leader of the Opposition in the West Pakistan Assembly that the British Scotland Yard should conduct the investigation (PT 1958 May 17).

Abdul Hameed Khan's (of Ferozsons) driver, Ibrahim, - who had driven Khan Qayyum to Mashraqi's house on April 28, 1958 - is again questioned in Lahore in regards to Dr. Khan Sahib's trial (PT 1958 May 17; C&MG 1958 May 17).

1958 May 17

Ch. Hassan Mohammed Randhawa (D.S.P. Crime and Investigating Officer) brings Mohammed Khursheed Khalid before the Lahore Additional District Magistrate (A.D.M). The A.D.M. grants Khalid a pardon. Later Khalid is taken to Lahore First Class Magistrate Qazi Hafizullah to record his statement. After the statement, he is taken to Borstal Jail (PT 1958 Sept. 24; PT 1958 Sept. 25; PT 1958 Oct. 10; PT 1958 Oct. 11, 1958; C&MG 1958 Jun. 12; C&MG 1958 Jun. 18; C&MG 1958 Oct. 10; C&MG 1958 Jun. 15; C&MG 1958 Sept. 24; C&MG 1958 Oct. 11).

Editor's comments: The A.D.M. granted Mohammed Khursheed Khalid a pardon because he had turned approver in Dr. Khan's murder case.

Medical Officer Mir Muhammad Riaz of the Borstal Institute examines Muhammad Khursheed Khalid (C&MG 1958 Jun. 17).

Dawn, Karachi May 17, 1958, publishes reports from the interview of Mashraqi son, Inamullah Khan:

"Mr. Inamullah Khan, Allama Mashriqi's son, told 'Dawn' today that his father told Wali Mohammad, a local advocate who had an interview with the Khaksar leader, that police did not let him have food, sent from his home, nor provided food from the police kitchen for the first two days of arrest.

Allama Mashriqi said to his advocate that police had been using abusive language and had stopped it only two days back. He said he had been provided with a filthy room.

According to his son Allama Mashriqi said to his advocate: 'May God grant me courage to bear this trouble and torture. History shows how innocent persons have always been prosecuted.'

Allama Mashriqi in his statement to the advocate said that the Government wanted to involve him in a conspiracy against Dr. Khan's murder so that 'I may not be able to create public opinion for Kashmir and thus the Pakistan Government may avoid any displeasure of Mr. Nehru.'

Continuing his statement, as Allama's son dictated, the Khaksar leader said that his followers under detention with him have been beaten up by the police and severely tortured during the past six days. 'The Government are trying to defame us in public by making fabricated accusations against us,' the Allama reportedly told his counsel.

Mr. Inamullah Khan said that that his father was running temperature at 102 deg and 103 deg.

Allama's advocate is likely to file a bail application on behalf of Khaksar leader tomorrow in the High Court.

Earlier in the morning, the Additional District Magistrate, Syed Hasanat Ahmad, granted permission to the advocate to see Allama Mashriqi in Lahore Fort and represent him. The permission was granted in response to an application submitted by Allama's son, Mr. Inamullah Khan, stating that at the time of his arrest his father had told him that since he was innocent and had no hand in any conspiracy legal aid should be provided.

The ADM also received this morning the report from Mr. Shaukat Tarar, a local magistrate, who was yesterday deputed by Mr.

Hasanat Ahmad to meet Allama Mashriqi and ascertain if he had engaged the advocate Wali Mohammad to plead his case" (*Dawn* 1958 May 17).

1958 May 18

The Punjab Muslim League criticizes the interrogation of Khan Qayyum (PT 1958 May 19).

1958 May 19

The Provincial Government bans the Khaksar Muslim League and a large number of armed police raid their offices in Lahore at midnight. The offices are thoroughly searched and Khaksar Muslim League materials are confiscated. Police interrogate individuals present at the premises. Police also conduct raids in other cities. The Government issues the following order:

"In exercise of the powers conferred by Section 16 of the Criminal Law Amendment Act, 1908, the Government of West Pakistan has declared unlawful the association known as the Pakistan Muslim League founded by Mr. Inayat Ullah Mashriqi, since it interfered and had for its objects, interference with the administration of law and with the maintenance of law and order and constituted a danger to the public peace" (PT 1958 May 20; *Dawn* 1958 May 21; PT 1958 Sept. 03; C&MG 1958 May 20; C&MG 1958 Sept. 20).

The Jamaat-i-Islami condems the ban on the Khaksar Muslim League. *Dawn*, Karachi of May 21, 1958, would report:

"Mian Tufail Mohammad, Secretary General, Jamaat-i-Islami, Pakistan in a statement yesterday strongly condemned the action of the Government in banning the [Khaksar] Muslim League founded by Allama Mashriqi.

He characterised the action as a weapon to harass political workers and a means to cure political activity in the country which, he reminded, was a 'blow to the oft-repeated promises made by those in power to have free and fair elections.'

Mian Tufail said if the 'Government thought there was sufficient material to justify such an extreme measure against a political party it was incumbent to take public into confidence and place all the relevant facts before it.'

He said that before an organisation was declared unlawful 'it must be shown at least prima facie that it was founded for an illegal purpose or as a whole supporting or engaged in it. Merely the fact that a few persons of any organisation were interrogated or even charged of some unlawful activity,' he emphasised, 'did not provide sufficient ground for declaring the entire organisation to which they belong as an unlawful association.'

The Jamaat leader has advised the supporters of the banned organisation to challege in a court of law 'this dictorial order as a well as the notorious provision of the law itself which empowered the Government to behave in such a ruthless manner in a democratic country.'

Mian Tufail also asked those in power 'not to behave in an irresponsible manner and exercise restraint especially when the elections are shortly going to be held. Putting curbs on the political activity of any person or organisation at this stage cannot fail to create the impression on the people's mind that the Government want to eliminate those who are opposed to the present leadership and who want to unseat them through the coming elections'" (*Dawn* 1958 May 21; PT 1958 May 21).

Mashriqi and three of his partymen remain imprisoned in Lahore Fort. Meanwhile, two other Khaksar leaders, Khurshid Khalid and Sami Khan, are sent to judicial lockup and moved to Lahore Central Jail after being detained for about nine days in Lahore Fort. (*Dawn* 1958 May 20; PT 1958 May 20).

Qazi Muhammad Hafizullah (Lahore First Class Magistrate) sends Muhammad Khursheed Khalid's statement to Syed Hasnat Ahmed (Lahore Additional District Magistrate [ADM]). The police also take a copy of the statement before it is sent to the ADM (C&MG 1958 Oct. 11).

Editor's comments: The police examined the copy of Muhammad Khursheed Khalid's statement prior to sending it to the Additional District Magistrate. They wanted to ensure that the statement was in accordance with their plans to implicate Mashraqi.

Police raid the Khaksar Muslim League's office in Quetta. A strong, armed police contingent along with a tear gas squad is present. Police thoroughly search the premises and confiscate Khaksar materials. After the search, the office is sealed and an armed police guard is posted at the location (PT 1958 May 21; C&MG 1958 May 20).

Police raid the Khaksar Muslim League's office in Rawalpindi. During the raid, armed police are posted in the area while police thoroughly search the premises. After the search, the office is sealed (PT 1958 May 21).

Heavily armed police raid various places in Sukker and search the houses of local leaders/organizers of the Khaksar Muslim League. Party documents, materials, and movable property are confiscated. The houses of Akhtar Qureshi and Malik Mehmood are sealed and armed police are posted (C&MG 1958 May 21).

Police raid the Khaksar Muslim League office in Campbellpur at night. The office is throughly searched. Party documents, materials, and movable property are confiscated and the office is sealed. An armed guard is posted at the office premises (C&MG 1958 May 21).

1958 May 20

Heavily armed police raid the Khaksar Muslim League's offices in Peshawar. They remove Khaksar party documents, materials, and movable property, including the party flags (C&MG 1958 May 21; PT 1958 May 21).
Editor's comments: The police were conducting raids on the Khaksar Muslim League offices in the hopes of finding objectionable materials that could be connected to the murder of Dr. Khan Sahib. However, nothing was found.

The Central Office of the Khasksar Muslim League in Ichhra (adjacent to Mashraqi's house) is sealed by the police. All types of materials are seized, including two jeeps and one private car (*Dawn* 1958 May 21; *Dawn* 1958 May 22; C&MG 1958 May 22).

Lahore Magistrate Qazi Hafizullah records Inayatullah Akhtar (a member of the Khaksar Muslim League) and Asghar Ali's statement regarding Dr. Khan Sahib's murder (*Dawn* 1958 Jun. 16; PT 1958 Jun. 17; *Dawn* 1958 Jun. 18; C&MG 1958 Jun. 17)
Editor's comments: Inayatullah Akhtar was originally produced in court as a prosecution witness, but later turned hostile. He stated that he was tortured to make a statement against Mashraqi.

Allama Mashraqi's son, who had been released on bail, is again arrested (*Dawn* 1958 May 21).

1958 May 21

Dawn, Karachi reports on the recent activities of the Government:
"As a sequel to the imposition of a ban on Allama Mashriqi's Muslim League widespread searches have been launced

by police of premises occupied by branches of the organisation in various cities.

Besides the Central Office of the organisation in Lahore, 34 branch offices of the Mashriqi League in West Pakistan have been declared unlawful places.

The ban was imposed last night [May 19, 1958] by a special notification issued by the Provinical Government under Section 16 of the Criminal Law (Amendment) Act 1909.

The Central Office of the organisation, adjacent to Allama Mashriqi's residence, was today [May 20, 1958] sealed by the police after seizing property of every description found in it including two jeeps and a car.

Allama's son, Mr. Inamullah Khan, who was released on bail was again taken into custody today [May 20, 1958] for interrogating him in connection with the activities of the Khaksar organisation.

The police claimed that recovery of helmets and uniforms from the organisation's offices provided an indication about its militaritistic tendency which they considered prejudicial to peace.

Meanwhile some political circles have expressed resentment over the imposition of ban on an organisation on the eve of general elections.

Indications available from Khaksar circles are that the ban is likely to be challeneged in a court of law.

According to latest reports some more arrests have been made by the police following searches of Khaksar League offices. Exact number of persons hauled up was unascertainable till late in the night" (*Dawn* 1958 May 21).

Allama Mashraqi is brought under heavy escort to the court of the Lahore Additional District Magistatre (ADM). *Dawn*, Karachi of May 22, 1958 would report, "A big crowd had gathered in court premises to have a glimpse of the Allama and his followers who were brought under heavy escort. Armed police had been posted at various points in court premises to prevent any possible untoward happening" (*Dawn* 1958 May 22). The Lahore Additional District Magistrate sends Mashraqi, along with other accuseds, to judicial lock-up. They are to be produced again in front of the Magistrate on May 26, 1958. Meanwhile, Khaksar Ali Mohammad is granted bail (C&MG 1958 May 22; PT 1958 May 22).

Editor's comments: *Dawn*, Karachi of May 22, 1958 reported that Mashraqi and five accuseds were sent to judicial lockup.

The Khaksar Muslim League office in Hyderabad is sealed. *Dawn*, Karachi of May 22, 1958 would report, "The office of the Khaksar ML [Muslim League] in Hyderabad was sealed by the police after search of its premises for about three and a half hours under the orders of the District Magistrate Hyderabad today [May 21, 1958]. A big posse of armed police stood by when the search was made by the police. Later the police also raided the office of the Khalid Memorial School and after search sealed the office. Armed guard is said to have been posted at both the offices" (*Dawn* 1958 May 22).

Mashraqi's son who was re-arrested on May 20, 1958 is released (*Dawn* 1958 May 22).

Police raids continue at Khaksar offices throughout the country. Khaksar documents and materials are confiscated (*Dawn* 1958 May 22).

Editor's comments: The police were struggling to prove that the Khaksar Muslim League was a militant body. Thus, they continued their rigorous searches for any materials implicating the Khaksars in Dr. Khan Sahib's case.

1958 May 22

Syed Hasnat Ahmed (Lahore Additional District Magistrate) rejects the bail application of Mashraqi and three prominent Khaksars (Inayat Ullah Akhtar, Malik Fateh Muhammad, and Pir Rehan Shah). Mashraqi is brought to court handcuffed and under extremely heavy police guard. A large crowd is present to catch a glimpse of Mashraqi (*Dawn* 1958 May 23). Syed Hasnat Ahmed also announces that Mohammed Khursheed Khalid, President of the Khaksar Muslim League (arrested on May 10, 1958 in connection with the Dr. Khan murder case), has turned approver. The A.D.M. states in his order:

"Mohammad Khurshid Khalid s/o Ch. Karam Dad has turned approver in case F.I.R. No. 186 dated 9-5-58 (Dr. Khan Sahib's murder case) under Section 302 read with Section 120 P.P.C., Police Station, Civil Lines.

He has made an application that he be treated as 'B' class prisoner due to the fact that he belongs to a respectable family and that his way of living is definitely superior to an ordinary person.

I have taken the evidence of two person, namely, Ch. Gul Nawaz, M.P.A., and Mr. Mohammad Rafi…He [Mohammad Khurshid Khalid] was the Sadar [President] of Khaksar Muslim League of which Mr. Mashriqi was naib Sadar [Vice President] at the time of his arrest. His status otherwise also justified his being placed in a better class. I, therefore, order that he should be treated as 'B' class prisoner till the pendency of the case."

Atta Mohammed (Dr. Khan Sahib's assassin) is also produced in the A.D.M.'s court. He is remanded to police custody until May 25, 1958 (PT 1958 May 23).

Editor's comments: How sad it is that Mashraqi, a Muslim and a national hero, at age 70 was handcuffed. His stature and reputation were ignored, and he was treated like a criminal, all based on fabricated charges.

A police officer records Khan Saadullah Khan's (son of Khan Sabib) statement (PT 1958 Oct. 16).

The ban on the Khaksar Muslim League is vehemently condmened. *The Civil & Military Gazette*, Lahore of May 24, 1958 would report:

"Syed Aziz-ul Huq, President of the East Pakistan Krishak Sramik Party, in a statement here yesterday [May 22, 1958] said: 'It is most unfortunate that the West Pakistan Government could find way to ban Allama Mashriqi's [Khaksar] Muslim League. This is a sin of democracy in the crudest form.'

Prof. Golam Azam, General Secretary, East Pakistan Jamat-i-Islami, said: 'The Republican Government of West Pakistan has threatened the existence of democracy by banning a political party without proving anything against it in any court of authority.

The simple arrest of the leader and some workers of Allama Mashraqi's [Khaksar] Muslim League by police for investigation does not at all justify this severe action against a party.

If this kind of despotic move of a party Government is tolerated, democracy can hardly thrive.

I appeal to all democratic forces to condemn this action with all force at their comand" (C&MG 1958 May 24; *Dawn* 1958 May 23).

In Peshawar, Malik Habib Ullah (Assistant Inspector General) questions Khan Abdul Ghaffar Khan (Dr. Khan Sahib's brother) and Dr. Khan Sahib's sons (*Dawn* 1958 May 24; *Dawn* 1958 Jul. 06).

1958 May 23

Dawn, Karachi reports:

"Sameen Khan and Fateh Mohammad who are also in judicial lock-up in connection with Dr. Khan's murder case are reported to be on fast for one week as a protest against what they claim to be their unjustified involvement in the matter...

Warrants of arrest have been issued againt the President of the Local Branch of the Mashriqi League [Khaksar Muslim League], Haji Ashraf, and Mr. Ishaq Zafar and Haji Allah [Khaksars from Rawalpindi]..." (*Dawn* 1958 May 23).

In Lahore, Hussain Shaheed Suhrawardy expresses grave doubts about the fairness of the forthcoming elections in Pakistan (*Dawn* 1958 May 24).

Editor's comments: Suhrawardy and other leaders had grave doubts about the fairness of the upcoming elections in Pakistan. On May 23, 1958, the Prime Minister of Pakistan, Malik Firoz Khan Noon, declared that the elections would be fair and free. But how could the elections possibly be fair and free when Allama Mashraqi was imprisoned on a fabricated case and his party was completely banned?

1958 May 24

Dawn, Karachi reports that Malik Habibullah (Assistant Inspector General) questioned Maulana Maudoodi (*Dawn* 1958 May 24).

1958 May 26

The Lahore Additional District Magistrate remands Allama Mashraqi and five followers to judicial custody for another 12 days. Allama Mashraqi complains of police torture. *Dawn*, Karachi of May 27, 1958 would report:

"Allama Mashriqi, when produced in the court, complained to the ADM that he was not receiving proper treatment in jail. He stated that he was subjected to oppressive treatment while in police custody in the Lahore Fort and added that his clothes were torn as under, the papers on which he had noted instructions for his counsel were confiscated and several persons were made to stand on his chest. He had not received any relief even on his transfer to judicial custody and was locked up in a cell intended for condemned prisoners, he went on, and said that he was not allowed to smoke 'huqqa,' nor other necessary things were supplied to him. The Allama complained that the jail authorities had ordered that if he got his meals from his house he would not be allowed to have anything from the jail and that all he needs must come from his house. Such restrictions on B Class prisoners were unprecedented, he added.

Making a plea for being lodged in A Class the Allama said that the treatment which he was expected to receive in B class was not being given to him" (*Dawn* 1958 May 27).

1958 May 28

Police continue their raids on Khaksar houses (PT 1958 May 29).

Police raid various houses in Lahore, including the house of an old Khaksar (Muhammad Latif), in connection with Dr. Khan Sahib's murder case (*Dawn* 1958 May 30).

Khan Abdul Qayyum Khan, President of the Pakistan Muslim League, makes the following announcement:
"A news item has appeared in the local Press this morning to the effect that in my statement to the police in connection with Doctor Khan Sahib's murder case I am alleged to have stated that I had met the alleged murderer Ata Muhammad, at Allama Mashriqi's residence. This is absolutely untrue. I never made such a statement to the police. As a matter of fact I have never met Ata Muhamad at all. As regards the statement purporting that the police will summon me as a witness, I have no knowledge of such a possibility" (C&MG 1958 May 29).

The Lahore Additional District Magistrate passes an order stating:
"The case [of] the State versus Alama Mashriqi and others under Sec. 302 read with Sec. 120-B/PPC should be put up before Mr. M.N. Rizvi for commitment proceeding. In future all papers for remand should also be produced before him. The challan may be put in the court before Mr. Rizvi well ahead of the 9th June as he intends to take up this case from that date" (C&MG 1958 May 29).

1958 May 29

In Lahore, police raid the office of Yasin Butt, editor of the daily *Waqt*. They remove papers from the office (PT 1958 Oct. 15).

1958 May 30

Dawn, Karachi reports that the Government has appointed M.N. Rizvi (a Lahore First Class Magistrate) as a Special Judge to hear the murder case of Dr. Khan Sahib. According to the newspaper, the Lahore Additional District Magistrate had been hearing the case thus far (*Dawn* 1958 May 30).

1958 June 02

Dawn, Karachi reports that police have filed an application against the daily *Nawa-i-Waqat* for publishing details of the Dr. Khan Sahib murder investigation. *Nawa-i-Waqat* had reported on May 28, 1958 that Khan Abdul Qayyum Khan would be produced as a prosecution witness and that the investigating officer felt that the Muslim League was not involved in the murder of Dr. Khan Sahib (*Dawn* 1958 Jun. 02).

1958 June 05

The Inspector General of Police (I.G.) announces in a press conference in Lahore that Mashraqi is behind Dr. Khan Sahib's murder. The Investigating Officer and Assistant Inspector General of Police (A.I.G., Crime) is also present at the conference. The I.G. of Police further narrates Ata Mohammed's background and states that Ata Mohammed was never a Khaksar (PT 1958 Jun. 06).

1958 June 06

Mashraqi and the others are brought to court. In the court of the Special Judge M.N. Rizvi in Lahore, police put up challans in connection with Dr. Khan Sahib's murder. Those challaned are Ata Mohammad, Mashriqi, and three of Mashraqi's followers (Sameen Jan, Mohammad Rafi, and Fateh Mohammad). The Judge also discharges four previous suspects (Rehan Shah, Asghar Haider, Zafar Haider, and Ali Mohammad) due to a lack of evidence against them. Mashraqi is challaned under Section 302/120 P.P.C. *The Pakistan Times*, Lahore of June 07, 1958 would report:

"Mr. Mashriqi submitted a written complaint to the Judge saying that he was badly treated by the jail authorities. He alleged that about a fortnight back when he was preparing a statement of certain facts for his counsel, three persons pounced upon him and snatched away the paper and read it. He further alleged that those persons were made to sit on his chest and his shirt was torn…Mr. Mashriqi said he would submit another statement.

A heavy contingent of armed police was present in the court premises. The police had cordoned off the courts and people were not allowed to come near the court room.

A large number of supporters of Mr. Mashriqi who had gathered in the court premises were pushed back by the armed policemen. Even the Press photographers were not allowed to stand in the verandah outside the court room.

When Mr. Mashriqi and his companions were being taken out of the court under a heavy guard, his followers and admirers shouted slogans, 'Allama Mashraqi Zindabad.' They greeted their leader with 'Ya Amir Salam-O-Alaikum'" (PT 1958 Jun. 07).

The prosecution is represented by P.I. Syed Fayyaz Hussain while S.M.Nasim, Ghulam Qadir, and Khawaja Wali Muhammad act as defence counsels for Mashraqi and the other Razakars accused. Muhammad Khursheed Khalid (an approver) is not present in the court room. The defense counsel asks the Magistrate for 10 days to study the case, but he refuses and fixes June 10, 1958 as the date of the next hearing. He also announces that next hearing will be held in Borstal Jail and that entry will be restricted (*Dawn* 1958 Jun. 07; C&MG 1958 Jun. 06; C&MG 1958 Jun. 07).

Editor's comments: The public showed tremendous enthusiasm and support for Mashraqi. Many were in tears because certain individuals with vested interests had wrongfully involved this great leader in a murder case. Others were angered by those who had dragged Mashraqi into court and made his life miserable for no reason. When Mashraqi arrived at the court on June 06, 1958, a large crowd had gathered; they shouted slogans and saluted Mashraqi as he was taken in and out of the court.

1958 June 07

An appeal filed by Allama Mashraqi and nine others comes up for hearing in the court of the Additional Sessions Judge. Their appeal is in regards to a ruling by a Lahore Magistrate, who sentenced them to different terms of imprisonment for allegedly assaulting an ASI and a constable and keeping them in wrongful confinement at Wahgah border. (*Dawn* 1958 Jun. 09; PT 1958 Jun. 08).

Editor's comments: This was another case against Mashraqi. This appeal was in connection with a judgement against Mashraqi on October 22, 1957 when Ch. Mohammed Zafar Yasin, a First Class Magistrate of Lahore, had sentenced Mashriqi to two years of imprisonment and a fine of Rs.1200 (PT 1957 Oct. 23; PT 1957 Oct. 29; PT 1958 Jan. 11). This sentence was for a false charge and was imposed solely to prevent Mashraqi from organizing a million-man march to seek freedom for Kashmir in 1957. The Government was constantly implicating Mashraqi with false charges in an attempt to keep him out of politics.

1958 June 10

A hearing for Dr. Khan Sahib's murder case is held in Borstal Jail, Lahore in front of Special Magistrate (Trial Magistrate) M.N. Rizvi. Mashraqi is brought to the court handcuffed and his plea to conduct an open trial is rejected. The prosecution is represented by Mohammed Anwar (Assistant Advocate General) and others while Mashraqi and the other defendants (except Atta Mohammed) are represented by S.M. Nasim, Barrister Ijaz Hussain Batalvi, and Khawaja Wali Mohammed.

Mohammed Khursheed Khalid (approver) records his statement in court. He informs the court that he was elected President of the Khaksar Muslim League by the Majlis-i-Shura of the party. He further states that he had five Vice Presidents: Allama Mashraqi, Sheikh Fazal Elahi, Yasin Butt (editor, *Waqt*), Mohammad Rafi, and Zafar Haider.

Mohammed Khursheed Khalid informs the court that the name of the Islam League was changed to Muslim League in 1956 at a meeting in Minto Park (PT 1958 Jun. 11; PT 1958 Jun. 12) "because Mr. Nehru had ridiculed Pakistan in the Indian Parliament by saying that Muslim League had weakened and that Pakistan was sure to become weak." He also informs the court that the Idara-i-Aliya had proclaimed that if 300,000 Khaksars assembled in Delhi on June 30, 1947, they would conquer India. He further states that Allama Mashraqi had founded the Islam League to secure areas including Kashmir, Punjab, and Bengal (which were treacherously given to India). Khalid adds that the Khaksar Muslim League has the same objectives as the Islam League. Khalid states that they had decided to march towards India with one million people on October 21, 1957.

Khalid also informs the court that Allama Mashraqi and Khan Qayyum met on April 28, 1958 at Ichhra, and discussed the merger of the [Khaksar] Muslim League and the All Pakistan Muslim League. Khalid states that he was present at the meeting and that Allama Mashraqi had arranged the meeting with his consent. Prior to the meeting with Khan Qayyum, Mashriqi had informed Khalid that Sardar Abdur Rab Nishter had not accepted Mashraqi's offer to amalgamate the [Khaksar] Muslim League and the Nishtar Muslim League. Khan Qayyum had issued a statement asking Sardar Abdur Rab Nishter to merge the two Leagues.

Mohammed Khursheed Khalid states that in January, 1958, he suggested to his deputies to contest the forthcoming elections of the National and Provincial Assemblies (PT 1958 Jun. 11; C&MG 1958 Jun. 11; C&MG 1958 Sept. 23; *Dawn* 1958 Jun. 11).

1958 June 11

Mohammed Khursheed Khalid, an approver in Dr. Khan Sahib's case, turns hostile. He states in court that the police at Lahore Fort gave him a severe beating and his statement in court on June 10, 1958 was under police coercion. He further adds that the police had threatened "to set him right" if he did not act according to their instructions. Khalid states that he did not know Ata Mohammad and saw him for the first time in court. He informs the court that Mashraqi had never consulted him about the murder of anybody (PT 1958 Jun. 12; PT 1958 Sept. 26). He also states that it was wrong for the Magistrate to give him one hour to consider whether he wanted to make a statement as an approver. According to Mohammad Khursheed Khalid, "The Magistrate started writing my statement as soon as I was produced before him..." (*Dawn* 1958 Jun. 12).

The Public Prosecutor declares that the approver has turned hostile. He then cross-examines Muhammad Khursheed Khalid with the permission of the court. The defence doesn't object (C&MG 1958 Jun. 12).

1958 June 12

Muhammad Khursheed Khalid continues his statement in Dr. Khan Sahib's murder case in the court of Special Magistrate M.N.Rizvi in Lahore. Muhammad Khursheed Khalid states that the police forced him to memorize a statement, which he would then repeat in front of the Magistrate. Police wanted him to say that Allama Mashraqi was a dictator and abetted his devotees in the murder of Dr. Khan Sahib (*Dawn* 1958 Jun. 13). He further adds that he had correctly stated previously in court that Allama Mashraqi gave the same conditions of amalgamation (of the Khaksar Muslim League and the Muslim League) to Khan Abdul Qayyum Khan that he had given to Sardar Abdur Rab Nishtar. However, Khalid had omitted the fact that Mashraqi had asked his permission prior to sending the same conditions to Khan Abdul Qayyum Khan. *The Civil & Military Gazette*, Lahore of June 13, 1958 would report:

"The approver [Muhammad Khursheed Khalid] stated that he did not say before that the Allama had asked his permission to put before the Khan [Khan Abdul Qayyum Khan] the same conditions which the Allama had offered to Sirdar Nishtar [Sardar Abdur Rab Nishtar] and that he [Muhammad Khursheed Khalid] had agreed. He said that he had omitted to do so because the police wanted him to make a statement that would show the Allama as a dictator" (C&MG 1958 Jun. 13; PT 1958 Jun. 13; *Dawn* 1958 Jun. 13).

Editor's comments: As Mashraqi told Khan Abdul Qayyum Khan and others, he wanted power to be shared with the masses. It is also important to note that Muhammad Khursheed Khalid came from an ordinary family. This again shows that Mashraqi believed in empowering the masses, and not just the rich. Furthermore, Mashraqi sought permission from Muhammad Khursheed Khalid to send conditions to Khan Abdul Qayyum Khan. This action in itself proves that Mashraqi was not at all a dictator, as some anti-Mashraqi elements have suggested. If Mashraqi had been seeking power for himself, he could have easily done so by taking advantage of various opportunities throughout his lifetime.

In a different case, Mashraqi's appeal comes up for a hearing in the court of Mirza Bashir Ahmed, Additional Sessions Judge. The judge reserves judgement, which is to be announced on June 30, 1958. (Here, Mashraqi was sentenced to two years of imprisonment and Rs. 1200 fine). (PT 1958 Jun. 13).

Editor's comments: The government did whatever they could to keep Mashraqi out of politics; they did not even leave him alone when he was old and sick. They implicated him in different court cases and arrested his followers and family members. The CID department and police constantly chased Mashraqi, his family, and other Khaksars/Razakars and raided their property. The government gave no regard to Mashriqi's stature, handcuffed him, tortured him, and treated him like an ordinary criminal.

1958 June 13

The Pakistan Times, Lahore reports that the prosecution is to produce Maulana Abul Ala Maududi, Khan Abdul Qaiyum Khan, and Col Abid Hussain as witnesses in Dr. Khan Sahib's murder trial (PT 1958 Jun. 13).

Ata Mohammed, the alleged assassin of Dr. Khan Sahib, cross-examines Mohammed Khursheed Khalid in the court of Special Magistrate (Trial Magistrate) M.N. Rizvi in Lahore. During the cross-examination, Khalid informs the court that police had shown him a tonga-wala in the Lahore Fort and had asked him to identify the tonga-wala when needed (PT 1958 Jun. 14). Khalid also states that Allama Mashraqi was the acknowledged leader of the Khaksar Movement and that everyone respected him. He further informs the court that Ehsanullah Khan Aslam (Allama Mashraqi's son) was killed in 1940 (*Dawn* 1958 Jun. 14; C&MG 1958 Jun. 14)

Editor's comments: Ehsanullah Khan Aslam (Mashraqi's son) died in May 1940 after being badly injured by police during their raid on the Khaksar Tehrik Headquarters (adjacent to Mashraqi's house) on March 19, 1940.

1958 June 14

Cross-examination of Muhammad Khurshid Khalid concludes in the court of Special Magistrate M.N. Rizvi in Lahore. Khalid informs the court that his statement as an approver was made under fear of police violence and that the statement was actually given to him by the police. Khalid describes the police torture on May 11 and 12, 1958:

"They [the police] made me stand up with a stick between my feet, another stick was on my shoulders and my handcuffed hands were raised above it with one man holding the chain. Others were beating me on my shoulders, back, buttocks and thighs.

When I fell down they made me sit down and gave me water and asked me whether it was not true that the murder of Dr. Khan Sahib was perpetrated during the meeting between Khan Qayyum and Allama Mashriqi. Six or seven men were inflicting violence on me. They locked me up at four in the morning and took me out in the afternoon.

Again violence was committed on me on the night between May 12 and 13, and I was beaten after being laid down on the ground. They beat me with a 'lither' (made of leather) which was 1½ feet long and nine inches wide and was quite heavy and hard. The men were of the same number and they took turns at beating me. The night had not gone far when I agreed to say what they wanted me to say because I could not bear more violence" (C&MG 1958 Jun. 15).

Khurshid Khalid also informs the court that no friends or relatives were allowed to meet him in jail. He states that his remand on May 11, 1958 was given at Lahore (C&MG 1958 Jun. 15). Continuing, Khalid says that the doctor who came to jail only took his body weight and did not examine him. Khalid further alleges that while he was being taken to the court of Qazi Hafizullah, the Superintendent of Police threatened him to give his statement as instructed by the police or face further police custody (PT 1958 Jun. 15). On May 16, 1958, police told Khurshid Khalid that his relatives had been arrested. Khalid states that the police violence against him was meant to make him say what the police wanted (*Dawn* 1958 Jun. 15).

Muhammad Khurshid Khalid further states that on May 16, 1958, the police showed a tongawala (who was a prosecution witness) to him at Lahore Fort so that he (Khalid) could recognize him during an identification parade. Khalid also states that police took him to Wazirabad, where he was shown to a shopkeeper so that the shopkeeper could identify him. According to Khalid:

"At the fort Bashir was shown to me and it was mentioned that he was a resident of Ichhra. At Wazirabad several attempts to procure a witness, who would say that he had sold the daggers to me, were made but failed. Then the DSP [Randhawa] in my presence talked to a shopkeeper and assured him that no harm would be done to him if he became a witness. He was told that I was also a witness.

On this the shopkeeper agreed to become a witness.

The DSP told me when he was leaving me at the jail that the Inspector-General of Police had planned to procure an approver at the cost of Rs. 20,000 so that all of us should be hanged and that I was fortunate to become an approver. He also told me that it had been arranged by the I.G. that the case would be heard by the Sessions Judge Aslam, who had promised to sentence us to death if an approver could be procured" (C&MG 1958 Jun. 15).

Regarding the Khaksar Movement, Khurshid Khalid informs the court that it was a peaceful movement and its aim was public service, discipline, and establishing the supremacy of Islam (through exemplary conduct). He further states that the Khaksar Muslim League is also a peaceful organization and its aim is not to have political opponents assassinated. He states that the Khaksars do not consider any other political party to be as strong as the Khaksar Muslim League and they don't believe that the Republican Party would have won the elections if Dr. Khan Sahib were still alive (*Dawn* 1958 Jun. 15).

The court also examines Lahore Magistrate Qazi Hafizullah, who had recorded Muhammad Khurshid Khalid's statement on May 17, 1958. Qazi Hafizullah informs the court that he gave a copy of Khurshid Khalid's statement to the police on May 19, 1958. Qazi Hafizullah is cross-examined by Barrister Ijaz Hussain Batalvi and S.M. Nasim. Replying to a question, Qazi Hafizullah states that Asghar Ali's (a prosecution witness) statement was recorded on May 20, 1958, but it did not occur to him (Qazi Hafizullah) to verify whether the statement was memorized. Qazi Hafizullah further admits that he didn't examine Muhammad Khurshid Khalid for police torture, though he knew that Khalid had been detained in Lahore Fort (*Dawn* 1958 Jun. 16).

Editor's comments: Also see September 25, 1958 of this work for details of police torture to Mohammed Khurshid Khalid.
1958 June 15

The Pakistan Times, Lahore publishes news under the following title: "Police had planned to get Mashriqi hanged." The newspaper further reports, "Explaining the details further, the approver said that the D.S.P. who accompanied him while he was being taken to the jail told him that the Inspector General of Police had planned to procure an approver at the cost of Rs. 20,000, so that all of them (the approver and other accused Khaksars) should be hanged" (PT 1958 Jun. 15).

1958 June 16

In the case of Dr. Khan Sahib's murder, another prosecution witness turns hostile. Inayatullah Akhtar, a member of the Khaksar Muslim League and a prosecution witness, informs the court that he never saw Ata Muhammad with Mashraqi and Muhammad Khurshid Khalid, or at Allama Mashraqi's Mehmankhana (guesthouse) in Ichhra, Lahore. He also states, "Neither did I see Ata Muhammad at the meeting between Allama Mashriqi and Khan Abdul Qayyum Khan" (C&MG 1958 Jun. 17). Inayatullah Akhtar discloses that police kept him in Lahore Fort for eleven days and tortured him. He further states that his earlier statement in the court of Qazi Hafizullah on May 20, 1958, was a result of this torture. He adds that while he was giving his statement before the Magistrate, the police were present in the courtroom (*Dawn* 1958 Jun. 18).

The Pakistan Times, Lahore of June 17, 1958 would report further about the police torture: "He [Inayatullah Akhtar] said they [the accuseds] were not allowed to sleep for two or three days and were beaboured. He deposed that they walked on his thighs, jumped on his chest, made him hold his ears from underneath his legs for three hours and wanted him to make the statement that he made on May 20 [1958]. He further deposed that the statement was taught to them first orally and then they were made to take a dictation of the statement which remained with them till just before the Magistrate examined them. 'It was taken from us outside his Court room'…they [the police] had been telling him that if he did not give the statement which they wanted him to give they would have him imprisoned for seven years. 'I have the fear even now that I will be maltreated,' the witness told the Court" (PT 1958 Jun. 17).

Dawn, Karachi of June 18, 1958 would also state, "he [Inayatullah Akhtar] stated that now he had been brought from the [Lahore] Fort, where he had been kept since the 10th of this month. During this period, the police had not allowed him to see his relations or friends. 'No one told me that my mother had come to see me or had applied for that purpose'" (*Dawn* 1958 Jun. 18).

Regarding Allama Mashraqi, Inayatullah Akhtar states that the Khaksars respect him, "but the whole world respects him" (C&MG 1958 Jun. 17).

Also see *Dawn*, Karachi of June 18, 1958 for a report on Karam Bibi's story about her son, Inayatullah Akhtar.

The other witnesses examined in court are Lt. Col. Syed Ejaz Hussain (Superintendent of the Borstal Institute and Juvenile Jail), Dr. Khalid Mehmood (Deputy Medical Superintendent, Unit Hospital, Lahore), and Dr. Mir Muhammad Riaz (Medical Officer of Borstal Institute, Lahore). Mir Muhammad Riaz informs the court that he medically examines everyone admitted to Borstal Jail. In response to the question of whether he checked Muhammad Khurshid Khalid's shoulders, buttocks, and thighs for any marks of police violence, he responds that he was "only searching for identification marks and not for injuries." Mir Muhammad Riaz further states that he did not examine Khurshid Khalid's shoulder, back, or thighs. He admits that it was his duty to look for injuries during the medical examination, but he failed to do so. The court then examines Mir Muhammad Riaz's Medical Register and notices that column 14, where injuries are supposed to be noted, was left blank (C&MG 1958 Jun. 17).

Outside the courtroom, police forcibly abduct Inayatullah Akhtar's mother, despite her protests and cries. Barrister Ijaz Hussain Batalvi reports the incident to the court.

Editor's comments: The inquiry was conducted in a deplorable manner. Muhammad Khurshid Khalid's injuries due to police violence were not recorded on purpose. Furthermore, police abducted Inayatullah Akhtar's mother because Akhtar had turned hostile. The witnesses turning hostile is glaring proof of loyalty to Mashraqi; despite fear of police, people came out with the truth.

1958 June 17

In the court of Special Magistrate (Trial Magistrate) M.N. Rizvi, Ata Mohammad concludes his cross-examination of Inayatullah Akhtar in Dr. Khan Sahib's murder case. The statements of three Magistrates are also recorded.

Inayatullah Akhtar, a prosecution witness who had turned hostile on June 16, 1958, informs the court that he risks danger to his life at the hands of the police. Inayatullah Akhtar also submits that his old mother is missing and was taken by police on June 16, 1958. The

Magistrate, however, says he is not competent to take any action against those responsible.

Ata Mohammed's confessional statement, which he had previously made before Magistrate Mohammed Shaukat Tarar, is read in court. In the statement, Ata Mohammed confesses to the murder of Dr. Khan Sahib.

Syed Hasnat Ahmed, the Lahore Additional District Magistrate, states that "Allama Masharaqi had once complained that the police had snatched from him some papers after getting upon his chest" (PT 1958 Jun. 18).

In response to a question, Syed Hasnat Ahmed states that "if someone stands behind the curtain in my retiring room I will not be able to see him" (C&MG 1958 Jun. 18; *Dawn* 1958 Jun. 18; C&MG 1958 Jun. 19).

Editor's comments: Additional District Magistrate was referring to the police listening to the statement of witnesses. DSP Randhawa was present behind the curtain when Mohammad Khurshid Khalid recorded his statement to Syed Hasnat Ahmed. Randhawa was listening to ensure that Khalid's statement was in accordance with what the police wanted him to state.

1958 June 18

The court proceedings in the murder case of Dr. Khan Sahib continue. Mashraqi files an application stating that he is about 70 years old and has been feeling sick, and that the long court proceedings are adversely affecting his health. He also continues to suffer from severe mental and physical strain. Keeping this in mind, he requests exemption from the long court proceedings. However, the judge denies this exemption

Mashraqi also requests that he be allowed to smoke a huqqa in jail, but the judge states that this is a matter for the jail authorities to decide. However, the judge permits him to smoke a huqqa in the courtroom. And keeping in mind Mashraqi's extremely poor health, the judge allows him to sit in an easy chair and permits Mashraqi's son to take care of him. The court also provides a bed outside the courtroom for Mashraqi to use.

Editor's comments: Mashraqi was an old man and was under tremendous pressure of all kinds. His family was also under grave stress, but the Government remained unconcerned. It is unfortunate how authorities treated a man of Mashraqi's stature in his own country. He was a man who devoted his life to uplift the masses and revive the lost glory of the Muslims.

Dawn, Karachi reports on Karam Bibi's story about her son, Inayatullah Akhtar:

"Earlier, in the morning, on Monday [June 16, 1958] Karam Bibi, the mother of Inayatullah Akhter...presented an application to the Magistrate for the return of her son.

In the application, she stated that on June 10 [1958] her son was suddenly taken away from her house by some police officials in a jeep without telling any reason and had not returned him till Monday.

Inayatullah, it may be recalled, was held up for interrogation by the police on May 10, but was discharged on May 20.

From then onwards till June 10 he stayed at home until he was allegedly brought from there by some police officials and held up in the Shahi Qilla [Lahore Fort] till Monday, when he was allowed by the Special Magistrate to go with the defence counsel, Khawja Wali Mohammad, after having been bound down to attend the Court today" (*Dawn* 1958 Jun. 18; *Dawn* 1958 Jun. 17).

1958 June 19

In the court of Special Magistrate M.N.Rizvi, more witnesses are examined in Dr. Khan Sahib's murder trial. Barrister Ijaz Hussain also cross-examines the witnesses (PT 1958 Jun. 20; C&MG 1958 Jun. 20; *Dawn* 1958 Jun. 20).

The Civil & Military Gazette, Lahore reports that the Pakistan Safety Act will be extended for another two years (C&MG 1958 Jun. 19).

1958 June 20

In the court of Special Magistrate M.N.Rizvi, more witnesses are examined in Dr. Khan Sahib's murder trial.

One witness, a police officer, informs the court that the Islam League held a public meeting at Chiniot near Lyallpur (now Faisalabad) on June 08, 1956 (PT 1958 Jun. 21; PT 1958 Oct. 03).

Another police officer states (about another meeting) that the Islam League held a public meeting at Minto Park, Lahore from November 23 to November 25, 1956. He further states that at the meeting (on November 25, 1956), Allama Mashraqi gave an address known as *Khitab-i-Aam*. According to the police officer, Mashraqi stated in this address, "This Dr. Khan Sahib has imposed restrictions on us for these three days [November 23-25, 1956] during which we are holding a military camp, a restriction that we should not walk straight but should walk like the dead." On this there were shouts from the crowd: "Death to the stooge of Bharat" (*Dawn* 1958 Jun. 22; C&MG 1958 Jun. 21)

1958 June 21

In the court of Special Magistrate M.N.Rizvi, more witnesses are examined in Dr. Khan Sahib's murder trial. A Sub Inspector, C.I.D Police, informs the court that Allama Mashraqi delivered a speech on November 11, 1956 outside Mochi Gate, Lahore. (PT 1958 Jun. 22; PT 1958 Jun. 23)

The Police Surgeon also testifies in court. He states that he conducted Dr. Khan Sahib's post mortem examination on May 09, 1958 at 8:30 a.m. He also states that he examined Ata Mohammad (accused) on May 09, 1958. The Surgeon provides details of both examinations to the court (C&MG 1958 Jun. 22).

1958 June 23

There are no court proceedings on this day on Dr. Khan Sahib's murder trial (PT 1958 Jun. 24).

1958 June 24

Proceedings resume in Dr. Khan Sahib's murder trial in the court of Special Magistrate M.N. Rizvi. The prosecution adds two more witnesses, bringing the total to 130. Maulana Abul Ala Maududi (Amir of the Jamaat-i-Islami) makes the following statement in court:

"I am the Amir of the Jama'at-i-Islami, which is a well-known party of Pakistan. I hold *dars* of Quran-i-Majid and *Hadis* on every Sunday in Barkat Ali Hall or in the Y.M.C.A. Hall. This we had been doing before the murder of Dr. Khan Sahib also. After dars I receive chits [piece of paper with question(s)] asking questions from me and I answer them in the meeting on the loudspeaker. The chits are not kept but are destroyed as unnecessary. I remember that either on Sunday, April 27, or on Sunday, May 4, one of the questions received by me was whether it was permissible for one to become a Shia if that was the only way to recover his wife. I had replied on the loudspeaker that it was reasonable to stick to a religion if one had faith in it, but to change religion for acquiring a woman was not good. I do not remember if anyone discussed the matter with me after the meeting. As is usual many people after the meeting asked me to give them time to meet me at my house for discussion of questions which were in their minds and I gave them time for that. Usually, I give the time between *Asar* [afternoon prayers] and *Maghrib* [evening prayers]. After the murder of Dr. Khan Sahib the police contacted me and asked me the questions which the Special P.P. has put today" (PT 1958 Jun. 25).

Barrister Ijaz Hussain Batalvi cross-examines other witnesses, but does not cross-examine Maulana Abul Ala Maudoodi (*Dawn* 1958 Jun. 25; C&MG 1958 Jun. 25).

Editor's comments: The prosecution had increased the number of witnesses from 124 to 128 on June 15, 1958. It now added two more for a total of 130 (PT 1958 Jun. 25). The prosecution found its case to be very weak, and thus kept adding witnesses in an attempt to ensure that Mashraqi and his followers could somehow be convicted.

1958 June 25

Another witness, Asghar Ali, turns hostile in Dr. Khan Sahib's murder trial in the court of Special Magistrate M.N. Rizvi. He informs the court that his statement before Lahore Magistrate Qazi Hafizullah was incorrect and that he gave the statement because of threats from the police. *Dawn*, Karachi of June 26, 1958 would report:

"He [Asghar Ali] told the Court his previous statement before a Magistrate, Mr Hafizullah, was made at the instance of the police. He alleged he was made to stand for hours with his arms raised up and that he was beaten with a leather 'durra' [a leather tool used by police for beating criminals] and his private parts were pulled.

The witness further deposed after his statement under Section 164 police had been threatening him that if he did not stick to that statement the police would blacklist him and would forfeit the pension of his father and grandfather" (*Dawn* 1958 Jun. 26).

Asghar Ali also states that Mashriqi was a leader of the Movement, but it was wrong to say that it was incumbent upon every Khaksar to obey his orders.

The prosecutor requests that Asghar Ali be arrested for giving a divergent statement under oath and prosecuted under Section 476 Cr.P.C. (PT 1958 Jun. 26).

Other prosecution witnesseses also record their statement in court. Allama Mashraqi himself cross-examines prosecution witness Mohammad Bashir (C&MG 1958 Jun. 26).

The Civil & Military Gazette, Lahore of June 26, 1958 would further report, "The number of prosecution witnesses to turn 'hostile' so far has risen to three. The previous two being Mr. Khurshid Khalid, the approver, and Mr. Inayat Ullah Akhter. Both these witnesses in their evidence told similar stories of alleged police violence and coersion" (C&MG 1958 Jun. 26).

Editor's comments: It is disgusting that the police tried to implicate Mashraqi in a conspiracy to murder Dr. Khan Sahib. All of these events prove that Mashraqi's family and the Khaksar circle were correct in stating that the government wanted to implicate Mashraqi in the murder in order to have a justification to hang him. This is the third witness that turned hostile.

A bail application filed on behalf of Mashriqi and three others' (Sameen Jan, Mohammed Rafi, and Fateh Mohammed) in the court of Lahore Sessions Judge Malik Mohammed Aslam Khan is returned. The application is returned on the grounds that the counsel filing the application does not have power of attorney from the petitioners. Earlier, Sh. Mohammed Nasim, counsel of the petitioners, sought permission to withdraw the bail application as per his clients' instructions. He informed the court that the four petitioners want to consult Manzur Qadir (who later became a Foreign Minister in Ayub Khan's cabinet) prior to pursuing the application and reserve the right to apply for bail again (PT 1958 Jun. 27).

1958 June 26

A.R. Changez (Justice of the West Pakistan High Court) issues a notice to Mohammad Sharif (S.H.O., Ichhra Police Station, Lahore) to explain why he should not be punished for being in contempt of the court of Magistrate M.N.Rizvi (who is hearing Dr. Khan Sahib's murder case). The notice comes following a petition filed by Barrister Ijaz Hussain on behalf of Karamat un Nisa (also known as Karam Bibi, mother of Inayatullah Akhtar). In the petition, it is alleged that the police abducted Karamat un Nisa from outside Borstal Jail on June 16, 1958 after her son turned hostile in Dr. Khan Sahib's murder case. In the petition, Karamat un Nisa narrates the story of her abduction and the torture of her son by police (PT 1958 Jun. 27; *Dawn* 1958 Jun. 27).

Dr. Khan Sahib's murder case continues in the court of Special Magistrate M.N.Rizvi in Lahore. Amiran Bibi (Ata Muhammad's former wife) is produced as a prosecution witness. Other witnesses are also examined (C&MG 1958 Jun. 27; *Dawn* 1958 Jun. 27).

1958 June 27

Dr. Khan Sahib's murder case continues in the court of Special Magistrate M.N.Rizvi in Lahore. The Special Public Prosecutor informs the court that the prosecution has dropped three more witnesses. Other prosecution witnesses are examined in court (*Dawn* 1958 Jun. 28).

1958 July 01

Dr. Khan Sahib's murder case continues in the court of Special Magistrate M.N.Rizvi in Lahore. More prosecution witnesses are examined. The witnesses include Khan Sher Bahadur Khan (Officer on Special Duty in the West Pakistan Law Department, Lahore), servants of Dr. Khan Sahib's son (Khuda Bakhsh, Baptist Perlea, and Jalal Din), and Ch. Abdul Majeed Bajwa (Deputy Suprintendent of Police, Civil Lines, Lahore) (C&MG 1958 Jul. 02; *Dawn* 1958 Jul. 02)

1958 July 02

Dr. Khan Sahib's murder case continues in the court of Special Magistrate M.N.Rizvi in Lahore. More prosecution witnesses are examined. The witnesses include M.A.K. Chaudhri (Assistant Inspector General of Police and a neighbor of Dr. Khan Sahib's son) and Muhammad Shamaz Khan (an MPA from Naushera, NWFP) (C&MG 1958 Jul. 03). Muhammad Shamaz Khan narrates the incident of the attack by Red Shirts in 1939. He states:

"In 1939 I was Salar of the Khaksars of Teh. [Tehsil] Naushera [NWFP].

On June 10, 1939, I had led a a jash [contingent] of the Khaksars consisting of some 45 persons to village Dangarzai where we had to set up the flag at the residence of Ghaus Muhammad, who had been appointed Salar of that village.

On our way back we tried to enter a mosque at Azamgarh to say our evening prayers, but the mulla did not allow us to enter the mosque. Then we started saying our prayers on the roadside.

On this many Red Shirts of village Azamgarh and village Akora [Akhora] surrounded us and started shouting. The Red Shirts then attacked us. They were armed with lathis and pitchforks.

We retreated but one of our men was killed and four or five of us were injured. I lodged the report of this incident and on this report some 25 persons were challaned from amongst the Red Shirts. But the total sentence imposed against them was a fine of Rs. 700.

At that time there was a Red Shirt Government in office in our province. Dr. Khan Sahib was the leader of the Red Shirts and Chief Minister of the province and his brother Khan Abdul Ghaffar Khan was the leader of the Red Shirts...

They [Red Shirts] did not tolerate the Khaksars..." (*Dawn* 1958 Jul. 04; *Dawn* 1958 Jul. 03).

1958 July 03

Dr. Khan Sahib's murder case continues in the court of Special Magistrate M.N.Rizvi in Lahore. Allama Mashraqi cross-examines Ch. Muhammad Sharif (S.H.O., Ichhra Police Station, Lahore). Khan Saad Ullah Khan (Dr. Khan Sahib's son) and Begum Safia Saad Ullah Khan (Dr. Khan Sahib's daughter-in-law) also record their statements in court (*Dawn* 1958 Jul. 04; C&MG 1958 Jul. 04).

1958 July 04

Dr. Khan Sahib's murder case continues in the court of Special Magistrate M.N.Rizvi in Lahore. More prosecution witnesses are examined. Malik Habib Ullah Khan (Assistant Inspector General of Police, Crimes), who supervised the investigation, gives details of the raid on Allama Mashraqi's house. Mashraqi himself also cross-examines Habib Ullah Khan for over one hour. The Inspector of the Civil Lines Police Station informs the court that he recorded Maulana Abul Ala Maududi's (Amir of Jamaat-i-Islami) statement on May 24, 1958 (C&MG 1958 Jul. 05; *Dawn* 1958 Jul. 05).

1958 July 05

Dr. Khan Sahib's murder case continues in the court of Special Magistrate M.N.Rizvi in Lahore. Investigating Officer Ch. Hassan Mohammed Randhawa (D.S.P., Crime) records his statement. According to Randhawa, a letter written by Mashraqi to President Iskandar Mirza was confiscated during the raid on Mashraqi's house on May 10, 1958 (PT 1958 Jul. 06; C&MG 1958 Jul. 06).

1958 July 06

Dawn, Karachi publishes court proceedings of Dr. Khan Sahib's murder trial (*Dawn* 1958 Jul. 06).

1958 July 07

Dr. Khan Sahib's murder case continues in the court of Special Magistrate M.N.Rizvi in Lahore. More prosecution witnesses are examined. Investigating Officer Ch. Hassan Mohammed Randhawa (D.S.P., Crime) is cross-examined. Tazi Khail (Dr. Khan's son's driver), who chased Ata Mohammed after the murder, is also examined. The prosecution evidence comes to a close (C&MG 1958 Jul. 08).

The Civil & Military Gazette, Lahore of July 08, 1958 would report: It took the court exactly four weeks to examine a total of 124 witnesses put up by the prosecution. The original list of prosecution witnesses stood at 140, but 16 of them were given up.

They included the Muslim League chief, Khan Abdul Qayyum Khan, the West Pakistan Minister for Communications, Col. Abid Hussain, and Malik Noor Muhammad father of Ata Muhammad, the alleged assassin" (C&MG 1958 Jul. 08; PT 1958 Jul. 08).

1958 July 08

M.N.Rizvi gives the prosecution and defense counsels a list of additional points on which to address the court in regards to Dr. Khan Sahib's murder trial. M.A.K. Chaudhry (Assistant Inspector General of Police) and Ch. Hassan Muhammad Randhawa (Deputy Suprintendent of Police, Crimes) record their statements in court. Three of the five accused (Khawaja Samin Jan, Fateh Mohammed Awan, and Mohammad Rafi) are also examined. They are Mashraqi's followers and deny having conspired with Mashraqi or Khurshid Khalid to murder Dr. Khan Sahib. *Dawn*, Karachi of July 09, 1958 would report:

"One of the accused, Khawaja Samin Jan, deposed that while in police custody he was subjected to violence. He further deposed that the police then offered him Rs. 10,000 and two squares of land if he gave a statement against Allama Mashriqi according to the wishes of the police.

Another accused, Fateh Muhammad Awan, stated that police had promised to free him and reward him if he would implicate Khan Qayyum Khan [President of the Pakistan Muslim League] in the murder of Dr. Khan. Fateh Mohammad also complained of police torture while he was in Lahore Fort for interrogation" (*Dawn* 1958 Jul. 09).

Mohammad Rafi states that police had been harassing his sister and other relatives. Thus, he decided to appear in court and was arrested. Mohammad Rafi denies any connection with the assassination and states that he was not even in Lahore when the incident took place. He further reports that police continually pressured him to give a statement against Mashraqi, and they promised to set him free if he acted according to their wishes (PT 1958 Jul. 09; C&MG 1958 Jul. 09).

Editor's comments: Police brutally tortured the accused in an attempt to coerce them to make statements according to police wishes.

1958 July 09

Allama Mashraqi's statement is recorded in the court of Special Magistrate M.N.Rizvi in Lahore. When asked if he regards Dr. Khan as one of the biggest internal enemies of Pakistan and an agent of Nehru, Mashraqi replies, "I never bothered about Dr. Khan or his party" (C&MG 1958 Jul. 10). *Dawn*, Karachi of July 10, 1958 would report:

"Replying to court questions throughout today's hearing, Allama Mashriqi said it was correct that the movement was based on the principal of obedience of the leader (Ittat-e-Amir), but the obedience was to be of the immediate officer in accordance with the Quran...

Q. It has been stated that your organization clashed with the Government on March 19, 1940 at Lahore?
A. Yes, but the clash occurred during my absence at Delhi, when Sir Shah Muhammad Suleman and I were having a talk with the Viceroy.
Q. It has been said in evidence that before the establishment of Pakistan you toured the Indo Pakistan sub-continent villifying the Quaid-i-Azam and the Muslim League.
A. This is entirely wrong. I had toured some parts of the sub-continent in 1945 and the purpose of the tour was to establish a Pakistan from Calcutta to Peshawar in one piece so that there should not be a Pakistan with two pieces...
Q. Is it correct that after the establishment of Pakistan you started the Islam League with the object of securing the freedom of Kashmir, the parts of Bengal, and the Punjab and Assam, which have gone over to India, and a territory linking the two parts of Pakistan?
A. After the genocide and the holocaust that followed the establishment of Pakistan and the ruination of one crore Muslims and the murder of 15 lakh of Musalmans all the big leaders of West Pakistan gathered and pleaded to me and implored me to start an organization for protecting the five crore Muslims of India. Then I

and 13 others laid foundation of the Islam League. This happened in July 1948.
Q. Is it correct that the object of the [Islam] League was that mentioned in the previous question?
A. No, not immediately. At the foundation of the party, the object was to show to the Hindus that a strong organization has been set up in Pakistan to protect the Muslims in India. The object stated in the question may have been the object later..." (*Dawn* 1958 Jul. 10).

Mashriqi also refers to the disbandment of the Khaksar Tehrik in 1947 after 300,000 Khaksars could not assemble in Delhi. He states that he issued the order to disband the Movement from Lahore. Mashraqi also discusses the appointment of Khurshid Khalid as President of the Khaksar Muslim League (PT 1958 Jul. 10). *The Pakistan Times*, Lahore of July 10, 1958 would report:

"[Mashraqi said that] It was not correct that [Muhammad] Khurshid Khalid, the approver was appointed the president of Khaksar Muslim League as a reward for performing some herioc deed. He was not appointed by anybody but he was elected unanmously when he (Mr. Mashriqi) relinquished the office in 1958...

He admitted that Fateh Mohammad, Samin Jan and Khurshid Khalid stayed in his Mehman Khana [Guesthouse]. They stayed in the Mehman Khana because they were entangled in various cases ...He said he never heard of Rehmat, a prosecution witness, who was stated to be a Khaksar...

It was also wrong that Mir Manzoor Mohammad Warsi had any family relations with him. He did not know whether Mr. Warsi was a Khaksar.

Continuing his statement Mashriqi said that he remembered that the Khaksar had a clash with the Red Shirts in 1939 in the former N.W.F.P. but he did not remember the details and the results of the incident. He only knew that the incident was of local nature in which Red Shirts were the aggressors and the Khaksars simply defended themsleves as the Khaksar Movement at that time had no desire to come into conflict with any Musalman. He did not remember whether Dr. Khan Sahib was the Chief Minister of the N.W.F.P. at that time...The Red Shirts Movement was founded by [Barrister] Mian Ahmad Shah [who joined the Khaksar Tehrik and became a prominent leader in the Khaksar Tehrik]" (PT 1958 Jul. 10).

Mashriqi further states states that the Government took action against the Razakars (for the peaceful march of one million people towards India in 1957 in order to seek Kashmir). However, Mashriqi states that he avoided a confrontation between the Razakars and the Government, which might have pleased Nehru. He also states that he was prosecuted in a fabricated case where he was accused of detaining policemen at Wagah border (also see April 21, September 20, and October 22, 1957 in this chronology). Mashriqi adds that police incited villagers near the camps to attack the Khaksars and prevent water from being delivered to Razakars in the area (PT 1958 Jul. 10).

The court also asks Mashraqi a question regarding the confiscation of his land in Lahore:

"Is it correct that during the time when Dr. Khan Sahib was the Chief Minister of the province [West Pakistan] about 20 kanals of your land [Wahdat Colony, Lahore] was acquired by Government without your consent and against your wishes? – Yes, it was forcibly possessed by the Government without my consent and without any notification and without sending me any notice and without giving me any compensation" (C&MG 1958 Jul. 10).

1958 July 10

Mashraqi's statement continues in Dr. Khan Sahib's trial. Mashraqi denies any involvement in Dr. Khan's murder or having ever met Ata Muhammad (the assassin). His statement takes almost 9 hours and is the longest statement recorded in the case thus far. *Dawn*, Karachi of July 11, 1958 would report:

"The 70-year-old Allama...stated that some members of the Republican Party had a hand in the murder of Dr. Khan Sahib and in order to shield them the blame was shifted on him and his followers...

Allama Mashraqi further said that the Government wanted that his organisation should not be able to participate in the forthcoming general elections. Therefore on the false charge against three or four of them the Government had banned the whole of their organisation" (*Dawn* 1958 Jul. 11).

Mashraqi states that the police tortured Ata Mohammed to implicate him (Mashraqi). He also informs the court that only 8 or 10 days prior to his (Mashraqi's) arrest, the Government of India bitterly criticized his activities in the Lok Sabha (Parliament). A warning was also received by the Government of Pakistan. Mashriqi further states that police had been harassing Khaksars for a couple of months prior to Dr. Khan Sahib's murder (PT 1958 Jul. 11). Mashriqi also states that while he was under detention, police snatched four manuscripts from him by getting on his chest. He had prepared the manuscripts to obtain his counsel's advice (C&MG 1958 Jul. 11).

Dawn, Karachi of July 11, 1958 would further report the proceedings of the trial:

"*Q:* I draw your attention to those parts of this letter [Mashraqi's letter addressed to President Iskandar Mirza from his home during the police search and was discussed in the court] which purport to show that you wanted President Iskander Mirza 'to arrange to come over to Lahore as early as he could.' If he accepted 'the rather extraordinary proposal' put forward by you, so that 'you could have further talks and frame the sort of government which will be effective enough to save Pakistan from the destruction that it is drifting towards.'

Do you want to comment on this?

A: Yes, that was the purpose of my talks" (*Dawn* 1958 Jul. 11)

Regarding the question of why Ata Muhammad chose to involve him in the case, Mashraqi replies, "I do not know him so how can I say why he made such a statement. My guess is that the police has tortured him to make such a statement" (*Dawn* 1958 Jul. 11). *Dawn*, Karachi of July 11, 1958 would also publish other questions posed to Mashraqi:

"Q. Do you wish to disclose why you have been incriminated in this case?

A. Yes. According to my calculations there were four reasons behind it.

Firstly, the Government wanted that we should not be able to participate in the elections. Therefore, on the false charge against three or four of us they have banned the whole of our organization, and caught hold of the whole of my property. This is what they did to me in 1951 also.

Secondly, eight or 10 days before my arrest serious allegation had been made in the Indian Lok Sabha that my activities had increased since my release since January 1958. A mild warning to our Government had also come from India...

Two or two and a half months before the murder of Dr. Khan Sahib the police called our four or five Khaksars again and again to the police sation. They were so tired of going to the police station that they at last complained to me about this trouble.

They told me that the police wanted to entangle them in the murder of Liaquat Ali Khan and were also saying that another murder was going to take place and that they would be in complicity in that murder plan. They also told me that the police were bothering them and wanted them to furnish securities" (*Dawn* 1958 Jul. 11).

Mashraqi also refers to the press statements of Khan Abdul Ghaffar Khan and Saad Ullah Khan (Dr. Khan Sahib's brother and son respectively). In their statements, they mention a conspiracy that was known to the police three months prior to the murder. The fourth reason Mashraqi gives is that according to the police case, Ata Mohammad had to go to the house of Rafi after committing the murder. But the fact of the matter was that Rafi was not there. During this period, Rafi was in Rawalpindi. Therefore, the whole structure of the police case failed. According to Mashraqi, all these factors show that he and his followers were incriminated to shift the blame on to them (*Dawn* 1958 Jul. 11).

Atta Mohammed also makes a statement in court. He states, "I did my duty by killing Dr. Khan" (PT 1958 Jul. 11).

1958 July 11

Ata Mohammed (accused) records his statement in the court of Special Magistrate M.N.Rizvi (PT 1958 Jul. 12; C&MG 1958 Jul. 12).

Mashraqi's health continues to deteriorate. Mashraqi's son visits him in jail.

Editor's comments: Mashraqi's health was deteriorating with every passing day. He was not receiving proper treatment in jail and his family was very concerned. When Mashraqi's son went to see him in jail, he found Mashraqi's health to be in serious condition. However, the Government remained unconcerned; they didn't even excuse Mashraqi from attending court proceedings (*Dawn* 1958 Aug. 19).

1958 July 12

Ata Muhammad (the accused) continues his statement in the court of Special Magistrate M.N.Rizvi in Lahore. Ata Muhammad praises Mashraqi in his statement, referring to him as the "biggest leader of our nation, who has taken upon himself voluntary organisation of the Mussalmans." However, Ata also attempts to wrongly implicate Mashraqi in the murder of Dr. Khan Sahib. During the court proceedings, Mashraqi shouts at Ata Muhammad for making false statements (C&MG 1958 Jul. 13; PT 1958 Jul. 15; *Dawn* 1958 Jul. 14).

1958 July 14

Ata Mohammed continues his statement in the court of Special Magistrate M.N.Rizvi (PT 1958 Jul. 15; C&MG 1958 Jul. 15; *Dawn* 1958 Jul. 15).

1958 July 15

Ata Mohammed continues his statement in the court of Special Magistrate M.N.Rizvi. He explains his state of mind prior to killing Dr. Khan Sahib (C&MG 1958 Jul. 16; PT 1958 Jul. 16).

1958 July 16

Ata Mohammed concludes his statement in the court of Special Magistrate M.N.Rizvi (PT 1958 Jul. 17; C&MG 1958 Jul. 17; *Dawn* 1958 Jul. 17).
Editor's comments: Ata Mohammed's statement took six days to complete (PT 1958 Jul. 17).

1958 July 17

Dr. Khan Sahib's murder case continues in the court of Special Magistrate M.N.Rizvi.

1958 July 18

Dr. Khan Sahib's murder case continues in the court of Special Magistrate M.N.Rizvi. The prosecution concludes it's arguments, doing its best to implicate Mashraqi in Dr. Khan Sahib's murder (PT 1958 Jul. 19). The prosecution charges Mashraqi with instigating the murder of Dr. Khan Sahib (C&MG 1958 Jul. 19; *Dawn* 1958 Jul. 20).

1958 July 19

Dr. Khan Sahib's murder case continues in the court of Special Magistrate M.N.Rizvi. The Defence Counsel, Ijaz Hussain Batalvi, states that the only evidence against Mashraqi is the statement of Ata Mohammed, which isn't even supported by any other evidence. According to Batalvi, "The statement of Ata Muhammad cannot be made a basis for conviction of the Allama [Mashraqi] and is sure to die its own death since it is not corroborated by independent evidence" (C&MG 1958 Jul. 20).

Batalvi also declares that the prosecution's argument is a "cock and bull" story and that they miserably failed to prove anything against Mashraqi. He informs the court that the police had tried to prove a charge of conspiracy against Mashraqi and therefore had made a completely false story. The Defence concludes its arguments (PT 1958 Jul. 20).

1958 July 20

There are no proceedings on this day in the case of Dr. Khan Sahib's murder.

1958 July 21

Three of the accused in Dr. Khan Sahib's murder case (Samin Jan, Fateh Mohammed, and Mohammed Rafi) are discharged by Special Magistrate M.N.Rizvi as the prosecution failed to produce any evidence against them. However, M.N.Rizvi commits Mashraqi and Ata Mohammed to the Court of Session for trial. Mashraqi also informs the court about his treatment in jail. *The Civil & Military Gazette*, Lahore of July 22, 1958 would report, "The Allama later told the court in reply to a question that no doctor had ever visited him in the jail during his two-month stay there and that he was suffering from chest and other diseases which could not be properly treated if he remained in jail" (C&MG 1958 Jul. 22). *The Pakistan Times*, Lahore of July 22, 1958 would further report:

"The prosecution examined in all 124 witnesses [of whom three turned hostile] in support of its case. It gave up eight witnesses and added six more to the calendar of witnesses to be examined in the Court of Session…The prosecution case was conducted by Khan Mushtaq Hussain Khan, Special Public Prosecutor, assisted by Mr. M. Anwer, Assistant Advocate General (who later resigned) and Syed Fayyaz Hussain, Prosecuting Inspector.

Mr. Ijaz Hussain [Batalvi], Sheikh Mohammad Nasim and Khwaja Wali Mohammad represented the accused" (PT 1958 Jul. 22; *Dawn* 1958 Jul. 22).

Editor's comments: There were some discrepancies regarding the number of witnesses produced in court in the different sources used. *The Pakistan Times*, Lahore of November 18, 1958 reported that Mashraqi and Ata Mohammed were committed to the Court of Session on July 22, 1958 and the prosecution presented over 130 witnesses to prove their case against Mashraqi (PT 1958 Nov. 18). *The Civil & Military Gazette*, Lahore of July 22, 1958 reported that the prosecution dropped six witnesses (C&MG 1958 Jul. 22). *The Civil & Military Gazette*, Lahore of August 11, 1958 reported that 125 witnesses were produced by the prosecution (C&MG 1958 Aug. 11).

Ch. Nazir Ahmed Khan files a bail application on behalf of Allama Mashraqi in the court of Lahore Sessions Judge Sheikh Anwar-ul Haq (who later became Chief Justice of the Supreme Court of Pakistan).

The application states that Mashraqi is over 70 years old and has been suffering from chest and intestinal diseases for the past few years. The application further states that he is not getting the proper treatment in jail. The application also points out that there is no direct evidence against Mashraqi in Dr. Khan Sahib's murder case and that the evidence presented against him is purely circumstantial (C&MG 1958 Jul. 22).

Editor's comments: Chaudhry Nazir Ahmed was the Central Minister for Industries in Prime Minister Liaquat Ali Khan's Cabinet from Sept. 1949 to Oct. 1951. Chaudhry Nazir Ahmed also held the position of Attorney General of Pakistan. He was Zakia Sultana's (Mashraqi's niece) brother-in-law.

1958 July 24

A.H Qureshi's (secretary of the banned Khaksar Muslim League) writ petition comes up for hearing before Justice Shabbir Ahmed of the West Pakistan High Court. The petition is against the West Pakistan Government's order to seal Qureshi's business and residential premises in Sialkot. Prior to the hearing, the Government Counsel submits that the Government is considering releasing the premises and a final decision may be taken within a week. Justice Ahmed states that the respondent should file a written statement on August 06, 1958 if no final decision by the government has been made by that date (PT 1958 Jul. 25).

1958 July 29

Mashraqi's bail application is presented before Lahore District and Sessions Judge Sheikh Anwar ul Haq. Ch. Nazir Ahmed Khan argues that the prosecution has failed to prove anything against Mashraqi in Dr. Khan's murder case. Furthermore, he states that three others accused in the murder case have been released. He also argues that Mashraqi was not involved in any conspiracy, as there is no direct proof against him. Ch. Nazir Ahmed Khan submits that Mashraqi is over 70 years old and is not in very strong physique; he is infirm and sick. Concluding his argument, he states that the jail conditions have caused considerable deterioration in Mashraqi's poor state of health. The District and Sessions Judge requests the Principal of King Edward Medical College to examine Mashraqi and send the medical report by July 31, 1958. The court fixes August 01, 1958 as the date of the next hearing (PT 1958 Jul. 30; C&MG 1958 Jul. 30).

1958 July 30

Dr. Sadiq examines Mashraqi (PT 1958 Aug. 19).

1958 August 01

Mashraqi's bail application hearing in the court of Shaikh Anwar-Ul-Haq (District and Sessions Judge, Lahore) is postponed until August 02, 1958 because of the absence of the prosecuter. However, *The Civil & Military Gazette*, Lahore of August 02, 1958 would report that the Principal of King Edward College, Col. Dr. Ilahi Bakhsh, has submitted his medical report. The report states, "I have today examined the Allama. He complains of debility, loss of appetite, dry tongue and irregularities of his bowels. Clinical examination alone suggests that the Allama is suffering from amoebic infection of his large intestine and liver for which he should have adequate treatment under expert medical supervision" (C&MG 1958 Aug. 02; PT 1958 Aug. 02).

Editor's comments: *The Civil & Military Gazette*, Lahore of August 03, 1958 reported that Mashraqi was medically examined by Dr. Sadiq, Assistant Professor of Medicine and Therapeutics at King Edward Medical College.

1958 August 02

Mashraqi's bail application is rejected by Lahore District and Sessions Judge Sheikh Anwar ul Haq. The Judge accepts the prosecution's argument that the case of Dr. Khan's murder would collapse if Mashraqi is released. *The Pakistan Times*, Lahore of August 03, 1958 would report: "Dr. Sadiq...in his report he submitted...The stools were reported to be occasionally soft with blood and mucus accompanied by abdominal griping...About the alimentary system the doctor noticed tenderness in the region of the caecum and ascending colon and the descending colon was palpable. The liver was enlarged by two fingers and was very tender...Mr. Mashriqi was suffering from amoebic infection of his large intestine and liver for which he should have adequate treatment under expert medical supervision" (PT 1958 Aug. 03).

Arguing on behalf of Mashraqi, Ch. Nazir Ahmed Khan states that there is hardly any case against Mashraqi. He further argues that Mashraqi is 70 years old and suffering from several ailments (C&MG 1958 Aug. 03). However, the District and Sessions Judge does not accept his argument and states:

"The medical report does not give any indication that the Allama is infirm inspite of his years. It does however seem to me that he is sick and this is a factor which requires serious consideration. The sickness has to be viewed seriously in view of his age...

It appears to me the apprehensions expressed by the prosecution are not without foundation and accordingly it will not be in the interest of justice if the Allama is enlarged on bail at this stage. It may be observed that the trial is likely to commence in the very near future.

At the same time I think it is a duty of the state to make arrangements for adequate looking after the health of the Allama. The learned P.P. has stated on behalf of the State that the Government would be prepared to make reasonable arrangements for medical attention to the Allama according to his own choice" (PT 1958 Aug. 03).

Editor's comments: Mashraqi's old age and his serious illness were completely ignored. The Judge suggested that Mashraqi could get proper treatment under government supervision. This was cruelty of the highest order; the offer of treatment and care by the Government was ridiculous as none ever gets proper care under police supervision. The court even ignored the fact that the case against Mashraqi was weak and three of the others accused in the murder were acquitted. Mashraqi and his family were going through a tremendous ordeal, but the eyes and ears of the authorities in power remained closed. Mashraqi's health continued to deteriorate and no adequate medical arrangements were made.

1958 August 09

Special Magistrate M.N.Rizvi, who conducted the preliminary trial in connection with Dr. Khan Sahib's murder, announces the reasons for his decision to commit Allama Mashraqi and Ata Muhammad to Sessions (PT 1958 Aug. 11). One reason given by Rizvi is Mashraqi's speeches, which condemned Dr. Khan Sahib's policies favoring India (C&MG 1958 Aug. 11).

Editor's comments: *The Pakistan Times*, Lahore of August 11, 1958 stated that the Special Magistrate announced his reasons on August 09, 1958.

1958 August 18

Barrister Ijaz Hussain Batalvi files a bail application on behalf of Mashraqi in the court of Justice Shabbir Ahmed of the West Pakistan High Court. The application is filed due to Mashraqi's deteriorating health (PT 1958 Aug. 29; PT 1958 Aug. 19). Ijaz Hussain Batalvi informs the court that Mashraqi is having lung and bronchial trouble. Batalvi also states that Mashraqi is suffering from ameobic dysentry and other ailments and that his health is deteriorating at an alarming rate. *Dawn*, Karachi of August 19, 1958 would further report, "The Allama, he [Ijaz Hussain Batalvi] said, possessed considerable property and had a certain political status. It was not likely that he would abscond and destroy for ever the political reputation he had built up and worked for all his life and allow to be confiscated the property...in order to avoid facing a trial based on hardly any evidence at all" (*Dawn* 1958 Aug. 19).

Justice Shabbir Ahmed calls for the opinion of Lt. Col. Ilahi Bakhsh (Principal of King Edward Medical College, Lahore) regarding Mashraqi's health. Lt. Col. Ilahi Bakhsh is to report on whether Mashraqi's health has worsened since Dr. Sadiq (of King Edward Medical College) examined him on July 30, 1958 (*Dawn* 1958 Aug. 19; C&MG 1958 Aug. 19)

Editor's comments: *The Civil & Military Gazette*, Lahore of August 02, 1958 reported that Col. Dr. Ilahi Bakhsh examined Mashraqi (on July 30, 1958).

Mashraqi's was 70 years old when he was falsely implicated in Dr. Khan Sahib's murder case and was sent to jail. His health had deteriorated considerably in jail. In the bail application, Mashraqi's son referred to a meeting with his father in jail on July 11, 1958. He narrated that when he met his father, he found him to be pale and in extremely poor health. Clearly, Mashraqi was not being looked after in jail and the medical facilities he needed were not available. Mashraqi's counsel further informed the judge that during the court proceedings of Dr. Khan Sahib's murder case, Mashraqi had to be sent back to jail on multiple occasions because he was about to collapse due to illness and exhaustion.

1958 August 19

The Pakistan Times, Lahore reports that Mashriqi's bail application of August 18, 1958 was accompanied by an affidavit by Mashraqi's son. The newspaper writes:

"...on his [Mashraqi's son] last interview with his father on July 11 he found him extremely weak, pale and infirm and that he had informed him that he was not receiving proper medical facilities...

Mr. Ijaz Hussain Batalvi, counsel for Mr. Mashriqi submitted that during the last fortnight the health of Mr. Mashriqi had considerably deteriorated and symptoms of physical feebleness had increased.

Mr. Batalvi further said that Mr. Mashriqi had been suffering from bronchial dilatation and lung trouble. He has also been suffering from amoebic dysentery and these and other ailments have greatly increased causing an alarming deterioration in his health...

Mr. Mashriqi, he [Ijaz Hussain Batalvi] said possessed considerable property and had a certain political status. It was not likely that he would abscond and destroy for ever the political reputation he had built up and worked for all his life and allow to be confiscated the property that was so necessary for his family in order to avoid facing a trial based on hardly any evidence at all" (PT 1958 Aug. 19).

1958 August 20

Two Khaksars, Mohammed Siddique and Mohammed Rafi, are acquitted by Lahore First Class Magistrate Mirza Azam Beg. Mohammed Rafi had been a defendant in Dr. Khan Sahib's murder case, but was acquitted (PT 1958 Aug. 21).

1958 August 26

The Principal of King Edward Medical College, Lt. Col. Ilahi Buksh, examines Mashraqi in Lahore (PT 1958 Aug. 29).

1958 August 28

Lt. Col. Ilahi Buksh (Principal of King Edward Medical College) states in his report to the West Pakistan High Court that Mashraqi is seriously ill. *The Pakistan Times*, Lahore of August 29, 1958 would report:

"Lt. Col. Ilahi Bakhsh, Principal, King Edward Medical College, Lahore, who was ordered by Mr. Justice Shabir Ahmed of the West Pakistan High Court to examine Mr. Inayatullah Khan Mashriqi said in his report on Thursday [August 28, 1958] that Mr. Mashriqi was seriously ill and needed immediate and proper treatment...The report further said that 'the patient looked emaciated and very weak with sunken eyes, dry tremulous, somewhat furred tongue. He has also recorded a loss of weight by 10 lbs.'

Continuing the report said: 'Allama Inayatullah Khan Mashriqi is seriously ill and he needs immediate and proper treatment. If his condition is only pneumonic which may be tuberculosis, virus or bacterial, the progress is more hopeful than if the condition turns out to be neoplasm (cancer). In the latter case taking his age and other factors into consideration the outcome is very gloomy and practically hopeless" (PT 1958 Aug. 29).

The Civil & Military Gazette, Lahore of August 29, 1958 would further state, "Mr. Ejaz Ahmed [Ijaz Hussain Batalvi], Advocate, who appeared for Allama Mashriqi, submitted that in view of the depressing and hopeless condition of health of Allama Mashriqi as depicted in the medical report," the court should grant interim bail to Mashraqi (C&MG 1958 Aug. 29).

1958 September 01

Justice Shabbir Ahmed of the West Pakistan High Court dismisses Mashraqi's bail application. *The Pakistan Times*, Lahore of September 02, 1958 would report:

"Earlier on Monday, Mr. Ijaz Hussain who argued the bail application on behalf of Mr. Mashriqi, submitted that the medical report submitted by Lt. Col. Ilahi Bakhsh had established beyond doubt that the petitioner was ill and infirm. He had lost ten pounds of weight during one month of his detention. His lungs were not functioning properly and the pulse had gone down from 120 to 108.

Mr. Ijaz Hussain further submitted that Mr. Mashriqi's condition was precarious and he lay handcuffed in a ward of the Mayo Hospital with six constables standing guard on him. He was not taking any medicine. The atmosphere, he said, was not conducive to proper treatment and he needed his own men to look after him.

Continuing his arguments, Mr. Ijaz Hussain submitted that Mr. Mashriqi was involved in the alleged conspiracy to murder Dr. Khan Sahib upon the evidence of witnesses who had been tortured by the police. He said that fears of the prosecution that if Mr. Mashriqi was released on bail he would influence the witnesses were quite baseless. Mr. Mashriqi was confined to bed and there was no possibility of his tampering with the witnesses. He further submitted that Mr. Mashriqi enjoyed a certain political status in the country and owned considerable property. It was not likely that he would allow his property to be confiscated by the Government" (PT 1958 Sept. 02).

The Civil & Military Gazette, Lahore September 02, 1958 would also report:

"The Counsel [Mashraqi's Counsel] said that after the petitioner's admission into hospital his health had further deteriorated and the doctor had expressed the opinion that the patient would develop cancer or tuberculosis…

The counsel said that the chances of the petitioner's absconding were practically non-existent. Moreover the petitioner was so ill that he could not be expected to run away" (C&MG 1958 Sept. 02).

Editor's comments: It is unfortunate that despite Mashraqi's poor health, the Judge dismissed his bail application. This could have happened only in a country like Pakistan where the judiciary is not independent. Its decisions are influenced. Mashraqi's case speaks of the status of the judiciary. In the West, there could have been a lawsuit against the government based on Mashraqi's circumstances and the government would have been made responsible for his rapidly deteriorating health (which led to his death after a few years). Yet it is so unfortunate that justice cannot be expected even today. Who is responsible for this mess in Pakistan and when will real accountabilty prevail? Are people's lives valueless that the authorities can play havoc with them without being held accountable?

All this drama was a result of vindictiveness that prevails in Pakistan. Mashraqi was punished for not supporting the people that held power. They wanted to eliminate Mashraqi by either hanging him or ensuring that he dies of poor health.

The public has been cheated from the very beginning. There was talk of free and fair elections, yet the government left no stone unturned to prevent Mashriqi and his party from playing any political role. Mashraqi was falsely charged in this murder case so that he and his party could be prevented from taking part in elections. Read the following:

According to *The Civil & Military Gazette*, Lahore of September 13, 1958, Qizilbash (Chief Minister of West Pakistan) "said the Republican Government was determined to hold free and impartial elections and 'we will do it'…

Mr. Qizilbash attacked the Muslim League and its leaders and said that they did nothing concrete when they were the rulers of this country for nine years. Now when the elections were nearing they had started a campaign to win public support. He assured the League leaders that they would not be able to make fools of the people in the name of the Muslim League and the two-nation theory" (C&MG 1958 Sept. 13).

But how could the Chief Minister even talk about fair and free elections when every endeavor was made to keep Mashraqi under detention? On the other hand, Qizilbash's criticism of the Muslim League was valid, as the Muslim League had not accomplished anything since the creation of Pakistan. This again shows that the Muslim Leaguers had supported the division of India for their own vested reasons.

1958 September 02

Justice Shabbir Ahmed of the West Pakistan High Court admits a writ petition challenging the order of the West Pakistan Government of May 19, 1958 (which declared the Khaksar Muslim League as an unlawful association). The petition is filed by Rehan Shah, Secretary General of the Khaksar Muslim League. Barrister Ijaz Hussain Batalvi appears for the petition. The petitioner also challenges the order of the Provincial Government for his externment from Lahore and Rawalpindi divisions. The externment notice was served to him on September 1, 1958 (PT 1958 Sept. 03).
Editor's comments: *Dawn*, Karachi of September 03, 1958 stated that the order of the Government was dated May 18, 1958.

1958 September 09

The Pakistan Times, Lahore reports that the hearing of Dr. Khan Sahib's murder case will commence on September 22, 1958 before Lahore District and Sessions Judge Sheikh Anwar ul Haq. The proceedings are to be held in Borstal Jail, Lahore. A list of 56 prosecution witnesses is submitted. This list includes two First Class Magistrates, an Additional Magistrate, and a number of police officials (PT 1958 Sept. 09).

1958 September 17

The Central Cabinet approves a draft Ordinance banning the formation or maintenance of parties of a military or semi-military nature. Persons found guilty under this Ordinance would be fined and imprisoned for up to two years (C&MG 1958 Sept. 18).

1958 September 19

A writ petition filed by Rehan Shah (Secretary General of the Khaksar Muslim League) is admitted by a Division Bench of the West Pakistan High Court (PT 1958 Sept. 20). The petition challenges the Home Secretary's decision of May 19, 1958 to ban the Khaksar Muslim League (C&MG 1958 Sept. 20).
Editor's comments: *Dawn*, Karachi of September 03, 1958 stated that the order of the Government was dated May 18, 1958.

1958 September 21

The Civil & Military Gazette, Lahore reports that the President of Pakistan has passed an Ordinance banning the wearing of uniforms by volunteers of political parties. According to the newspaper:

"The Ordinance prohibits the wearing of uniforms in connection with political purposes and the maintenance by private persons of associations of a military or semi-military character and the matters connected therewith.

Offences under the Ordinance shall be cognizable and non-bailable, punishable with imprisonment for two years or with fine which may extend to Rs. 1,000 or with both" (C&MG 1958 Sept. 21).

1958 September 22

Dr. Khan Sahib's murder case commences before Lahore District and Sessions Judge Sheikh Anwar ul Haq. Mashraqi and Ata Mohammed plead not guilty. The case is conducted in Borstal Jail, Lahore (PT 1958 Sept. 23; PT 1958 Nov. 18). Attendance in the courtroom is restricted and a heavy police posse armed with rifles and lathis stands guard around the court premises. *The Civil & Military Gazette*, Lahore of September 23, 1958 would report:

"The Allama, who was brought in the court handcuffed, looked pale and haggard due to his recent illness and requested the court to provide him an easy chair in the court room. The court promised to do so.

His handcuffs were removed and he was permitted to lie down on a bench in the court room." Mashraqi asks the court to postpone the case for three weeks... However, the judge rejects Mashraqi's plea to postpone the case.

The court also records the evidence of prosecution witnesses, including Muhammad Khurshid Khalid. Khalid states that prior to independence in 1947, Allama Mashraqi made an announcement that 300,000 Khaksars must assemble in Delhi by June 30, 1947, or he would disband the Khaksar Movement. The number of Khaksars who assembled in Delhi was less than 300,000 thousand, and therefore Mashraqi disbanded the Khaksar Movement. Khalid further states that in 1957, the name of the Islam League was changed to the Khaksar Muslim League. This was in response to Nehru's statement that the [original] Muslim League was finished and therefore, Pakistan was also finished. Khalid further informs the court that in 1957, Mashraqi made an announcement of a million-man march to liberate Kashmir. According to Khalid, Mashraqi stated that if the Indian Prime Minister did not settle the Kashmir issue, one million people would march peacefully into India on October 21, 1957. Khalid states that he, along with other Khaksars, was arrested in this connection and the police prosecuted them.

Muhammad Khurshid Khalid also informs the court that he was elected President of the Khaksar Muslim League at a meeting in 1958. Mashraqi participated in this meeting. He further states that a Majlis-e-Shura consisting of five people, including Allama Mashraqi, was established. A few days after his election, he called a meeting of the Majlis-e-Shura and they decided to participate in the West Pakistan Assembly elections. The Khaksar Muslim League published posters announcing its decision to participate in the forthcoming elections. Other arrangements for contesting the elections were also made (C&MG 1958 Sept. 23; *Dawn* 1958 Sept. 23).

Editor's comments: According to the statement in the newspaper (C&MG 1958 Jun. 11), the Khaksar Muslim League was named in 1956 instead of 1957.

It is deplorable that Mashraqi – a patriotic man with tremendous stature – was purposely implicated on a false charge and made to suffer. He was handcuffed at an old age (70 years) and was not even granted bail, despite the doctor's report stating that he was seriously ill. Such cruelty on the part of the Government is inexcusable.

1958 September 23

Dr. Khan Sahib's murder case continues in the court of Lahore District and Sessions Sheikh Anwar ul Haq. Muhammad Khurshid Khalid remains in the witness stand for almost five hours. He informs the court that his statement before the Additional District Magistrate (Syed Hasnat Ahmed) on May 17, 1958 was under police pressure. He also informs the court that he was tortured while in police custody. He adds that while he was making his statement to the Additional District Magistrate, he could see a D.S.P. (Randhawa) sitting in the adjoining room through the open door. After his statement, he was taken to Borstal Jail where a doctor examined him. However, the doctor never asked about the torture meted out to him by the police (C&MG 1958 Sept. 24).

Muhammad Khurshid Khalid further states that prior to making a statement before the First Class Magistrate (Qazi Muhammad Hafiz Ullah) on May 17, 1958, he was first taken to the D.S.P.'s office, where police threatened him to make a statement according to their instructions. Khalid also states that the First Class Magistrate never read back his questions and answers after he had recorded his statement. Instead, the Magistrate silently obtained Khalid's thumbprint on the statement. Khalid informs the court that some portions of his statement are false. The Public Prosecutor reads Khalid's statement and Khalid clarifies which portions are correct. Continuing his statement, Khalid states that the police told him not to tell the Magistrate (Qazi Muhammad Hafiz Ullah) whether they had offered him any promise or benefit or threatened him in connection with his confession. Khalid states that he complied with the police instructions under fear of police torture (C&MG 1958 Sept. 24; PT 1958 Sept. 24; PT 1958 Oct. 02).

Editor's comments: Mohammed Khursheed Khalid, an approver in Dr. Khan Sahib's case, turned hostile on June 11, 1958. Mohammed Khursheed Khalid was questioned rudely on September 23, 1958 in the court of Sheikh Anwar ul Haq. Allama Mashraqi didn't accept this. *The Pakistan Times*, Lahore of September 24, 1958 reported that Mashraqi "rose from the bench and stated that he could not tolerate his President being questioned rather rudely."

The Civil & Military Gazette, Lahore publishes a photo of Mashraqi lying on a bench during the proceedings in the court of Lahore District and Sessions Judge Shaikh Anwar-Ul-Haq (C&MG 1958 Sept. 23).

Editor's comments: It is unfortunate to note that Mashraqi – a true hero of Pakistan – was treated in this manner. Mashraqi's treatment was the work of those who did not care about the democracy, but instead had only personal gains in mind.

Unpatriotic people have plundered the nation and misled the public with flowery statements and speeches seeking personal glorification. One of the best ways of guaging the sincerity of a leader is to monitor his/her personal lifestyle. I urge the nation to reject leaders who maintain a high profile lifestyle while their nation lives in poverty. These leaders are not sincere to the people. It is high time that Pakistanis thought about what kind of leaders they have had and what criteria they need to fix prior to electing these leaders to powerful positions.

Should political tolerence prevail in the country or should people continue to suffer at the hands of selfish leaders?

"Discard those leaders who live in luxury while the nation lives in poverty. "

– Nasim Yousaf

Malik Firoz Khan Noon (Prime Minister of Pakistan) issues a statement defending the ban on uniformed volunteers of political parties (C&MG 1958 Sept. 24).

1958 September 24

Dr. Khan Sahib's murder case continues in the court of Lahore District and Sessions Judge Sheikh Anwar ul Haq. Muhammad Khursheed Khalid is cross-examined by the Special Public Prosecutor. Khalid again rejects the statement he had made as an approver, as it was the result of intense police pressure. He points out the portions of his earlier statement that are false. He informs the court that his earlier statement had been given to him by D.S.P. Randhawa. He also states that Allama Mashraqi was supposed to address a public meeting on May 10, 1958, but the meeting was postponed to May 18, 1958 due to Dr. Khan Sahib's murder (C&MG 1958 Sept. 25). According to Khalid, "Allama Mashriqi was the acknoweledged leader of the Khaksar movement. All the Khaksars respected him. I respected the Allama in my capacity as a Khaksar at that time and I respect him even now" (PT 1958 Sept. 25).

1958 September 25

Mohammed Khurshid Khalid's cross-examination concludes in Dr. Khan Sahib's murder case in the court of Lahore District and Sessions Judge Sheikh Anwar ul Haq. Khalid describes the police pressure and torture while he was in jail. He states that police told him that during an earlier investigation, a man had died in Lahore Fort and nothing was done about it (police told this story to create fear in Khurshid Khalid's mind). Police also informed him that it had been settled with the Additional Sessions Judge that he would convict all of them (including Mashraqi) in Dr. Khan Sahib's murder case. Khalid further states, "On May 17 [1958] I was informed by the police that my relatives had been taken into custody" (C&MG 1958 Sept. 26). *The Pakistan Times*, Lahore of September 26, 1958 would report:

"During his [Mohammed Khursheed Khalid] cross-examination...the witness [Mohammed Khurshid Khalid] deposed that he was subjected to great torture by the police on the night between May 11 and 12. He said 'They [the police] made me stand up with a stick holding my feet apart. Another stick was placed on my shoulders and my hand, which were chained, were raised above it with one man holding the handcuffs. Others were hitting me on my shoulders, back, buttocks and thighs.

On my falling down they would make me sit, give me water and ask me whether it was not true that the murder of Dr. Khan Sahib 'was the result of a conspiracy hatched during the meeting between Allama Mashriqi and Khan Abdul Qaiyum Khan.'…

Continuing, the witness [Mohammed Khurshid Khalid] said that at about 4 a.m. on the same night he was locked in a cell but in the afternoon he was again brought out from his cell and was severely beaten with a leather sheath…this torture continued till he lost all his resistance and offered himself to make the statement as dictated by the police" (PT 1958 Sept. 26).

Muhammad Khurshid Khalid further states that he was informed by the police that he was lucky to have been saved because the police had almost managed the services of an approver against all of them by paying Rs. 20,000 (*Dawn* 1958 Sept. 26).

Muhammad Khursheed Khalid also states, "During my detention in the [Lahore] Fort, the police asked me to write on a blank paper that I had not engaged any counsel. I was told that this would be forwarded to a magistrate, who could not, however, enter the Fort according to the I.-G.P's [Inspector General of Police] order.

One day a doctor came to the Fort and he was supposed to see me in the presence of Malik Sahib, but the doctor appeared to be terribly frightened and did not ask me a single question" (C&MG 1958 Sept. 26).

Khalid also informs the court that on May 15, 1958, police took him to Wazirabad. While he was in the police car, many people were brought to see him "So as to become witnesses against me." Continuing his statement, Khalid says that during the identification parade in Borstal Jail, on May 24, 1958, "I picked out a tongwala in the presence of a magistrate…" (C&MG 1958 Sept. 26). Police had previously shown the tongawala to Khurshid Khalid and had told him to identify the tongawala when needed.

Regarding his decision to tell the truth, Khalid deposes that while he was in Borstal Jail, his conscience began to prick and on June 04, 1958, he decided to speak the truth. He states that he saw Ata Muhammad for the first time on June 10, 1958 when he appeared before the committing Magistrate (C&MG 1958 Sept. 26).

With respect to the Islam League, Khurshid Khalid states that a meeting was held in Lahore (at Metro Hotel) to form the Islam League. A committee of 51 members (Mashraqi included) managed the party. Later, the Islam League was changed to the Khaksar Muslim League. According to Khalid, "I became its [Khaksar Muslim League's] President. After I became President, Allama Mashraqi did not issue any order to any individual or branch of the Muslim League.

I permitted Allama Mashraqi to negotiate with Khan Qayyum Khan for the merger of the two Leagues" (C&MG 1958 Sept. 26). Mohammed Khursheed Khalid also states that he was advised by the police to omit the name of Khan Abdul Qaiyum Khan from his statement (PT 1958 Sept. 26).

The Defense Counsels were Barrister Ijaz Hussain Batalvi, Khawaja Wali Muhammad and Abdus Sami Pal (*Dawn* 1958 Sept. 26).

Editor's comments: Mohammed Khursheed Khalid's statement nullifies the accusation that Allama Mashriqi was a dictator. Mashraqi had no inhibition or ego problem in acting as a normal member of his party, even under any elected leader of the party.

1958 September 29

Prosecution witnesses including M.A.K. Chaudhry (Assitant Inspector General of Police) are examined in Dr. Khan Sahib's murder case in the court of Lahore District and Sessions Judge Sheikh Anwar ul Haq (PT 1958 Sept. 30).

1958 September 30

Dr. Khan Sahib's murder case continues in the court of Lahore District and Sessions Judge Sheikh Anwar ul Haq. Four prosecution witnesses are examined. A prosecution witness from Peshawar talks of the tragic incident when Red Shirt members attacked the Khaksars in NWFP. He states that on June 10, 1939, a batch of Khaksars went to Danagar Zai village (NWFP) in order to hoist the Khaksar flag at the house of Ghaus Muhammad (a newly elected Salar of the village). On their way back, they stopped for Maghreb prayers at Azam Garh (NWFP). The imam of the mosque declared the Khaksars *kafirs* [pagans] and so the Khaksars had to pray on the road-side (instead of in the mosque). Meanwhile, a large number of people belonging to the Red Shirts Movement, and armed with weapons and lathis, had gathered. The Red Shirts attacked the Khaksars. As a result, one Khaksar was killed and many more were injured. This incident was tried by a *jirga* [unofficial local court], which fined the accused a collective sum of Rs. 700. The prosecution witness also states that Dr. Khan Sahib was the Chief Minister of the NWFP province at the time. He adds that the Red Shirts did not like the Khaksar Movement.

The next prosecution witness, a retired Deputy Superintendent of Police, states that in 1939, he was the Inspector of Police in Peshawar. He investigated the attack on the Khaksars by the

Red Shirts. He further states that 66 Red Shirts were challaned. A case was registered with the Akhora Police Station (NWFP), but the Khaksars were not prosecuted.

Another prosecution witness states that one of Allama Mashraqi's sons, Ehsanullah Khan Aslam, was killed during the Khaksar agitation in (March) 1940 (C&MG 1958 Oct. 01; PT 1958 Oct. 01; *Dawn* 1958 Oct. 01).

Editor's comments: Dr. Khan Sahib was Chief Minister of the NWFP province and leader of the Red Shirts at the time. He did not want the Khaksar Movement to have influence in the North-West Frontier Province.

1958 October 01

More prosecution witnesses are examined in Dr. Khan Sahib's murder case in the court of Lahore District and Sessions Judge Sheikh Anwar ul Haq. One of the witnesses informs the court that Mashraqi had addressed a public meeting under the auspices of the Islam League in Chiniot near Lyallpur (now Faisalabad) on June 08, 1956 (PT 1958 Oct. 02). The defence counsel produces a copy of Ch. Qadir Bakhsh's (Special Judge) judgement, in which the main prosecution witness against Allama Mashraqi was described as a stock witness. The defence counsel submits an application for a perjury case against this witness, Muhammad Bashir (C&MG 1958 Oct. 02).

Editor's comments: The court was holding its proceedings in Borstal Jail in Lahore.

1958 October 02

Thirteen more prosecution witnesses, including Maulana Abul Ala Maududi (Amir Jama'at-i-Islami) and Amiran Bibi (the wife of Ata Mohammad, the alleged assassin), are examined in Dr. Khan Sahib's murder case in the court of Lahore District and Sessions Judge Sheikh Anwar ul Haq. Sub-Inspector Saeed Ahmed (Stenographer, C.I.D. Police) informs the court that he covered a public meeting held under the auspices of the Islam League in Minto Park, Lahore from November 23-25, 1956. On November 25, 1956, Mashraqi delivered an address entitled *Khutbai-am* (PT 1958 Oct. 03). In the speech, Mashraqi talked about the restrictions imposed by Dr. Khan Sahib's government on the Islam League's three-day camp. The Sub-Inspector also states that slogans were raised against Dr. Khan Sahib during the public meeting. Regarding the forced occupation of Mashraqi's land, the Sub-Inspector states that Mashraqi said: "I cannot give my land in Wahdat Colony [Lahore], which is registered with the Government, at any cost. Because of the fact that the Government did not issue any notice about the acquisition of this land, and has not notified it in any Gazette, therefore, there is no justification for the Government to usurp my land - through the Chief Minister" (C&MG 1958 Oct. 03).

Mashraqi cross-examines Saeed Ahmed in court. Another C.I.D. stenographer, Mohammed Mirza, informs the court that Mashraqi also addressed a public meeting in Mochi Gate, Lahore on November 11, 1956 (PT 1958 Oct. 03).

1958 October 03

Five more prosecution witnesses are examined in Dr. Khan Sahib's murder case in the court of Lahore District and Sessions Judge Sheikh Anwar ul Haq (PT 1958 Oct. 04). The Judge rejects an insanity plea filed by Ata Mohammad's divorced wife (C&MG 1958 Oct. 04).

1958 October 06

Eight more prosecution witnesses are examined in Dr. Khan Sahib's murder case before Lahore District and Sessions Judge Sheikh Anwar ul Haq (PT 1958 Oct. 07).

1958 October 07

Seven more prosecution witnesses, including Khan Saad Ullah Khan (Dr. Khan Sahib's son), are examined in Dr. Khan Sahib's murder case before Lahore District and Sessions Judge Sheikh Anwar ul Haq. Other witnesses include Khan Saad Ullah Khan's wife (PT 1958 Oct. 08).

Martial Law is imposed in Pakistan (PT 1958 Oct. 08).

1958 October 08

Fifteen more prosecution witnesses are examined in Dr. Khan Sahib's murder case before Lahore District and Sessions Judge Sheikh Anwar ul Haq (PT 1958 Oct. 09).

1958 October 09

Ten more prosecution witnesses, including Syed Hasnat Ahmed (A.D.M., Lahore) and Mohammed Shaukat Tarar (Magistrate), are examined in Dr. Khan Sahib's murder case in the court of Lahore

District and Sessions Judge Sheikh Anwar ul Haq. Syed Hasnat Ahmed informs the court that on May 17, 1958, DSP Randhawa brought Muhammad Khurshid Khalid before him. After listening to Khurshid Khalid, Syed Hasnat Ahmed sent him to First Class Magistrate Qazi Muhammad Hafizullah to record his statement.

During cross-examination, Syed Hasnat Ahmed admits that he did receive an application from Khawaja Wali Muhammad (Advocate) regarding the police torture of the accused persons. He further states:

"At the fourth or fifth appearance for remand in my court, Allama Mashriqi complained to me that some police officials had forcibly snatched some papers from him and during the scuffle two or three buttons of his shirt had been torn off. He showed me his shirt.

I found one of the buttons missing. There were, however no injury marks of any kind on his person...The shirt of Allama Mashriqi was slightly torn in the front.

Allama Masriqi did say that the other co-accused as well as the approver were being tortured" (C&MG 1958 Oct. 10; PT 1958 Oct. 10; *Dawn* 1958 Oct. 11).

1958 October 10

More prosecution witnesses, including Qazi Mohammed Hafizullah (First Class Magistrate) and Mohammed Shaukat Tarar (Magistrate), are examined in Dr. Khan Sahib's murder case in the court of Lahore District and Sessions Judge Sheikh Anwar ul Haq. Qazi Muhammad Hafizullah, who recorded Khurshid Khalid's statement on May 17, 1958, informs the court that he didn't examine Khurshid Khalid for police violence. Ch. Muhammad Shaukat Tarar (Magistrate) also states that he did not ask Muhammad Khursheed Khalid whether he had been tortured. Qazi Muhammad Hafizullah further informs the court that police had taken a copy of Muhammad Khursheed Khalid's statement before it was sent to the Additional District Magistrate on May 19, 1958.

Another prosecution witness (an A.S.I. of Police) informs the court that on April 21, 1957, while serving in the Criminal Investigation Department (CID), he was assigned to monitor the activities of the Khaksar Camp at Wahgah Border (C&MG 1958 Oct. 11; PT 1958 Oct. 11).

1958 October 13

Sixteen more prosecution witnesses, including Yasin Butt (editor of the daily *Waqt*), are examined in Dr. Khan Sahib's murder case before before Lahore District and Sessions Judge Sheikh Anwar ul Haq. The court has examined 101 witnesses out of 120 to be produced by the prosecution (PT 1958 Oct. 15).

1958 October 14

Dr. Khan Sahib's murder case resumes before Lahore District and Sessions Judge Sheikh Anwar ul Haq. Malik Habib Ullah (Assistant Inspector General of Police, Crimes) states that prior to raiding Allama Mashriqi's house, he informed the West Pakistan Government, Chief Secretary, Inspector General of Police (I.G.), Deputy Inspector General of Police (D.I.G.), and Senior Superintendent of Police (S.S.P) (PT 1958 Oct. 16).

1958 October 15

Dr. Khan Sahib's murder case continues in the court of Lahore District and Sessions Judge Sheikh Anwar ul Haq. Prosecution witnesses are examined. Police continue to deny the use of violence against Allama Mashraqi during investigations (C&MG 1958 Oct. 16; PT 1958 Oct. 17; *Dawn* 1958 Oct. 16).

1958 October 17

Dr. Khan Sahib's murder case continues in the court of Lahore District and Sessions Judge Sheikh Anwar ul Haq. The prosection closes its evidence. Initially the prosecution had submitted a list of 130 witnesses to be produced in court, but after producing 104 witnesses, they declared two of them hostile and the rest unnecessary. The C.I.D. Inspector informs the court that he was part of the raiding party that searched Mashraqi's house and the Khaksar headquarters (adjacent to Mashraqi's house). Items confiscated included a letter addressed to President Iskandar Mirza (PT 1958 Oct. 18; C&MG 1958 Oct. 18).
Editor's comments: *The Civil & Military Gazette*, Lahore of October 18, 1958 reported that the prosecution produced 114 witnesses.

The prosecution saw no stength in the case and dropped the idea of producing any more witnesses.

1958 October 21

Dr. Khan Sahib's murder case continues in the court of Lahore District and Sessions Judge Sheikh Anwar ul Haq. Ata Mohammed, the alleged assasin, informs the court that he murdered Dr. Khan Sahib by himself and that Allama Mashraqi was not involved in the murder. In response to a question, Ata Mohammad states, "The fact is that I never mentioned anything regarding the participation of Allama Mashriqi or Khurshid Khalid in any of my activities connected with the present offence during my statements before the two magistrates and if they have recovered anything in this connection they must have done it on their own." In reply to another question, he says, "My name is Ata Muhammad and I am the man who intentionally murdered Dr. Khan Sahib at 16, Aikman Road, on May 9, 1958, in full possession of my senses. I planned the whole thing myself without the assistance or instigation of any other person" (PT 1958 Oct. 22).

Dawn, Karachi of October 22, 1958 would also report, "Replying to a question by the Special Prosecuter the alleged assassin [Ata Mohammad] said it was wrong to suggest that on May 6 Allama Mashriqi called him through Khurshid Khalid and impressed on him that Dr. Khan Sahib was a great Kafir and was an enemy of Pakistan and that he should be liquadated" (*Dawn* 1958 Oct. 22).

The Civil & Military Gazette, Lahore of October 22, 1958 would further state that "...he [Ata Mohammad] told the District and Sessions Judge, Mr. Anwarul-Haq, that it was wrong to suggest that the conspiracy was hatched at the house of the Allama [Mashraqi] in the presence of Khurshid Khalid, who had turned approver, but was later declared hostile" (C&MG 1958 Oct. 22).

Earlier, Hassan Muhammad Randhawa (Deputy Superintendent of Police, Crimes) is asked to leave the courtroom on an application moved by Allama Mashraqi (C&MG 1958 Oct. 22).

Editor's comments: Ata Mohammad's statement reveals that Mashraqi was implicated on purpose.

1958 October 22

Dr. Khan Sahib's murder case continues before Lahore District and Sessions Judge Sheikh Anwar ul Haq. Ata Mohammed, the alleged assasin, concludes his statement. Ata Mohammed informs the court that financial problems and frustration, for which he held the Government responsible, were the reason for his murder of Dr. Khan Sahib. He states, "Keeing this purpose in view I came to Lahore twice in search of my victim and spent most of my time wandering through Gulberg and Aikman Road in order to get information about Dr. Khan Sahib. I had taken an oath before my arrival in Lahore that I will never go out of Lahore till I had fulfilled my sacred mission." Ata Mohammad repeats, "I planned the whole thing myself without the assistance or instigation of any other person." Concluding his statement, he says, "Financial troubles and frustration make a man brutal..."

1958 October 23

The Pakistan Times, Lahore October of 23, 1958 would report, "Replying to a Court question [of whether Mashriqi regarded Dr. Khan Sahib as an enemy of Pakistan and an agent of Nehru]...the Allama replied he never bothered about Dr. Khan Sahib..." (PT 1958 Oct. 23).
Editor's comments: Dr. Khan Sahib was the Chief Minister of the West Pakistan Government when Mashraqi's 20 kanals of land were forcibly acquired by the Government to construct the Wahdat Colony in Lahore (PT 1958 Nov. 19).

Dr. Khan Sahib's murder case continues before the Lahore District and Sessions Judge Sheikh Anwar ul Haq Districts. Mashraqi informs the court that police tortured Ata Mohammed to implicate Mashriqi. The Special Public Prosecutor asks Mashraqi some questions.
Editor's comments: See the following sources for more information: C&MG 1958 Oct. 24; PT 1958 Oct. 24.

1958 October 24

On this date, the following information was found in *The Pakistan Times*, Lahore (of October 24, 1958): Allama Mashraqi, Quaid-e-Azam and Allama Iqbal were photographed together and photo was published in daily *Shahbaz* (exact date of the photograph and its publication in *Shahbaz* is unknown).

1958 October 25

Dr. Khan Sahib's murder case continues before Lahore District and Sessions Judge Sheikh Anwar ul Haq. The prosecution reads extracts of the letter Mashraqi had written to Dr. Khan Sahib regarding the forcible takeover (without compensation) of 20 Kanals of Mashraqi's land in Wahdat Colony, Lahore. An extract of the letter read by the prosecution states, "I [Allama Mashraqi] had been offered about Rs. 30,000 for the land but did not sell it since I had decided to live there myself. The Government has forcibly taken possession of the land and thrown away iron girders posted on the boundaries. It will not be possible for me to agree to surrender at any cost and I shall resist such step to last ditch" (PT 1958 Oct. 27; PT 1958 Oct. 26).

Editor's comments: The prosecution again tried to implicate Mashraqi in the murder. The extracts from the letter were read in an attempt to prove that Mashraqi had personal enmity against Dr. Khan Sahib.

1958 October 26

The Pakistan Times, Lahore reports that the defence counsel pleaded before Lahore District and Sessions Judge Sheikh Anwar ul Haq to take a lenient view of the punishment for Ata Mohammed (PT 1958 Oct. 26; PT 1958 Oct. 27).

1958 October 27

Dr. Khan Sahib's murder case continues before Lahore District and Sessions Judge Sheikh Anwar ul Haq. Barrister Ijaz Hussain Batalvi argues that neither the retracted confession of Ata Mohammed nor the earlier statement of Mohammed Khursheed Khalid (an approver who later became hostile) make a case of conviction against Allama Mashraqi. According to Ijaz Hussain Batalvi, "They [the prosecution] had cooked up a fertile story of conspiracy in the Fort which they wanted to put through the mouth of the approver, but eventually they did not succeed." He argues that there is no evidence that "Allama Mashriqi and Ata Mohammad even ever met or came to know each other…The prosecution has tried their best by bringing in lot of irrelevant material, and repeatedly reading out extracts from the statements of Khursheed Khalid and Ata Mohammaad, under Sec 164 Cr. P.C., which are no more substantial evidence [Mohammed Khursheed Khalid turned hostile and Ata Mohammed admitted that he falsely implicated Mashraqi] to create a web of suspicion around the Allama" (PT 1958 Oct. 29).

1958 October 28

Dr. Khan Sahib's murder case concludes in the court of Lahore District and Sessions Judge Sheikh Anwar ul Haq. All the four assessors in Dr. Khan Sahib's murder trial unanimously express their opinion that Allama Mashraqi is not guilty of conspiracy or abetment to assassinate Dr. Khan Sahib. *The Civil & Military Gazette*, Lahore October 29, 1958 would further report:

"Mr. Batalvi said the first statement of Ata Muhammad is the same which he had given in the Sessions Court and in which he had stated that he was the only man responsible for the murder of Dr. Khan and no body instigated him to commit the murder. 'The whole prosecution story of conspiracy is nothing but a cock and bull story,' he added" (C&MG 1958 Oct. 29; PT 1958 Nov. 18; *Dawn* 1958 Oct. 29).

1958 November 17

Mashraqi is acquitted in the case of conspiring to murder Dr. Khan Sahib. Lahore District and Sessions Judge Sheikh Anwar ul Haq announces the judgement, which comprises of 129 pages. According to the Judge, the prosecution failed to establish a case of conspiracy against Mashraqi

Mohammed Khursheed Khalid (the approver who turned hostile) remains in police custody until the court has made a decision regarding his turning hostile.

Ata Mohammed is sentenced to death for murdering Dr. Khan Sahib (PT 1958 Nov. 18).

The Civil & Military Gazette, Lahore November 18, 1958 would report, "The court room was packed to capacity and those present heard the judgment in hushed silence" (C&MG 1958 Nov. 18).

Dawn, Karachi of November 18, 1958 would also report: "A pin drop silence was restored as the Judge took his seat. Soon after the Allama's acquittal was pronounced his admirers and followers, present in court premises in good strength, profusely garlanded him. The Allama was later taken in a procession to his Ichhra residence" (*Dawn* 1958 Nov. 18).

Editor's comments: The case initially went to the Special Magistrate court, where the prosecution presented over 130 witnesses in an attempt to prove their case against Mashraqi. The Special Magistrate M.N.Rizvi committed Mashraqi and Ata Mohammed to the Sessions on July 22, 1958.

In the court of the Lahore District and Sessions Judge Sheikh Anwar ul Haq, 114 prosecution witnesses were produced during a 40 day-long hearing. The proceedings of the trial were held in Borstal Jail, Lahore for security reasons and the judgment was made on November 17, 1958.

On the day of the decision, the premises were overflowing with a large number of people including Mashraqi's family members and followers who had gathered to hear the judgement. Before the judgement, there was pin drop silence, which reflected the fear that everyone had in their minds that this scholar of the East might be sentenced to death and taken to the gallows. This was a very emotional and touching moment and when the outcome was declared, Mashraqi's supporters breathed a sigh of relief. Slogans such as

"Allama Mashraqi Zindabad" and "Allama Mashraqi Long Live" were raised.

It is very sad to note that, at the age of 70, Mashraqi had to go through such tremendous physical and mental torture. His health had drastically gone poor in detention due to poor quality food, maltreatment and poor medical care. In jail, he remained sick and his health deteriorated fast. After his release, the doctors detected cancer. If he was at least granted bail and treated properly toward the beginning period of this disease, he might have survived for a longer period. However, he succumed to cancer and died within few a years. But who is accountable for all this?

1958 November 18

Mashraqi issues a statement following his release from jail.

"The indesirable torture I have been put to by the previous Government for uncommitted crimes will remain a landmark in the history of corruption and tyranny for all time...

It is fortunate that these Governments crashed under the weight of their own evil deeds overnight and the result is a benignant rule which promises well for the future. The striking event of the murder of Dr. Khan Sahib, however regrettable, had no doubt served as a precursor of this astounding revolution and such a revolution otherwise may not have come about for many years to come.

The dramatic and complete exit of Iskander Mirza from Pakistan and of his notorious satellites has struck the last nail in the coffin of that regime, which was signal in its iniquity and for which Mirza was so much to blame in later years.

I have no doubt that under the most well-conducted and intelligent regime of President Ayub, Pakistan will not only solve promptly the most vexed problems that it has had to face for the last 11 years through the criminal weakness of culprits at the helm of affairs, but that Pakistan will grow from strength to strength before the growing weakness of Bharat [India], which has started lately.

My suffering almost to the point of death that I had to face at the hands of the political tyrants, has not gone in vain and I am happy that truth and righteousness have at last won a battle like of which has, perhaps seldom happened in the history of the defeat of evil.

I have something more to say. During this career of seven months as a person charged with heinous crime, I had the first opportunity of meeting prisoners in jail. I have come to get the impression that the fate of a large number of them also has an inevitable tinge of that corruption, nepotism, dishonesty and especially the curse of false evidence in courts which characterised the previous Governments.

These unfortunates are rotting in badly-administered and corrupt jails as uncared-for victims throughout years.

It would be a rare feat of kindness and high-thinking if, on this occasion, when all iniquity is being purged away a sort of general amnesty, at any rate to first offenders, is given on some memorable occasion of the establishment of the present Government.

Such an action will assure people that the Government, not only has a keen eye on public welfare but that it has got a human touch. It is also apt to create a tremendous reform in the personal character of individuals" (C&MG 1958 Nov. 19; PT 1958 Nov. 19).

The Civil & Military Gazette, Lahore and *The Pakistan Times*, Lahore publish the Lahore District and Sessions Judge Sheikh Anwar ul Haq's judgement in Dr. Khan Sahib's murder case (C&MG 1958 Nov. 18; PT 1958 Nov. 18).

Editor's comments: The entire judgment is spread out over the course of a few days in *The Pakistan Times* and *The Civil & Military Gazette*, Lahore.

The Civil & Military Gazette, Lahore publishes a photo of Allama Mashraqi with his supporters and followers outside Borstal Jail, where Dr. Khan Sahib's murder trial was held (C&MG 1958 Nov. 18).

1958 November 19

The Civil & Military Gazette, Lahore and *The Pakistan Times*, Lahore publish the Lahore District and Sessions Judge Sheikh Anwar ul Haq's judgement in Dr. Khan Sahib's murder case (C&MG 1958 Nov. 19; PT 1958 Nov. 19).

Editor's comments: The entire judgment is spread out over the course of a few days in *The Pakistan Times* and *The Civil & Military Gazette*, Lahore.

1958 November 20

The Civil & Military Gazette, Lahore and *The Pakistan Times*, Lahore publish the Lahore District and Sessions Judge Sheikh Anwar ul Haq's judgement in Dr. Khan Sahib's murder case (C&MG 1958 Nov. 20; PT 1958 Nov. 20).

Editor's comments: The entire judgment is spread out over the course of a few days in *The Pakistan Times* and *The Civil & Military Gazette*, Lahore.

1958 November 21

The Pakistan Times, Lahore publishes the Lahore District and Sessions Judge Sheikh Anwar ul Haq's judgement in Dr. Khan Sahib's murder case (PT 1958 Nov. 21).

The Lahore District and Sessions Judge Sheikh Anwar ul Haq grants bail to Muhammad Khurshid Khalid (the approver who later turned hostile in Dr. Khan Sahib's murder trial) (C&MG 1958 Nov. 22).

1958 December 24

Dawn, Karachi reports that Sialkot District and Sessions Judge Ch. Sultan Khan has accepted the appeals filed by three former members of the Khaksar Muslim League and has set aside their sentence from a lower court of six months rigorous imprisonment each.

The Border Police of Sajjanpur had apprehended Zafar Haider, Asghar Haider, and Ali Muhammad on November 17, 1957 on charges of illegally entering into Pakistan from India. The accused stated that they were Pakistani nationals and that the charges against them were fabricated. They submitted that they had been camping at the border to participate in the million-man march that was supposed to take place on October 21, 1957.

In his order, the Judge states: "It appears that since the appellants had camped on the border to the annoyance of the Border Police and because the deadline fixed by the high command of that party for crossing into India was approaching, the Border Police being tired of the volunteers camping near their post, decided to implicate them in this case" (*Dawn* 1958 Dec. 24).

The newspaper further states, "Believing that the appellants were falsely implicated in the case he [the Judge] set aside their conviction and acquitted them all.

Mian Mohammad Ismail, advocate, represented the appellant" (*Dawn* 1958 Dec. 24).

1960, 1962

"Allama Mashraqi's life is a book to learn from"

– Nasim Yousaf

1960

1960 May 04

Mashraqi's book *Takmillah* (Volumes I and II) is published (Mashraqi [1931] 1997, 09).

1962

1962 May 06

Mashraqi is arrested in Lahore and the Government issues a press note. *The Pakistan Times*, Lahore of May 07, 1962 would report:
"Inayatullah Khan Mashriqi...and over a dozen of his followers, have been arrested and detained for a conspiracy of a violent nature and activities prejudicial to the interests of the State.
Editor's comments: May 06, 1962 is the approximate date of Mashraqi's arrest. The exact date of his arrest was not available in the sources used.
Mashraqi was arrested for allegedly conspiring to topple Ayub Khan's Government (Hussain 1988, 267). The Government could never prove anything against Mashraqi; he was always arrested on false, baseless charges. (Also see *Jang* 1962 May 08).

1962 May 08

The Civil & Military Gazette, Lahore reports that seventeen former Khaksars have been arrested in Rawalpindi under the Security of Pakistan Act. According to the newspaper, some of the Khaksars are being kept in Rawalpindi Jail, while others were sent to Lahore. The newspaper also states that police interrogated the Khaksars (C&MG 1962 May 08).

1962 May 10

The President promulgates an Ordinance prohibiting all political activities in the country (*Jang* 1962 May 12).

1962 June 18

Mohammad Ali Bogra informs the National Assembly that orders are being issued to release many political leaders (*Jang* 1962 Jun. 20).

1962 June 24

A large public meeting is held in Rawalpindi. At the meeting, the release of political leaders is demanded. Those addressing the meeting include Khaksar Sher Zaman (*Jang* 1962 Aug. 27).

1962 July 21

Khurshid Khalid announces the revival of the Khaksar Tehrik. *The Pakistan Times*, Lahore of July 22, 1962 would report:
"Mr. Khurshid Khalid, former President of the defunct Khaksar movement announced, on Saturday [July 21, 1962] the revival of the Khaksar organisation, which was dissolved in 1947 just before the creation of Pakistan. Mr Khurshid announced this decision in a Press conference...
Mr. Khurshid claimed that only movements like that of the Khaksars could ensure unity between East and West Pakistan, because, it was based on true Islamic principles and mainly aimed at strengthening the defence of the country.
His party, he said, would cooperate with any other organisation whose aim was to strengthen the country and to liberate Kashmir.
A convention of the Khaksar leaders from both the wings of Pakistan, he said, will be held on August 24, 25 and 26, in Rawalpindi" (PT 1962 Jul. 22).
The Civil & Military Gazette, Lahore of July 22, 1962 would also report that Khurshid Khalid said that with the revival of the Khaksar Tehrik, the Khaksar Muslim League and the Islam League would come to an end.
Editor's comments: According to *The Civil & Military Gazette*, Lahore of July 22, 1962, the convention of Khaksar leaders was to be held on August 25-26, 1962 (C&MG 1962 Jul. 22).

1962 July 28

Khaksars parade in Lahore. Police intercept them near Bhatti Gate and ask them to disperse (C&MG 1962 Jul. 29).

1962 August 03

Khaksars in Multan demand Mashraqi's immediate and unconditional release. They pass a resolution stating that Mashraqi should be released immediately due to his poor health or he should be tried in an open court of law (PT 1962 Aug. 06).

1962 August 04

Khaksar Muhammad Latif Butt is released from jail after completing three months of detention. He was arrested on May 06, 1962 (C&MG 1962 Aug. 05).

1962 August 23

The West Pakistan Government removes the restrictions on Allama Mashriqi (C&MG 1962 Aug. 24). However, the restrictions on the Khaksars/Razakars remain in place. Furthermore, a convention of Khaksars/ Razakars, which is to be held in Rawalpindi on August 24, 1962, is not allowed. Mashraqi was sick during this time. Mashriqi wrote to Ayub Khan to remove restrictions on the Khaksar/Razakar activities (Hussain 1994, 202-203).

1962 August 24

The Daily Jang, Karachi reports that Khaksar Muhammad Zakria died while traveling from Lahore to Karachi following his release from jail. The newspaper further reports that the Khaksars suspect that he died as a result of police torture. The newspaper also states that the Khaksar leaders and supporters have asked the President of Pakistan, Muhammad Ayub Khan, to order an inquiry into his death (*Jang* 1962 Aug. 24).

1962 August 25

The Government of Pakistan issues a Press Note. *The Pakistan Times*, Lahore of August 26, 1962 would report:

"The Khaksar organisation, under whatever name it might re-emerge, would still remain banned under Section 18 of the Criminal Law Amendment Act, it was officially announced in Lahore on Saturday.

A Press note said: 'Reports received from various parts of the Province indicate that Khaksars contemplate reviving their movement. Before the imposition of Martial Law the Khaksars were functioning first under the name of Islam League and then under the name of the Pakistan 'Muslim League'. The latter organisation (founded by Mr. Inayatullah Khan Mashriqi) was banned in May 1958 under Section 10 of the Criminal Law Amendment Act, 1908. That ban still continues. If the Khaksar organisation re-emerges in another name it will still stand banned under Section 18 of the Criminal Law Amendment Act. All concerned are, therefore, warned not to indulge in any activity in contravention of the law.'" (PT 1962 Aug. 26; *Jang* 1962 Aug. 27)

Editor's comments: The Khaksar Tehrik was outlawed despite the fact that on July 14, 1962, the National Assembly had passed a Bill removing the ban on all political parties in Pakistan (PT 1962 Jul. 17). Thus, the Khaksars/Razakars – who worked sincerely for the uplift of the country – were not allowed to exist under any circumstances.

The Civil & Military Gazette, Lahore reports that Mashraqi declared his intentions to defy the Government's ban on wearing a uniform and carrying a belcha. Mashraqi objected to the fact that these restrictions were imposed only on the Khaksar Tehrik. The newspaper states that Mashraqi said, "The law of the land demands that every citizen should be equally treated. Then why the Khaksars should be discriminated and persecuted by the authorities?

We shall not accept these restrictions and will continue to wear our uniforms" (C&MG 1962 Aug. 25).

Editor's comments: Mashraqi was a valorous and fearless person and despite his poor health, he took part in Khaksar/Razakar activities. He fought for the rights of the people until he died.

1962 August 27

The Civil & Military Gazette, Lahore reports that President Muhammad Ayub Khan didn't accept the offer to lead the Khaksar Tehrik. According to the newspaper:

"The President, who was replying to a letter from Mr. Khurshid Khalid, Nazim-e-Aala of the Khaksar Movement said that 'he cannot accept his (Khalid's) offer to assume the leadership of the Khaksar Movement.'

Explaining restrictions imposed by some local authorities on Khaksars using military-syle uniforms and doing parade, the President said there was no justification for a military-type private political organisation to function in an independent country.

President Ayub has advised the Khaksars that instead of assuming features similar to those of military the Khaksars would do best if they selflessly serve the people, according to the objectives of their own organisation.

PPA adds:

The President said the people needed selfless service and Khaksars could serve them more easily if they co-operated with the Union Councils.

The president, defending the ban imposed on Khaksar Movement, stated that in a free country military organisation of private and political nature could not have any room, for the obvious reason that such organisations either become an instrument of political pressure or a source of disturbance to the public peace and order.

He asked them that as citizens of a free country Khaksars should try to undersatnd and obey the law under which their movement had been banned" (C&MG 1962 Aug. 27; *Jang* 1962 Aug. 28).

Editor's comments: Only those nations who have discipline, unity, and character can prosper. The Khaksar Tehrik was working for this cause that its opponents either failed to understand or ignored for vested reasons.

1962 September 04

Muhammad Khurshid Khalid holds a press conference in Lahore. *The Pakistan Times*, Lahore of September 05, 1962 would report:

"Mr. Khurshid Khalid, Chief Organiser of the Khaksar movement, addressing a Press conference in Rawalpindi on Tuesday [September 04, 1962] stated...

The Kashmir problem, he added, could not be solved unless one crore people of Pakistan were organised into a disciplined force and the Khaksars alone could galvanise the people into a well-knit force...

President's [Ayub] suggestion that Khaksars should work in collabration with the Union Councils... Khaksars could assist the Union Councils in their development projects provided the Khaksars were allowed to function as an organisation.

But he continued the greatest problem before the country was the liberation of Kashmir to which the Khaksars would devote their entire energies.

Asked if the Khaksars would assist the Kashmir Liberation Movement proposed by veteran Kashmiri leader, Ch. Ghulam Abbas, he said that Kashmir could not be freed by 10,000 volunteers alone. Unless the entire nation was mobilized into a fighting force as a second line of defence one could not think of freeing Kashmir.

The Khaksar leader further urged the President to allow them to call on him to explain their programmes and policies" (PT 1962 Sept. 05).

1962 September 15

The Pakistan Times, Lahore reports that seventeen Khaksars were expelled from Rawalpindi for three months under the West Pakistan Maintenance of Public Order Ordinance, 1960. The order was issued by the Rawalpindi District Magistrate (PT 1962 Sept. 15).

1962 September 22

The Pakistan Times, Lahore reports, "Mr. Khurshid Khalid, a former Khaksar leader, has been arrested by the police...
　　He has been remanded to the judicial lock-up and will soon be produced before the Additional District Magistrate, Gujrat, for trial" (PT 1962 Sept. 22; C&MG 1962 Sept. 25).
Editor's comments: The Government of Pakistan had again pounced on the Khaksar Tehrik and arrested Muhammad Khursheed Khalid under fabricated charges.

1962 September 26

A bail application is presented on behalf of Muhammad Khurshid Khalid (Nazim-e-Aala of the Khaksar Tehrik) in the court of the Gujrat Additional District Magistrate. Muhammad Khurshid Khalid is also produced in court. Consideration of the bail application is postponed until September 28, 1962 (C&MG 1962 Sept. 27).

1962 November 10

A hearing is held for three Khaksars arrested in August, 1962. *The Pakistan Times*, Lahore of November 11, 1962 would report:
　　"No prosecution witness turned up in the Khaksars case when it came up for hearing on Saturday [November 10, 1962] for the third time...at the request of the police the date was extended on three occasions.
　　The three Khaksars, Ramzan Khokhar, Atta Mohammad Butt and Aslam Tariq, were arrested in August...
　　He [the Magistrate] ordered that the witnesses should be compelled to attend the court by issuance of warrants for attendance.
　　Hearing has now been fixed on November 21 [1962]" (PT 1962 Nov. 11).

Mashraqi's Son-in-Law Passes Away

1962 December 09

My father, Mohammad Yousaf Khan, was Mashraqi's son-in-law. He was married to my mother, Masuda Yousaf, who was Mashriqi's third daughter with his first wife. My father passed away at a young age on December 9, 1962 at 9 a.m. He was buried in a Rawalpindi graveyard; my mother was later buried in the same graveyard.

Mashriqi was shocked at the sudden and tragic death of his cherished son-in-law. My father was well respected in the community and people adored him for who he was. A large number of people visited our family and offered their condolences. Thousands of people from all walks of life, including civil and military dignitaries, attended his funeral. Mourners continued to visit our house for many months.

My father was an honorable man with a great sense of integrity. Although he passed away when I was a young boy, his personality left a tremendous impression on my mind which is still vivid after so many years.

I am who I am because of my parents.

1963, 1983

"A truly successful human: admired when alive, remembered after perished"

– Nasim Yousaf

1963

1963 January 06

The daily *Jang*, Karachi reports, Allama Mashraqi reveals that plans are being made to divide Jammu & Kashmir. He suggests that President Muhammad Ayub Khan adopt strict policies with India towards Kashmir (*Jang* 1963 Jan. 06; *Chitan* 1963 Mar. 09; Zaman 1988, 228).

1963 August 06

Imroze, Lahore reports that Allama Mashriqi is in critical health condition (*Imroze* 1963 Aug. 06).

The Pakistan Times, Lahore reports, "Mashraqi in Precarious Condition" (PT 1963 Aug. 06).

1963 August 07

The daily *Jang*, Karachi reports that Mashriqi is seriously ill (*Jang* 1963 Aug. 07).

Dawn, Karachi reports, "Allama Mashraqi in coma" (*Dawn* 1963 Aug. 07).

Mashraqi is admitted to Albert Victor Hospital in Lahore, Pakistan. Dr. Riaz Qadeer is his doctor at the hospital.

1963 August 08

The daily *Jang*, Karachi reports that Mashriqi is in a coma. (*Jang* 1963 Aug. 08).

Mashriqi comes out of the coma and delivers his message to the nation from the hospital (Hussain 1994, 204).

1963 August 09

The daily *Jang*, Karachi, reports that Mashriqi will be moved to Mayo Hospital (Lahore) today (*Jang* 1963 Aug. 09).

The Pakistan Times, Lahore reports, "Mashriqi admitted to AVH: Operation Planned" (PT 1963 Aug. 09).
Editor's comments: AVH stands for Albert Victor Hospital (also known as Mayo Hospital).

The Pakistan Observer, Dacca reports, "Mashraqi Removed To Hospital" (PO 1963 Aug. 09).

Morning News, Dacca reports, "Mashriqi's Condition Improving" (MN 1963 Aug. 09).

1963 August 10

The daily *Jang*, Karachi, reports, Mashriqi is admitted into Mayo Hospital, Lahore (*Jang* 1963 Aug. 10).

Imroze, Lahore, reports, Allama Mashriqi is not out of danger. He could not be operated on due to extremely poor health (*Imroze* 1963 Aug. 10).

The Civil & Military Gazette, Lahore reports that Mashraqi's health is progressing (C&MG 1963 Aug. 10).

Allama Mashriqi delivers an important message to the nation. He appeals to the nation to be prepared against the conspiracies of USA and Britain, who are supplying arms to India. In addition, Russia has an inclinication toward India, and all of this is a sign of danger for Pakistan. Mashraqi says that this might be his last message to the nation, and he advises Pakistan's people to stand united, give up personal gains, and sacrifice themselves for the nation. (Also see *Imroze* 1963 Aug. 10).
Editor's comments: Although Mashraqi was on his death bed, he was still concerned about the nation's wellbeing.

1963 August 11

The daily *Jang*, Karachi reports that Mashriqi continues to be seriously ill. (*Jang* 1963 Aug. 11).

Imroze, Lahore, reports, Allama Mashriqi remains in critical condition. He is in a coma. (*Imroze* 1963 Aug. 11).

The Civil & Military Gazette, Lahore reports "Mashraqi's condition critical" (C&MG 1963 Aug. 11).

The Pakistan Times, Lahore reports, "Allama Mashriqi Makes No Progress" (PT 1963 Aug. 11).

Dawn, Karachi reports, "Mashraqi unconscious" (*Dawn* 1963 Aug. 11).

1963 August 12

The daily *Jang*, Karachi reports, Mashriqi refuses to be operated on (*Jang* 1963 Aug. 12).

The Civil & Military Gazette, Lahore and *Imroze*, Lahore, report, President of Pakistan, Muhammad Ayub Khan, inquired about Mashraqi's health. The President asked the doctor to arrange for Mashraqi's treatment in Switzerland. (C&MG 1963 Aug. 12; *Imroze* 1963 Aug. 12).

Editor's comments: Although he appreciated President Ayub's gesture, Allama Mashriqi did not accept the offer because he did not want to use public funds for his personal treatment.

The Pakistan Times, Lahore reports, "Mashriqi shows signs of improvement" (PT 1963 Aug. 12).

Dawn, Karachi reports, "Mashriqi improves" (*Dawn* 1963 Aug. 12).

Morning News, Dacca reports, "Mashriqi improving" (MN 1963 Aug. 12).

1963 August 13

The daily *Jang*, Karachi, reports, Mashraqi's condition improves. Maulana Maudoodi (Amir of Jamaat-e-Islami) visits Mashriqi in the hospital (*Jang* 1963 Aug. 13).

The Pakistan Times, Lahore reports, "Ayub solicitude for Mashriqi's health." According to the newspaper, President Ayub expressed his anxiety about Mashraqi's health. The newspaper further reports, "Allama Mashriqi improving" (PT 1963 Aug. 13).

Dawn, Karachi reports, "Mashraqi may be sent to Switzerland" (*Dawn* 1963 Aug. 13).

The Civil & Military Gazette, Lahore reports that a Hakim has been permitted to treat Mashraqi (C&MG 1963 Aug. 13).

1963 August 14

The daily *Jang*, Karachi reports, President of Pakistan, Muhammad Ayub Khan, is concerned about Mashraqi's health. He talks to the doctor in Mayo Hospital and inquiries about Mashraqi's health. Mashraqi extends thanks to the President. The President offers to send Mashraqi to Switzerland for medical treatment on the government's expense. (*Jang* 1963 Aug. 14).

Editor's comments: Although appreciative of the President's gesture, the family does not accept the offer.

The Pakistan Times, Lahore August 14, 1963 reports that President Muhammad Ayub Khan has approved a foreign exchange grant for Mashraqi's medical treatment in Switzerland (PT 1963 Aug. 14).

Dawn, Karachi, reports "Ayub [President of Pakistan] approves grant of foreign exchange for Mashriqi's treatment." The newspaper further reports that Maluana Abdus Sattar Niazi and Amir Habibullah Khan Saadi called on Allama Mashriqi in the hospital on August 13, 1963 (*Dawn* 1963 Aug. 14).

1963 August 17

The Pakistan Times, Lahore reports, "The Central Home Minister, Khan Habibullah Khan, sent a telegram to Allama Enayatullah Khan Mashriqi on Thursday [August 15, 1963] inquiring about his health..." (PT 1963 Aug. 17).

1963 August 18

Morning News, Dacca reports, "Mashriqi making steady progress" (MN 1963 Aug. 18).

The Pakistan Times, Lahore reports "Allama Mashriqi shows progress" (PT 1963 Aug. 18).

1963 August 22

The Pakistan Times, Lahore reports, "Allama Mashriqi's condition worsens" (PT 1963 Aug. 18).

Dawn, Karachi reports, "Mashriqi's condition worsens" (*Dawn* 1963 Aug. 22).

The Civil & Military Gazette, Lahore reports, "Mashraqi's condition again worsens" (C&MG 1963 Aug. 22).

The Pakistan Observer, Dacca reports, "Mashriqi's condition worsens" (PO 1963 Aug. 22).

Morning News, Dacca reports, "Mashriqi's Condition Worsens" (MN 1963, Aug. 22).

1963 August 23

Dawn, Karachi reports, "Allama Mashriqi in a semi-conscious state" (*Dawn* 1963 Aug. 23).

1963 August 24

The daily *Jang*, Karachi, reports, Mashraqi is in a coma. The Khaksar leaders appeal to the public to pray for Mashraqi's recovery at the Juma prayers (*Jang* 1963 Aug. 24).

The Civil & Military Gazette, Lahore reports, "Allama Mashriqi in Coma" (C&MG 1963 Aug. 24).

The Pakistan Times, Lahore reports, "Allama Mashriqi still in coma" (PT 1963 Aug. 24).

The Pakistan Observer, Dacca reports, "Mashriqi's Condition Reported Grave" (PO 1963 Aug. 24).

1963 August 25

The Civil & Military Gazette, Lahore reports, "Ayub [President of Pakistan] Visits Mashriqi in Hospital" (C&MG 1963 Aug. 25).

Dawn, Karachi reports, "Ayub visits Mashriqi in hospital" on August 24, 1963 (*Dawn* 1963 Aug. 25).

The Pakistan Times, Lahore reports that President Muhammad Ayub Khan visited Allama Mashriqi in the hospital on August 24, 1963 (PT 1963 Aug. 25).

Morning News, Dacca reports that President Muhammad Ayub Khan and Provincial Governor Malik Amir Muhammad Khan visit Mashriqi in Mayo Hospital, Lahore. The newspaper further states that

Mashraqi thanked them both and said "Apka Bahoot Shukria" (MN 1963 Aug. 25).

The Eastern Examiner, Chittagong reports that President Ayub Khan visited Mashraqi in the hospital (EE 1963 Aug. 25).

The Pakistan Times, Lahore publishes an article by Abdullah Malik. In the article, Malik includes a quote from D.C. Smith stating: "Its [Tazkirah's] publication provoked a considerable and widespread commotion: it attracted attention not only in Muslim India but in European and American Orientalist circles and at the Azhar" (PT 1963 Aug. 25).

1963 August 26

Imroze, Lahore reports, Mashraqi's health is deteriorating (*Imroze* 1963 Aug. 26).

1963 August 27

The daily *Jang,* Karachi prints pictures of the President of Pakistan's visit to Mashraqi at the Mayo hospital, Lahore (*Jang* 1963 Aug. 27).

The Pakistan Times, Lahore reports, "Allama Mashriqi Grows Very Weak" (PT 1963 Aug. 27).

Dawn, Karachi reports, "Mashriqi's condition deteriorating" (*Dawn* 1963 Aug. 27).

The Civil & Military Gazette, Lahore reports, "Mashriqi Appears to Have Lost Power of Speech" (C&MG 1963 Aug. 27).

Allama Mashraqi Passes Away

1963 August 27

Allama Mashraqi dies at night in Lahore.

With Mashraqi's death, an important chapter of Indo-Pak history was closed. Pakistan had lost a selfless leader. A personality of his caliber, ability, and devotion is yet to emerge. Pakistan is in much need of such a leader.

Word of Mashraqi's death spread like wildfire across the world. Every newspaper in Pakistan printed headlines or news of his death on the front page. They published editorials paying tributes to Mashraqi, and printed messages from prominent people from all walks of life. Pakistan Radio, All India Radio, and the BBC (UK.) also announced the news.

Mashraqi's death was widely mourned and well over 100,000 people attended his funeral. People came from every corner of Pakistan and even from abroad to join the mourning and as a tribute to their leader. The funeral procession was over a mile long. He was buried at the headquarters of the Khaksar Tehrik (Lahore), where he began the Movement in 1930. Comprehensive details of Mashraqi's funeral are provided in my book *Allama Mashriqi & Dr. Akhtar Hameed Khan: Two Legends of Pakistan*.

1963 August 27

From this date forward, many tributes to Allama Mashriqi were received and some of them were published in various newspapers. The following is a listing of persons whose tributes were published:

- Khawaja Nazimud Din, President Muslim League and ex-Prime Minister of Pakistan
- Noorul Amin, Ex-Chief Minister of East Pakistan
- Sardar Mohammad Alam, President All Jammu and Kashmir Conference, Lahore Circle.
- Nawab Muzzafar Ali Khan, Chairman Provincial Muslim League Organizing Committee
- Saddar ud Din Ansari, Joint Secretary Convention Muslim League
- Nawab Yameen Khan, Joint Secretary Sind Muslim League Organising Committee
- Mian Mohammad Shaukat, Amir Jamat-I-Islami, Hyderabad.
- Abdul Waheed Khan, Minister of Railway, West Pakistan
- M.M. Shaheed, President Arab Tameer Tehrik
- Mir Ali Ahmed Talpur, Ex-Provincial Minister
- Khawaja Abdul Ghafoor, Convener Nizam Islam Party
- Commodore Khalid Jamil, Convention Muslim League, Karachi
- Ansar Ali, Joint Convener Pakistan Youth League
- Ahmed Hassan Quraishi, Vice President Rawalpindi Cantonment Board
- Ghulam Jilani Barq
- Hafiz Jalundhari
- Multan Bar Association
- Journalists of Sukkur and Khairpur condoled his death

Under All Parties Conference, a Julsa (Meeting) was conducted at Chowk Yadgar, Peshawar to condole over Mashriqi's death. (Zaman 1987, 454 - 482).

1963 August 28

The Pakistan Times, Lahore reports, "Allama Mahriqi passes away." The newspaper further states that leaders described Mashraqi as a "figure who played prominent part in the freedom movement of the Indo-Pakistan sub-continent" (PT 1963 Aug. 28).

Dawn, Karachi reports, "Mashriqi dies of cancer in Lahore hospital." The newspaper also publishes tributes to Mashraqi from various leaders. Paying tribute to Mashraqi, the newspaper states, "He was repeatedly offered many lucrative appointments by the princely states of India but he refused to accept the offers. In 1920 he was offered a knighthood with the post of Political Secretary to the Government of India but he declined to accept the appointment due to his high sense of patriotism and feelings for the Muslim people of the Indian Sub-Continent" (*Dawn* 1963 Aug. 28).

Imroze, Lahore, reports that Allama Mashraqi has died (*Imroze* 1963 Aug. 28).

The Civil & Military Gazette, Lahore reports of the death of Allama Mashraqi (C&MG 1963 Aug. 28).

Business Post, Karachi reports, "Mashriqi passes away" (BP 1963 Aug. 28).

The Times of India, Bombay reports Mashraqi's death (TI 1963 Aug. 28).

The Pakistan Observer, Dacca reports Mashraqi's death (PO 1963 Aug. 28).

Morning News, Dacca reports, "Allama Mashraqi Passes Away" (MN 1963 Aug. 28).

Morning News, Karachi reports, "Allama Mashraqi Passes Away" (MNK 1963 Aug. 28).

The Eastern Examiner, Chittagong reports, "Allama Mashraqi Passes Away" (EE 1963 Aug. 28).

1963 August 29

The Pakistan Times, Lahore reports the condolence messages from President Ayub and others throughout the country on the death of Allama Mashraqi. The newspaper also writes an editorial about Mashraqi entitled "A Brave Fighter" (PT 1963 Aug. 29).

The Civil & Military Gazette, Lahore reports, "Mashraqi's funeral today [August 29, 1963]." The newspaper further writes, "Ayub [President of Pakistan] Condoles Mashriqi's Death." The newspaper also publishes the condolences of various other leaders. The newspaper also states that Bashir Ahmed Siddiqui has been chosen as the acting Chief of the defunct Khaksar Movement (C&MG 1963 Aug. 29).

Morning News, Dacca reports that President Ayub sent a telegram to Mashraqi's widow. In the telegram, he states:

"I am very much grieved to learn that your husband has passed away. He was a great scholar and organiser, who had given up a brilliant academic future to serve the people as he thought right.

He was also a man with the courage of his conviction. May his soul rest in eternal peace. Please accept my heartfelt sympathy in your bereavement" (MN 1963 Aug. 29).

Dawn, Karachi reports, "'Mashriqi was eminent scholar:' More Condolence Messages" (*Dawn* 1963 Aug. 29).

Morning News, Dacca reports, "Mashriqi's Death Condoled." The newspaper further states that Bashir Ahmed Siddiqui has been accepted as the acting leader of the Khaksar Movement for the interim period (MN 1963 Aug. 29).

The daily *Jang*, Karachi reports, "Allama Inayatullah Khan Mashraqi Intiqal Kar Gai" (Allama Inayatullah Khan Mashraqi died) (*Jang* 1963 Aug. 29).

Morning News, Karachi reports, "Mashriqi's Death Shocks Leaders" (MNK 1963 Aug. 29).

Morning News, Karachi reports, "Mashriqi's Death Casts Pall Of Gloom Over Country" (MNK 1963 Aug. 29).

The Eastern Examiner, Chittagong publishes an editorial entitled "Allama Mashraqi" (EE 1963 Aug. 29).

The Statesman, India publishes an obituary for Allama Mashraqi (TS 1963 Aug. 29).

The Hindustan Times, New Delhi reports Mashraqi's death (HT 1963 Aug. 29).

The Hindu, India reports Mashraqi's death. The newspaper writes:

"A brilliant mathematician, educationist and author, Allama Mashriqi, a graduate of Christ['s] College, Cambridge, turned to

politics in 1930 ...he was imprisoned during the Second World War...
In 1957, he led 3,00,000 followers to the border of Pakistan and India threatening to launch what he said would be a fight for 'liberation of Kashmir'...Subsequently, his movement was disbanded" (*The Hindu* 1963 Aug. 29).

1963 August 30

The daily *Jang*, Karachi reports that Mashraqi was buried in Lahore. The newspaper publishes an article on Mashraqi as well as tributes from various leaders including the President of Pakistan, Muhammad Ayub Khan (*Jang* 1963 Aug. 30).

Imroze, Lahore reports 100,000 people attended Allama Inayatullah Khan Al-Mashraqi's funeral (*Imroze* 1963 Aug. 30).

The Pakistan Times, Lahore reports, "Allama Mashriqi laid to rest" on August 29, 1963 (PT 1963 Aug. 30).
Editor's comments: The newspaper also provides details of Mashraqi's funeral.

Dawn, Karachi reports, "Mashriqi's death condoled" (*Dawn* 1963 Aug. 30).

The Civil & Military Gazette, Lahore August 30, 1963 reports that Mashriqi's death was condoled (C&MG 1963 Aug. 30).

The Dacca Times, Dacca reports Mashraqi's death (DT 1963 Aug. 30).

The Eastern Examiner, Chittagong reports that Mashraqi's death was mourned and that he has been laid to rest (EE 1963 Aug. 30).

Morning News, Karachi reports, "Mashriqi Laid To Rest" (MNK 1963 Aug. 30).

Huriyat (Karachi), *The Statesman* (New Delhi), and *Anjam (Unjaam)*, (Karachi) wrote on Mashriqi's death (Zaman 1987, 471-472, 479-480).

1963 August 31

The daily *Jang*, Karachi reports Mashraqi is buried in Lahore. 100,000 people attended the funeral (*Jang* 1963 Aug. 31).

The Pakistan Times, Lahore reports, "Nation has lost an 'illustrious son': Mashriqi's Death Condoled" (PT 1963 Aug. 31).

The Civil & Military Gazette, Lahore reports, "Mashriqi's death condoled" (C&MG 1963 Aug. 31).

Morning News, Dacca publishes an editorial entitled "Allama Mashriqi." The newspaper also reports that Mashraqi's followers and sympathizers will hold a public meeting in Dacca to condole Mashraqi's death (MN 1963 Aug. 31).

1963 September 01

The daily *Jang*, Karachi reports on funeral prayers held for Mashraqi in Karachi and prints pictures of the funeral (*Jang* 1963 Sept. 01).

The Pakistan Times, Lahore reports, "Allama Mashriqi's wife thanks people" (PT 1963 Sept. 01).

Morning News, Dacca reports Mashraqi's death with condolence messages from various leaders (MN 1963 Sept. 01).

Morning News, Dacca reports, "Rich Tributes to Mashriqi: Paltan Meeting Condoles Death." The newspaper further writes:
"The death of Allama Enayetullah [Inayatullah] Khan Mashriqi, the founder of the Khaksar movement was condoled at a public meeting, held at Paltan Maidan [Dacca] here yesterday evening...
The speakers at the meeting paid tributes to the Khaksar leader for his patriotism selfless social service, love and devotion towards Islam.
The meeting by a resolution urged the people to follow the ideals of social service, upheld by the Allama during his life time" (MN 1963 Sept. 01).

Rawalpindi Jang Hafiz Jalundhary wrote about Mashriqi. (Zaman 1987, 465).

1963 September 02

The daily *Jang*, Karachi publishes an article on Mashraqi (*Jang* 1963 Sept. 02).

1963 September 03

The daily *Jang*, Karachi reports on funeral prayers for Mashraqi held at Larkana (Sind) and other news (*Jang* 1963 Sept. 03).

1963 September 06

The Pakistan Times, Lahore reports S.M. Miraj Din's message. He states, "With the sad demise of Allama Inayatullah Khan Mashriqi, our country has lost an honest and sincere leader. His services to the cause of the liberation of the Indo-Pakistan sub-continent from the clutches of the British are well known. He also attached great importance to the liberation of Kashmir and to the question of Punjab rivers. Besides, he was a man of rare scholarship..." (PT 1963 Sept. 06).

1963 September 10

The daily *Jang*, Karachi, reports new head, Mian Bashir Ahmed Siddiqui, of Khaksars to re-instate the Khaksar Tehrik (*Jang* 1963 Sept. 10).

1963 September 18

The daily *Jang*, Karachi reports Khaksar Tehrik will be re-organised (*Jang* 1963 Sept. 18).

1963 October 15

Khyber Mail, Peshawar of October 15, 1963 publishes a Jubilee Supplement listing the principals of Islamia College (Peshawar) up to 1961. *Khyber Mail*, Peshawar of October 16, 1963 would further report that President Muhammad Ayub Khan inaugurated the Golden Jubilee of Islamia College.
Editor's comments: Allama Mashraqi became Principal of Islamia College in 1917 (KM 1963 Oct. 15).
       Mashraqi died on August 27, 1963, only a couple of months prior to the College's Golden Jubilee. Some of the prominent personalities who studied at Islamia College include Lt. General

Azam Khan, Khan Abdul Qayyum Khan (President of the Muslim League), and Abdul Huq Jehanzeb (Wali of Swat).

1963 October 18

Khyber Mail, Peshawar reports that the next meeting of the city Khaksars will be held on October 19, 1963 in Karachi (KM 1963 Oct. 18).
Editor's comments: The date of the source newspaper is approximated.

1963 November 25

Khan Habibullah Khan, Interior Minister, makes a statement that Rafiq Sabir Mazangavi who attacked Quaid-e-Azam [on July 26, 1943] was not a Khaksar (*Al-Islah* 1997, 40).

1983

Mashraqi's Daughter Passes Away

1983 November 05

My mother, Masuda Yousaf (Mashriqi's third daughter with his first wife) passed away on November 5, 1983. She was buried in the same Rawalpindi graveyard as my father.

My mother always reminded us of the principled life that her father led, and the services that he rendered for his nation. She inculcated in our minds that one must follow his example and lead a life that makes a difference to benefit all of humanity.

It is probably these teachings which are driving me to write books – those on Mashraqi to enlighten the nation on what leadership is all about and those on trade to help people start their own businesses, thus contributing to job creation and alleviation of poverty.

My works on Allama Mashraqi would not have been possible without the insight I received from my mother.

My mother was a woman with a wonderful heart. She was very soft-hearted toward the poor and was always willing to help them. She was loved by everyone.

I am who I am because of my parents.

Photographs

"That nation suffers which fails to remember its martyrs"

– Nasim Yousaf

Jinnah visits Mashraqi. From left to right: Liaquat Ali Khan, Allama Mashraqi, Quaid-e-Azam, Barrister Mian Ahmad Shah, Dr. Sir Zia ud Din.

Mashraqi attends a dinner hosted by Ch. Mohammad Ali (Prime Minister of Pakistan) in November 1957. In this photo, the Prime Minister is standing on the left with Mashraqi. President Iskandar Mirza is standing on the right (in white coat/jacket).

Hussain Shaheed Suhrawardy (Prime Minister of Pakistan) invites Mashraqi for a dinner. In this photo, Mashraqi is talking to his host.

Allama Mashraqi (second from left) with foreign Ambassadors.

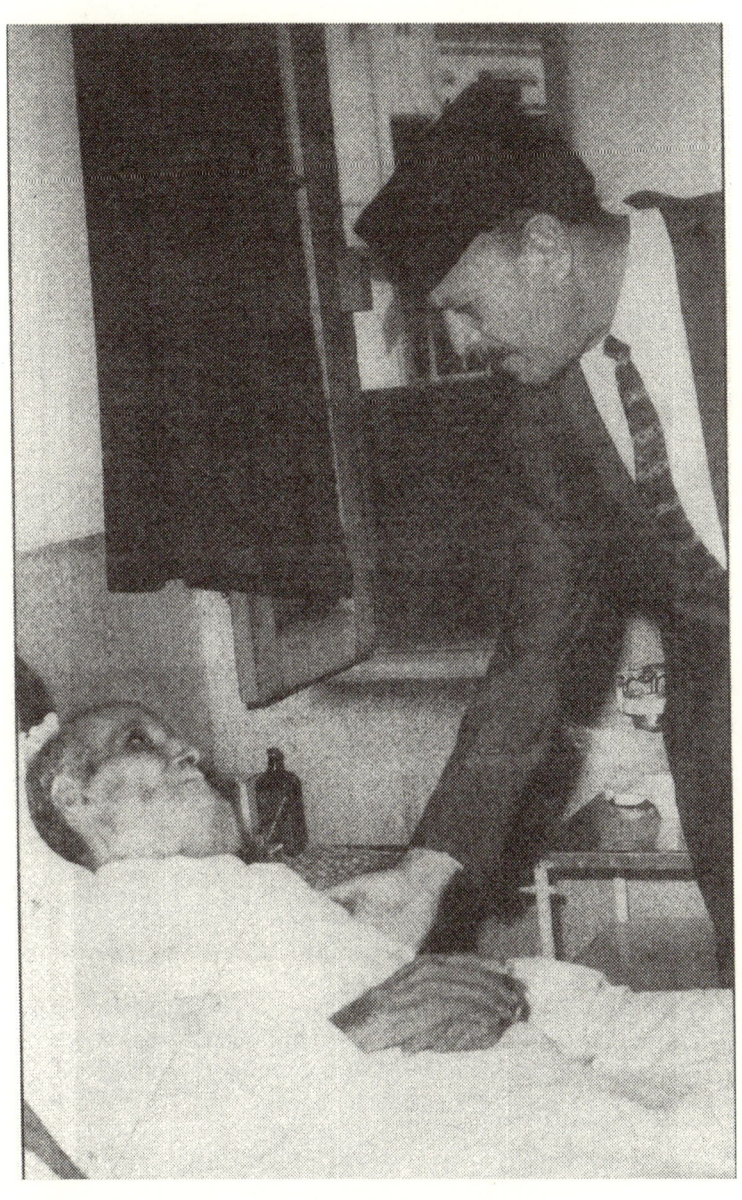

President Muhammad Ayub Khan visits Allama Mashriqi in Mayo Hospital, Lahore.

A historic photo!

From left to right:
Syed Younus Ali Shah (Mashraqi's son-in-law), Raja Mohammad Afsar Khan, Inamullah Khan Akram (Mashraqi's son), Raja Mohammad Akbar Khan (Mashraqi's granddaughter's husband), Mohammad Yousaf Khan (Mashraqi's son-in-law), Zawar Haider.

Allama Mashraqi addresses the public.

Allama Mashraqi gives an address to the people of Lahore.

Allama Mashraqi addresses a large crowd.

At another occasion, a large gathering listens to Mashraqi.

Dawn, Karachi and *The Pakistan Times*, Lahore of May 11, 1958 report Mashraqi and his son's arrest. They are arrested on fabricated charges in Dr. Khan Sahib's (Chief Minister of West Pakistan) murder case.

The Pakistan Times, Lahore of June 6, 1958 reports on Dr. Khan Sahib's murder case.
Editor's comments: Anti-Mashraqi forces falsely implicated him in Dr. Khan Sahib's murder case in order to subject him to the death penalty. However, Mashraqi was honorably acquitted.

Mashraqi is arrested in Dr. Khan Sahib's (Chief Minister of West Pakistan) murder case.
Editor's comments: Height of cruelty! At age 70, a great patriot was handcuffed on fabricated charges. Who is accountable for this?

Mashraqi is brought to the court in Dr. Khan Sahib's murder case under heavy police guard.

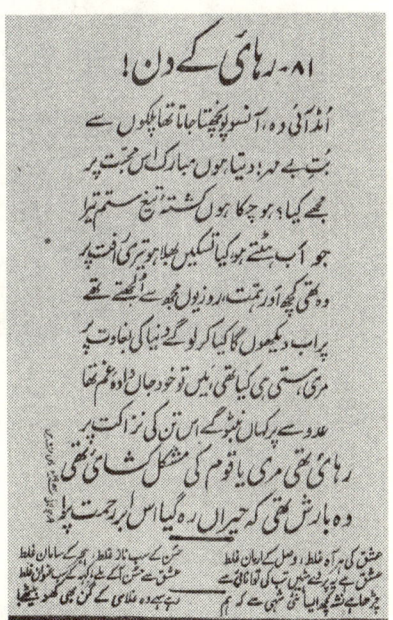

Editor's comments: Mashraqi was arrested on many occasions. On July 9, 1952, he was released from jail and wrote this poem to express his sentiments. See poem on page 205 of *Armughan-i-Hakeem* by Allama Mashraqi.

Mashriqi receives a warm welcome upon his return from Haj (Pilgrimage).

Mashraqi returns a salute in military style.

Mashraqi is adorned by flowers from his followers.
In this photo, his face can hardly be seen.

Mashraqi with his followers in Karachi.

After establishing his Khaksar Tehreek in 1930, Mashraqi adopts
the lifestyle of a commoner. Unlike many other leaders,
he maintains no gap between him and his followers.

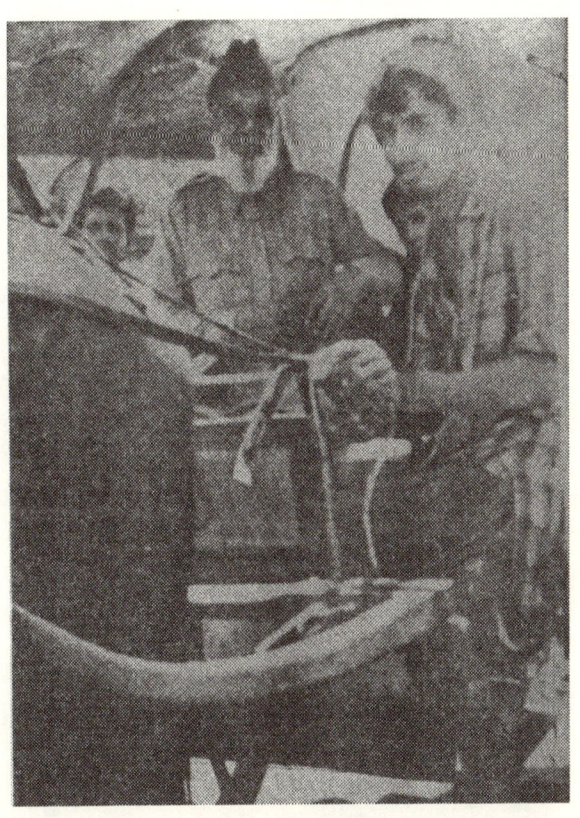

Mashraqi, a Cambridge University (U.K.) scholar, unlike his peers, does not feel belittled traveling on the transport of the common masses (*tonga*).

Mashraqi with his followers in Multan.

Mashraqi is surrounded by common people who adore him.

Mashraqi is on his way to address the public. He is followed by his admirers.

Mashraqi stands with his followers.

Mashraqi with his supporters.

Mashraqi is showered with flowers from his admirers.

President Muhammad Ayub Khan visits Mashraqi in Mayo Hospital in Lahore (C&MG 1963 Aug. 25).

Jang, Karachi of August 29, 1963 reports Allama Mashraqi's death.

Imroze, Lahore of August 30, 1963 reports that over 100,000 people attended Mashraqi's funeral.

Dawn, Karachi of August 28, 1963 reports on Mashraqi's tragic death.

The Eastern Examiner, Chittagong of August 28, 1963 reports Allama Mashraqi's sad demise.

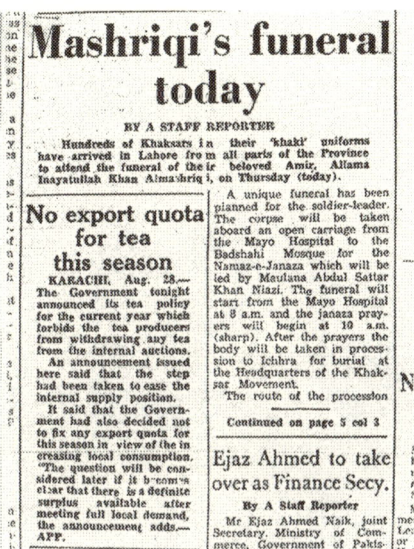

The Civil and Military Gazette, Lahore of August 29, 1963 reports on Mashraqi's funeral.

Jang, Karachi of August 30, 1963 reports on Mashraqi's funeral.

Imroze, Lahore of August 29, 1963 reports on Mashraqi's burial.

Mashraqi's funeral procession. The editor, Mr. Nasim Yousaf, is standing to the right of his paternal uncle, Raja Mohammad Afsar Khan, on the vehicle (see circle on the picture).

People fill the streets of Lahore to get a last glimpse of their beloved leader.

People crowd the streets along the entire route of the funeral to honor Mashraqi.

Another picture shows the crowd that had gathered to pay last tributes to their leader.

Photo taken at another point along the funeral procession.

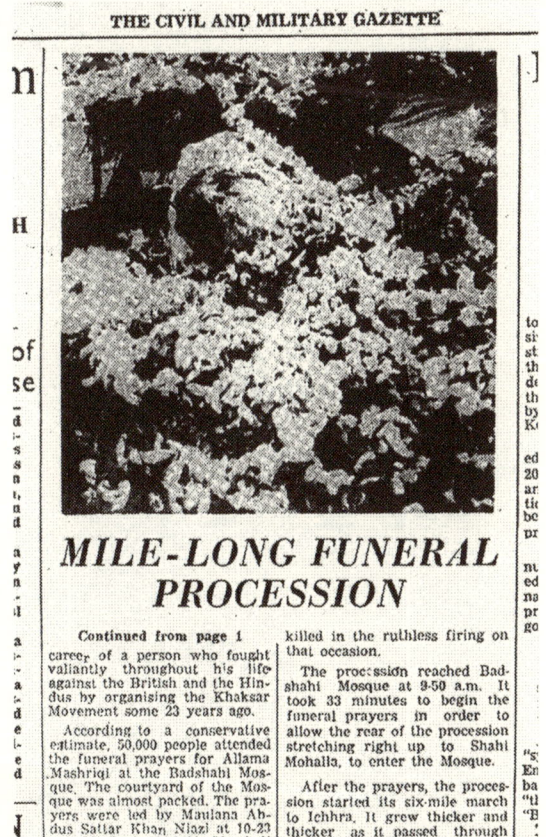

The Civil and Military Gazette, Lahore of August 30, 1963 reports on the mile long procession for Mashraqi's funeral.

VALIANT FIGHTER FOR FREEDOM

MASHRIQI'S DEATH CONDOLED

Political leaders and educationists have expressed their deep sense of sorrow over the death of Allama Mashriqi.

Ch Mohammad Hussain, MNA, said that the Allama was a great organiser and valiant freedom-fighter. After the establishment of Pakistan he concentrated his efforts on the liberation of Kashmir from the Indian yoke.

He expressed his sympathies with the bereaved family.

The Principal of the local Islamia College, Civil Lines, Prof. Hamid Ahmad Khan, said that he was shocked to hear the news of Allama Sahib's death.

PPA adds: The Speaker of the Provincial Assembly Mr Mohammed Anwar, when con- capital.

The Rawalpindi Bar Association at an emergency meeting condoled the death of Khaksar leader, Allama Mashriqi.

In a resolution the Association termed his death a great national loss.

Ch Ghulam Abbas, a veteran Kashmir leader, expressed a deep sense of grief on the death of a "great revolutionary" and a scholar.

HYDERABAD

Begum Tahira Agha, Chairman of the Sind Provincial Muslim League (Councillors), said in Hyderabad that Allama Mashriqi was a great soldier.

Muslim resurgence in the Sub-Continent.

Paying glowing tributes to the late Allama Ch Khaliquzzaman said that it was a sad loss for "the work of great men has to be judged not only by its success but even by failures in a laudable cause."

Mr Manzar-e-Alam, General Secretary of All-Pakistan Muslim League (Conventionists) said that he was deeply grieved to hear of the sad demise of an "old political worker". He sympathised with the bereaved family.

Mr Z. H. Lari, president of the Karachi Muslim League (Councillors) in a message of condolence said that in the death of Allama Mashriqi, the country had lost a distinguished and self-sacrificing leader. Allama Mashriqi, he said, was endowed with a great intellect. The Khaksar Party, which the late Allama founded in pre-partition days, Mr Lari said, was organised in a "marvellous way" which created in its followers a spirit of sacrifice which was unrivalled. He hoped that the spirit of the Allama

Indeed Mashraqi was a great freedom fighter!
The Civil and Military Gazette, Lahore, August 29, 1963.

A man with courage of convictions

President condoles Mashriqi's death

Continued from page 1.

said, "With his demise a chapter of the history of Indo-Pakistan Muslims has closed."

Maulana Maududi said at a time Allama Mashriqi's movement had brought into its fold the whole Muslim nation and had greatly aroused the Muslims to fight for their freedom. That he said, was the outcome of his ability as a great organiser.

He prayed for the eternal peace of his soul and offered sympathy with the bereaved family.

Political leaders and educationists expressed deep sense of sorrow over the death of Allama Mashriqi.

Ch. Mohammad Hussain, MNA, said that Allama was a great organiser and a valiant freedom fighter. After the establishment of Pakistan, he concentrated his efforts for the liberation of Kashmir from the Indian yoke, he added. He expressed his sympathies with the bereaved family.

The Principal of the local Islamia College, Civil Lines, Professor Hamid Ahmad Khan, said

i-Ahrar, Pakistan, Sheikh Hissamuddin, said Allama Mashriqi through his Khaksar Movement, considerably influenced the course of the Indian history. He had tremendous organising capacity which he fully utilised in influencing the Muslim youth, he added.

The Ahrar chief said Allama Mashriqi might not have been completely successful in his mission to organise Muslims to bring near the ideal of Islamic domination, but he did make mighty efforts to take Muslims of the Indian sub-continent towards that goal.

PINDI BAR'S RESOLUTION

APP continues from Rawalpindi:

The Rawalpindi Bar Association at an emergency meeting held today condoled the death of Allama Mashriqi.

In a resolution, the Association termed his death a great national loss.

A message from Hyderabad says:

Begum Tahira Agha, Chairman of the Sind Provincial Muslim League (Counciliors), said in her condolence message on

The Pakistan Times, Lahore of August 29, 1963 reports that President Muhammad Ayub Khan condoles Mashraqi's death.

Giant Among Men

Lahore, Aug. 27 (APP): Allama Inayetullah Khan Mashriqi, rose to fame in the thirties as the leader of the Khaksar Movement—a social service organisation.

The parades and camps of Khaksars aroused the suspicion of the British Government and soon after the beginning of the World War II action was taken to suppress the movement.

Allama Inayetullah Mashriqi, was born at Ghulamabad near Amritsar on August 25, 1888. He passed his M.A. in Mathematics in first class from the Punjab University at the age of ninteen.

Later Allama Mashriqi proceeded to United Kingdom During his stay abroad, he also took keen interest in journalism and wrote in the "Empire Views", "West-Minister Reviews "and London Times" mainly about the Indian political scene. It was perhaps there that seeds were sown, which took him into active politics despite his study of a disinterested and terse subject like mathematics. The A'lama was endowed with an amazing memory.

On return to India Allama Mashriqi joined the Indian Educational Service and was appointed Vice-Principal of Islamia College, Peshawar. He acted as Principal for sometime.

In 1917 Allama was appoin-

The Eastern Examiner, Chittagong, August 28, 1963.

Mashriqi's Death Shocks Leaders

Morning News, Karachi, August 29, 1963.

Leaders pay rich tributes to Mashriqi

Khwaja Nazimuddin, President of the Pakistan Muslim League, said in Dacca that Allama Mashriqi's death has ended the career of "a very interesting figure who took prominent part in the politics of the Indo-Pakistan Sub-Continent."

He said: "I pray to Allah that his soul may rest in peace and grant patience and courage to his children to bear the loss."

Maulana Abul Ala Maudoodi, Amir, Jamaat-i-Islami, condoling the death of Allama Mashriqi in Lahore said: "With the death of Allama Mashriqi a chapter in the history of the Muslims of the Indo-Pakistan Sub-Continent has closed today".

Maulana Maudoodi said that Allama Mashriqi possessed extraordinary organisational capabilities and inspired the Muslims of the Sub-Continent before partition.

Maulana Abdul Hamid Khan Bhashani, leader of the defunct National Awami Party, sent a condolence telegram to Mr Akhtar Hamid Khan, son-in-law of the deceased. He said that in the Allama's death the country had been deprived of a "Mojahid".

Maulana Bhashani said in Karachi that Allama Mashriqi had rendered great services for the cause of the country.

"I pray to the Almighty to grant peace to the soul of Allama Mashriqi," he added.

Mr Nurul Amin, a former Chief Minister of East Pakistan, said in Dacca that he was much grieved to learn the sad news of the passing away of Allama Inayetullah Khan Mashriqi.

He said: "I pray to Allah for his "Maghferat".

Chaudhri Ghulam Abbas, a veteran Kashmir leader, in Rawalpindi expressed a deep sense of grief on the death of a "great revolutionary" and a scholar.

Mr Akhtaruddin Ahmad, MNA, said in Dacca, Pakistan had lost a great patriot and it was a "great loss" for the nation. Allama Mashriqi, he said, was a devoted, selfless and sacrificing personality. Mr Akhtaruddin wished the nation had more people like him.

Shah Azizur Rahman, an NDF leader, said he was an intellectual leader with a thinking of his own and consistent in the pursuit of his ideals.

Large number of Chinese still detained in India

PEKING REJECTS DELHI ASSERTION

PEKING, Aug 27: China today rejected a reported Indian assertion that there were no longer any Chinese in India who wanted to return to China, according to the New China news agency.

In a Note delivered to the Indian Embassy here the Chinese Foreign Ministry recalled a Note handed over in New Delhi on July 31 saying China would send a ship for a fourth batch of repatriates.

The agency said India had replied that no Chinese in India wished to return, but today's Note described this as "an utterly baseless assertion".

The Note said India still held large numbers of Chinese in concentration camps and prisons and added that the Embassy in New Delhi had been instructed to discuss arrangements for shipping them to China.—Reuter.

Mobin's concern over move for Press curbs

LAHORE, Aug 27: Mr Mobinul Haq Siddiqui, ex-Speaker of the West Pakistan Assembly, today expressed great concern over the reported move to impose curbs on the freedom of the Press.

He said in a statement that freedom is the very essence of democracy. The Press has to play an important role in the national life of a country and therefore, it should be allowed to function in a free manner.

"The freedom of expression and freedom of thought will be mean-

Dawn, Karachi, August 28, 1963.

Imroze, Lahore, August 29, 1963 writes that Mashraqi was a brave soldier, a great scholar, and a superb patriot. Messages and tributes were received from all over upon Mashraqi's death.

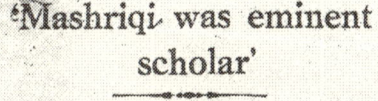

Dawn, Karachi, August 29, 1963.

The Pakistan Times, Lahore, August 30, 1963.

Jang, Karachi, of August 31, 1963 reports over 100,000 people attended Mashraqi's funeral. People cried hysterically and mourned their leader's demise.

Imroze, Lahore of August 29, 1963 writes an article on Mashraqi's life story.

Imroze, Lahore of August 31, 1963 writes another article on Mashraqi.

Jang, Karachi of August 30, 1963 writes an article on Mashraqi.

Jang, Karachi of Sept 2, 1963 publishes an article on Mashraqi's life.

Morning News, Karachi, August 30 1963.

IMPORTANT NOTE:

See more news, pictures, and editorials on Mashraqi's death in the aforementioned newspapers and many other newspapers of the time such as, *Tameer* (Lahore), *Kohistan* (Rawalpindi), *Nawai Waqt* (Lahore).

۱۹۔ میری تثلیث

تثلیث کا قائل تو نہ پہلے تھا نہ اب ہوں
لیکن مجھے اک آن نہ بھولے گی یہ تثلیث

اسلم تو ہوا اندر ستم ہائے فرنگی
میں قید تھا، اور یاد پہ لگتی تھی بڑی ٹھیس
بیٹا تھا وہ اک فردِ زماں، ماتے پہ جس کے
اک لاٹ عیاں علم کی جوں ہالہ جبیں پر
شرک اٹھتی تھی اس ظلم پہ گوحال سے مری سخت
دعوے ہے کر لگا کوئی کیا اس میں مری ریس
پھر خیر، وہ قصہ تو فرنگی کا ہوا پاک
سات ایک برس میں ہی کہ سن اس کا تھا چالیس (۲)

(۱۹۰)

Mashriqi mourns his son's (Ehsanullah Khan Aslam) death. His son was hit by a tear gas grenade during the police raid at the Khaksar headquarters in Lahore on March 19, 1940. He later died from this fatal injury on May 31, 1940. Mashraqi was in Vellore Jail in India at the time and was prohibited from attending his son's funeral. Mashraqi expressed his feelings of sorrow in this poem. For complete poem, see page 190 of *Hareem-e-Ghaib* by Allama Mashraqi.

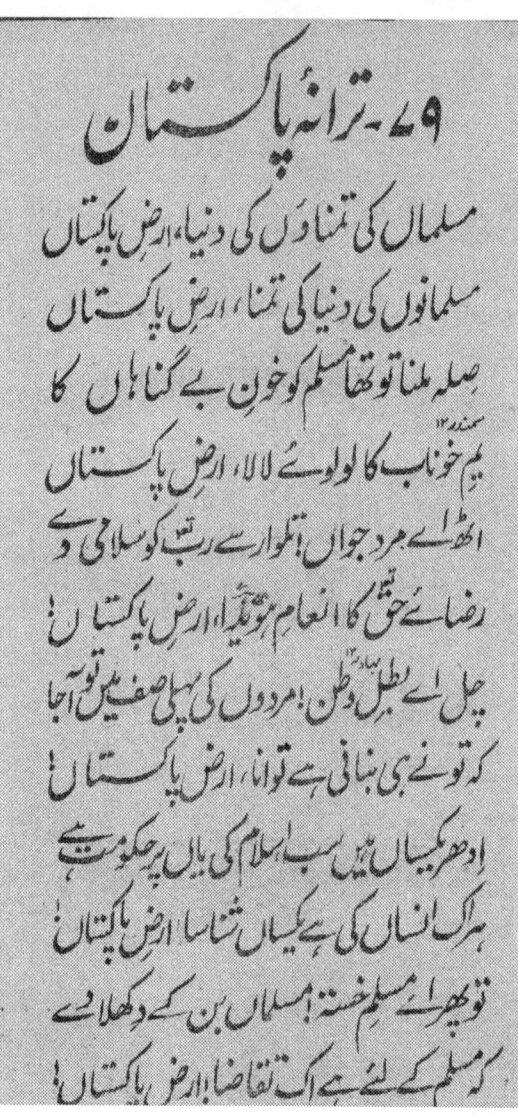

Mashraqi's poem on Pakistan. For complete poem, see page 201 of *Armughan-i-Hakeem* by Allama Mashraqi.

Some of My Efforts

"Leaders are not what they say, but what they do"

– Nasim Yousaf

Letters to Pakistani Dignitaries

Over the past few years, I have written many letters to President General Pervez Musharraf, Prime Minister Shaukat Aziz, and other dignitaries. These letters suggest to the Government of Pakistan to apprise the nation of Allama Mashraqi and his followers' services toward the freedom of the Pakistan, the liberation of Kashmir, and their countrymen.

Some of these letters are reproduced here. I have also included an acknowledgement if I have received a response.

A press release demanding the formation of an Allama Mashriqi Research Academy is also reproduced in this section.

Letters to the President of Pakistan

2000

I sent a letter to President General Pervez Musharraf on August 03, 2000, with a copy to Maliha Lodhi, Ambassador of Pakistan in Washington, D.C., USA.

I received a response letter from the Chief Executive Secretariat (vide letter No. 983/C&G/a-3/CES/2000) dated November 11, 2000. According to this letter, my proposal was sent to the Ministry of Education.

I received a second letter from the Ministry of Education No. F.1-2/2000-Coord (C.E) (Admn. Wing) dated November 22, 2000, informing me that my proposal was forwarded to the Curriculum wing.

I received a third letter from the Ministry of Education No. D. 324/2000-SS (Curriculum Wing) dated November 29, 2000,
informing me that my proposal was sent to H.E. & LB wing for examination, in consulation with the National Institute of Historical and Cultural Research.

I heard nothing further on this matter.

2001

I sent another letter to President General Pervez Musharraf on August 27, 2001.

I received a letter from the President's Secretariat letter No. 404/P/SO-C/2001 dated September 11, 2001 informing me that my proposal has been sent to the Ministry concerned.

2002

On January 30, 2002, I sent a letter to the Embassy of Pakistan in Washington, D.C. for an appointment with President General Pervez Musharraf during his upcoming visit to the USA.

I received a phone call followed by a fax (No. 6/2/2002-MT dated February 01, 2002) from the Trade Minister in the Embassy of Pakistan Washington D.C., USA:

"The Embassy will try to accommodate your request for a meeting with the President. However, the President's engagements have already been finalized. Owing to the short duration of the visit, it would be difficult to accommodate any more meetings. It is suggested that if you would like to meet ...[Federal] Minister for Commerce & Industries, who is accompanying the President, we can arrange a meeting."

I politely declined this appointment via fax dated February 02, 2002 to the Trade Minister because I did not feel that that meeting would bring desired results.

2003

On November 14, 2003, I sent a registered letter (certified mail) to President General Pervez Musharraf, via the Ambassador of Pakistan in Washington, D.C. USA. I also sent a similar letter to the Prime Minister, Mir Zafarullah Khan Jamali. In the letter, I made various requests including establishing a research academy in the name of Allama Mashriqi. This letter is reproduced here.

"Mohtarram President General Pervez Musharraf Sahib,

Assalam-u-Alaikum

I am delighted to send you the two books that I have authored in the recent past. I am sending these through Mohtarram Ashraf Jehangir Qazi, Ambassador of Pakistan in Washington, D.C.

My first book was published in 2001 in the U.S. and is entitled *Import & Export of Apparel & Textiles*. In Part I of this book, I tried to make a humble effort to apprise Pakistani exporters, particularly those who are new to international trade, on how to export to the USA. In Part II of this book, I made an attempt to assist and encourage importers of apparel and textiles from around the world to import from Pakistan. The second book titled, *Allama Mashriqi & Dr. Akhtar Hameed Khan: Two Legends of Pakistan* was published this year in the U.S.

The purpose of this letter is primarily to draw your attention to the tremendous sacrifices and contributions of two great patriots of Pakistan, Allama Mashriqi and Dr. Akhtar Hameed Khan, towards their countrymen. In my second book, I had promised to the nation that I would send a copy of my work to the President and Prime

Minister of Pakistan, so that they would have a chance to read it and take the necessary steps that are very important to the Pakistani nation.

The second book is divided into two parts on Allama Mashriqi and Dr. Akhtar Hameed Khan. This book sheds light on the selfless and exemplary lives that these two giants of our nation led. This book is a fraction of what could be written on them and what needs to be done to acquaint Pakistan with their lives and times. Various aspects of their personalities including distinguished valor and substance are an immense source of inspiration, learning, and guidance for every soul of humanity.

Allama Mashriqi and the Khaksars

The first part of my book discusses Allama Mashriqi's life and the role of the Khaksar Tehrik (Movement) that was founded in 1930 to re-build the nation and to achieve freedom. Mashriqi and the Khaksars mobilized the nation to rise for freedom. During this struggle, Mashriqi and Khaksars' sufferings were unmatched as they valiantly resisted against the rulers who did their best to eliminate the movement altogether.

The role of Allama Mashriqi and the Khaksars in the making of Pakistan has not been made public and in fact many history books have distorted and misquoted their role. The brutal massacre of the Khaksars on March 19, 1940 is a very important part of Pakistan's history, but the facts of this massacre are unknown to the majority of Pakistanis, since they have not been written or discussed in history books. This incident is also excluded whenever there is a discussion or program about Pakistan history on the radio, television, and even in the supplements of the newspapers that are published every year on important days such as March 23 and August 14. There are many other matters relating to Mashriqi and the Khaksar movement that have been ignored in Pakistan history. The nation needs to be apprised of the historical facts that are unknown to a vast majority. These include the following:

1. The massacre of the Khaksars on March 19, 1940 was one of the cruelest killings of innocent people in the history of India. It occurred only three days prior to the beginning of the historic Muslim League Session at Minto Park Lahore (March 22-24, 1940) which passed the Lahore Resolution (Pakistan Resolution).

2. Quaid-e-Azam Mohammad Ali Jinnah made a statement on the massacre of the Khaksars prior to coming to Lahore to attend the historic Muslim League Session held on March 22-24, 1940.
3. A large number of attendees at the historic Muslim League Session at Lahore (March 22-24, 1940) raised slogans in favor of the Khaksars and denounced the actions taken by the Punjab Government including the killing and injuring of innocent Khaksars, arrest of Allama Mashriqi, and ban on the Khaksar movement. The Muslim League had a difficult time controlling the emotions of the people in favor of the Khaksars. History is witness to the reality that this massacre was a turning point in the freedom struggle and the history of Pakistan.
4. The Pakistan Resolution (Lahore Resolution) was passed on the same day (March 24, 1940) when the Muslim League also passed a Khaksar resolution asking for an inquiry into the tragic killing of the Khaksars.
5. Mashriqi's determination and exemplary courage during his arrest for a long period as well as the resistance of the Khaksars during the ban on the Khaksar Tehrik further attest to the fact that the Khaksars' resistance to the British was the most unparalleled, toughest, and the longest fight in the Indian freedom struggle after the Khilafat movement. Mashriqi and the Khaksars remained steadfast despite the agony they faced and the unmatched atrocities that were inflicted on them.

It is not possible to cover all aspects and matters relating to Allama Mashriqi in depth -- his life, scholarly contributions, vision of our nation, and role in Pakistan history. However, in my book, I have made a modest endeavor to briefly shed light on him and have discussed some issues from Pakistan history that are foreign to the nation.

My Request

I feel extremely good to be presenting this work of mine, that was produced after years of research, in order to bring to your attention the importance of Mashriqi and the Khaksars' roles in the history of our nation. I am earnestly requesting to you to personally look into the matter and issue a directive to the concerned authorities to make Mashriqi and the Khaksars' roles known to the public as they are clearly important from Pakistan history's point of view. I am also requesting that you ask the relevant institutions not to eliminate or distort the facts of Pakistan history because such steps are very dangerous for the growth of any nation. By directing the appropriate authorities to take necessary steps in acquainting the nation about Allama Mashriqi and Khaksars' contributions and sacrifices, you will redress the grievances of the families of Mashriqi and the Khaksars, particularly families of those Khaksars who either laid their lives or suffered in prison for the cause. In the past, myself and members of my family have met heads of the state, federal ministers, etc, in order to apprise them of the injustice that has been done in the history books, but nothing has came out of these meetings. I hope you will take the following steps to address the neglected and unattended important issues pertaining to every Pakistani. Your positive action in this regard will go a long ways in revealing the consequential facts of our history that are still unknown. Of course, if needed, my services to follow through on the following steps shall always be available:

1. A research academy should be formed to conduct complete research on Mashriqi and his Khaksar Movement. A library exclusively for Khaksar literature should be formed. All Khaksar materials should be collected from the public, government departments, the India Office (U.K.), and historical resources in India. Mashriqi's books and speeches should be translated into English and other languages. An official and unbiased biography on Mashriqi should be published depicting his purpose of establishing the Khaksar Tehrik. His emphasis on equality, non-prejudicial or non-sectarian society, self-sacrifice, and community service, as well as his own exemplary life, including the fact that he did not seek personal glorification, are just a few points that are beneficial learnings for all of humanity.
2. Icchara in Lahore (where he laid the foundation of the Khaksar movement in 1930) as well as the Punjab University should be named after Allama Mashriqi. A monument should be erected in Lahore at the site of the massacre of March 19, 1940. March 19 should be declared "Martyrs Day" and special seminars should be held in major cities in remembrance of those Khaksars who laid their lives on that day. Official yearly seminars, on his death and birth anniversaries, should be held on the life and times of Mashriqi.
3. National media should be directed to broadcast/publish special programs on Mashriqi, particularly on his birth and death anniversaries. A film and television program should be made on Allama Mashriqi's life and the Khaksar Movement. Funds should be allocated for this purpose.
4. A national holiday should be observed on Mashriqi's birth or death anniversary.

In the end, I would like to add that well over a hundred thousand people attended Mashriqi's funeral on August 29, 1963. For months afterward, mourners kept visiting Mashriqi's family and phone messages from Pakistanis across the world kept pouring in. Thus, he must have done something significant for the nation that so many people came to pay their tributes upon his death.

Dr. Akhtar Hameed Khan

Dr. Akhtar Hameed Khan's services are well known to you, as such I will refrain from reminding you of his contributions. You have already vowed to carry Dr. Khan's mission when you inaugurated a symposium in the March 04, 2000 on his life and times. I thank you for recognizing his services to the nation. Keeping in view his services, I request you to consider the following for what he did for his countrymen:

1. Orangi Town in Karachi should be named after Dr. Khan. A road leading to Orangi Town should be named after him.
2. A monument should be erected at Orangi Town. An official biography on Dr. Khan should be published. Official yearly seminars, on his death and birth anniversaries, should be held on the life and times of Dr. Khan.
3. Dr.Khan's works should be translated into various languages so that they can help alleviate poverty that exists around the world. This will be a service to all of humanity.

Closing

I have enclosed the following books:

1. *Allama Mashriqi & Dr. Akhtar Hameed Khan: Two Legends of Pakistan*
2. *Import & Export of Apparel & Textiles - Part I: Export to USA, Part II: Import from Pakistan*

Please acknowledge that you have received these books. In addition, I would certainly appreciate your valuable comments after you have read my book.

Best Regards.
Allah Hafiz.

Nasim Yousaf

P.S. As per my promise in my second book, I will also be sending a copy of this book to the Prime Minister Mir Zafarullah Khan Jamali along with a similar request.

C.C: Ambassador of Pakistan (Washington D.C.)"

Letters to the Prime Minister of Pakistan

September 07, 2004

"To:
Excellency
Prime Minister Shaukat Aziz
Islamic Republic of Pakistan
Prime Minister's Secretariat
Islamabad, Pakistan

My Ref: PM./Books-1/ /2004

SUBJECT: Outstanding Services and Sacrifices of Allama Mashriqi (Inayatullah Khan) & Dr. Akhtar Hameed Khan Towards Pakistan

Mohtarram Prime Minister Shaukat Aziz sahib,

Assalam-u-Alaikum,

Please accept my heartiest congratulations on your appointment as the Prime Minister of Pakistan. There is great hope that your policies will turn the fate of poor people of Pakistan. For this reason, people like Allama Mashriqi and Dr. Akhtar Hameed Khan, two great men of Pakistan, laid their lives. Their dream is yet to come true.

I would also like to take this opportunity to extend to you my warm and sincere thanks for speaking of and honoring Dr. Akhtar Hameed Khan's services at different forums and at the Memorial Lecture in Islamabad.

I am very pleased to send you two books (out of the three) that I have authored in the recent past, as listed here:

1. *Allama Mashriqi & Dr. Akhtar Hameed Khan: Two Legends of Pakistan.*

2. *Pakistan's Freedom & Allama Mashriqi: Statements, Letters, Chronology of Khaksar Tehrik (Movement), Period: Mashriqi's Birth to 1947.*

The purpose of sending these books is primarily to draw your attention to the colossal sacrifices and services of two statesmen of Pakistan, Allama Mashriqi and Dr. Akhtar Hameed Khan, towards their countrymen. These books are a fraction of what could be written on them and what needs to be done to acquaint Pakistan with their lives and times. Various aspects of their personalities are indeed a great source of inspiration, learning, and guidance for every soul.

I invite your attention particularly to Pakistan's history in which Allama Mashriqi's role for mobilizing the nation towards freedom has been completely neglected. In many cases, it has been distorted and given a sense of negativity due to political controversies with the Muslim League. In Pakistan, a culture of tolerance has not yet been developed and it needs to be developed. This is extremely important for the progression of any nation.

I would like to bring to your attention that some of the historians, writers, and speakers have even deliberately or unintentionally tried to deform Allama Mashriqi's image. For example, many historians constantly quote that the man who attacked Quaid-Azam Muhammad Ali Jinnah on July 26, 1943 in Bombay (India) was a Khaksar. Writers and speakers who are not aware of the reality or for vested reasons are referring him to be a Khaksar. In fact, these learned writers and speakers have completely ignored the verdict of the Bombay High Court in this case. It is to be noted that the Justice of the Bombay High Court did not accept the evidence submitted that the assailant was a Khaksar. These authors and spokespersons have also ignored the book, **Jinnah Faces An Assassin**, authored by Quaid-e-Azam Muhammad Ali Jinnah's nephew, in which he has mentioned that the Bombay High Court's decision does not accept the attacker to be a Khaksar. Under the circumstance, there is no justification left for distorting the history and damaging Allama Mashriqi's likeness among the public.

Mashriqi's unprecedented services, pre and post creation of Pakistan, should not be transgressed and disregarded. It is greatly deplorable that the Pakistani nation is unaware of the truth that Allama Mashriqi founded the Khaksar Tehrik (Khaksar Movement) in 1930 with a definite purpose. Its objective was to revive the people from their deep slumber in order to bring independence to the sub-continent, uplift the suffering masses, and restore the glory of the Muslims. This Movement created history and successfully mobilized the people that led to freedom, but unfortunately the Khaksar Tehrik's services have been completely ignored, which is unjustifiable from the nation's point of view. The role of Allama Mashriqi and the Khaksars in mobilizing the public for independence needs to be made public. It is highly deplorable that many history books have distorted and misquoted Allama Mashriqi's role. The nation needs to be apprised of the historical facts that are unknown to a vast majority. I am certain that my books that have been published (in the USA) will surely be of source of information to everyone interested in the struggle towards liberty of the nation.

Keeping in view the services of Allama Mashriqi and Dr. Akhtar Hameed Khan, I candidly suggest to you to look into the following steps that need to be taken in regards to these distinguished men.

Proposals In Regards To Allama Mashriqi:

I propose, the following:

1. Allama Mashriqi Research Academy (AMRA) should be formed and should be responsible for the following functions:

    a. To collect Khaksar material from all sources including Quaid-e-Azam Muhammad Ali Jinnah's archives, Khaksars and the Khaksar Tehrik's archives, India Office (U.K.), Cambridge University, the archives of Mahatma Gandhi, Jawaharlal Nehru, and other leaders of the time.

    b. To provide research facilities including scholarships on Mashriqi and his Khaksar Movement.

    c. To translate all Khaksar material into English and other languages and properly index and catalogue them.

    d. To make Khaksar material available at public libraries within Pakistan and outside the country.

    e. To establish the Allama Mashriqi Library & Museum (AML&M).

    f. To publish a biography on Mashriqi.

    g. To arrange the production of film(s) on his life and the Khaksar Movement.

    h. To arrange seminars and lectures on his life and works.

i. Other functions.

2. A national holiday should be observed to honor Allama Mashriqi's services.

3. Ichhra in Lahore (where he laid the foundation of the Khaksar Movement in 1930) should be named Allama Mashriqi Town.

4. Allama Mashriqi University should be established.

5. Allama Mashriqi and the Khaksar Tehrik's role should be added to the academic curriculum.

6. National media should be directed to allocate adequate time to enlighten the public of his services.

7. Last but not least, a monument should be erected in Lahore at the site of the massacre of March 19, 1940.

I would like to stress with **great concern** that a lot of Khaksar materials have already disappeared for various reasons and many important people from Allama Mashriqi's time have died. Time is running out and many of the above steps need to be taken at once to secure Pakistan's national heritage and history. If action is not taken soon, Pakistan's history will forever remain incomplete.

Proposals In Regards To Dr. Akhtar Hameed Khan:

Dr. Akhtar Hameed Khan's services are well known to you. You have also attended lectures and symposiums where you have lauded Dr. Khan's services to the nation. At these forums, you have also heard speeches of Mr. Shoaib Sultan Khan (another great person), Chairman National Rural Support Program (NRSP), highlighting valuable services of Dr. Khan. As such, I will refrain from reminding you of Dr. Khan's contributions. Keeping in view his valuable services to alleviating poverty, I suggest the following for your consideration:

1. Orangi Town in Karachi should be named after Dr. Khan. A road leading to Orangi Town should also be named after him.

2. A biography on Dr. Khan should be published.

3. Seminars and lectures should be held on a regular basis on the life and times of Dr. Khan.

4. National media should be directed to allocate adequate time to enlighten the public of his services.

5. Dr. Khan's works should be translated into various languages so that his techniques can help alleviate poverty around the world. This will be a great service to the entire humanity.

Your actions in regards to Allama Mashriqi and Dr. Khan will make a significant difference and will enlighten the people on Pakistan's history as well as the teachings of Allama Mashriqi and Dr. Khan who worked for uplifting the masses. They both defined self-help as a great means to achieving the desired results. Their teachings are, as a matter of fact, a great source of eradicating terrorism. If we can remove poverty and exploitation of the poor, terrorism will indeed be eliminated from the face of this earth. Thus, their wisdom and guidance are extremely important to learn from.

May God bless Pakistan and its people.

With Warm Regards,

Allah Hafiz.

Nasim Yousaf

Enclosed the books listed above.

C.C: To the Officiating Ambassador of Pakistan, Washington D.C, USA.

Total pages 4 including this one"

Acknowledgement:

Prime Minister Shaukat Aziz sent a letter number 2(2) PSO(PM)/2004 dated October 18, 2004 thanking me for the two books I enclosed with the above letter.

"Fax Message page 01 of 01

July 04, 2005

Your Excellency, Prime Minister of the Islam Republic of Pakistan,
Mr. Shaukat Aziz,
Islamabad, Pakistan

Subject: Appointment during your forthcoming visit to the USA

Mohtarram Shaukat Aziz sahib,

Assalam-u-Alaikum,

I am seeking an appointment with you in order to discuss the following:

1) Matters pertaining to setting up an Allama Mashriqi Research Academy (AMRA)
2) Setting up a Non-Governmental Organization to promote exports from Pakistan

It would be appreciated if an appointment is confirmed on any date and time convenient to you.

I wish you and the people of Pakistan happiness and prosperity.

Thank You,

Best Regards,

Nasim Yousaf"

Acknowledgement:

In response to the above letter, Muhammed Sadiq, Deputy Chief of Mission of the Embassy of Pakistan in Washington D.C., USA telephoned me on August 22, 2005 and conveyed to me that the Allama Mashriqi Research Academy is under consideration. He also mentioned that my meeting with the Prime Minister is likely during his upcoming visit to the USA in 2005. My second proposal was also discussed.

Letter to the Minister for Science & Technology

"Fax Message: Page 1 of 3

November 08, 2004

Prof. Dr. Atta-ur-Rahman
Minister Incharge For Science & Technology
Chairman Higher Education Commission
Islamabad, Pakistan.

Subject: Allama Mashriqi and the Academic Curriculum.

Mohtarram Atta-ur-Rahman sahib,

Assalam-u-Alaikum,

I would like to begin by commending the Higher Education Commission (HEC) for taking steps to encourage higher learning and research in Pakistan. It was one of the dreams of Allama Mashriqi (Inayatullah Khan) to see Pakistan as a center of scientific development and research.

Keeping Higher Education Commission's initiative in mind, I would like to bring to your attention an extremely important matter related to the history of Pakistan, one, which has been neglected in the past due to political controversies. In Pakistan, a culture of tolerance has not yet been developed and this needs to change. This is extremely important for the progression of any nation.

Please note, anyone even with a little knowledge of Indo-Pakistan history does recognize the names of Allama Mashriqi and his Khaksar Tehrik (also known as the Khaksar Movement prior to partition of India). However, most people lack detailed knowledge of the Khaksar Tehrik and its founder (Allama Mashriqi). It is extremely important that people are made aware of Allama Mashriqi's contribution toward independence, his and Khaksars' suffering for the cause, and other valuable services to the nation.

Mashriqi not only emerged as a great leader in the last century, he was a world-renowned mathematician and scholar, a superb visionary and courageous freedom fighter. His academic and scholarly accomplishments, his exemplary personality, his religious outlook, and his adoption of a simple lifestyle as a leader of a poor nation need to be publicized for people to learn lessons from. Indeed, his life is a beacon for humanity to follow.

It is unfortunate that the majority remains ignorant of this giant among men. It is of the utmost importance that people today understand the purpose of the Khaksar Movement and Mashriqi's historic role in rebuilding the nation and mobilizing the masses toward independence. In addition to his active role in the freedom movement, Mashriqi was an internationally recognized mathematician and scholar. His monumental book, *Tazkirah* (nominated for Nobel Prize), equally deserves utmost attention of the scholars. In *Tazkirah*, Mashriqi scientifically examines the Holy Quran. It is extremely important that scholars are encouraged to carryout studies on this unprecedented book.

Keeping in mind the importance of the subject, I have been conducting independent research on Allama Mashriqi and the Khaksar Tehrik for many years. I have already documented some of the unexplored facts regarding Mashriqi's role in the Pakistan Movement in my recently published books in the USA. These are listed here:

1) *Allama Mashriqi & Dr. Akhtar Hameed Khan: Two Legends of Pakistan.*
2) *Pakistan's Freedom & Allama Mashriqi: Statements, Letters, Chronology of Khaksar Tehrik (Movement), Period: Mashriqi's Birth to 1947.*

In view of the importance of this subject, I request you to take immediate action. I would like to bring to your attention the fact that highly important and extensive Khaksar materials are missing. These materials, taken by the Government from the Khaksar headquarters and other offices during raids in the pre- and post- partition period, should be recovered and published. Much time has already been lost. Many important members of Mashriqi's family, his Khaksar lieutenants, and followers have passed away. Keeping the urgency of the situation in mind, a drive needs to be launched to collect these materials from all sources.

In my humble view, the Higher Education Commission, with its extensive budget and resources, needs to establish an Allama Mashriqi Research Academy (AMRA) to enlighten the nation about Mashriqi's scientific interpretation of the Holy Book and the role of Mashriqi and the Khaksar Movement.

The Allama Mashriqi Research Academy (AMRA) would accomplish the following:

a) Carry out studies on *Tazkirah* and arrange its translation in English and other international languages.
b) Collect Khaksar material from all sources including Quaid-e-Azam Muhammad Ali Jinnah's archives, Khaksars' and the Khaksar Tehrik's archives, India Office (U.K.), Cambridge University, the archives of Mahatma Gandhi, Jawaharlal Nehru, and other leaders of the time.
c) Provide research facilities, including scholarships on Allama Mashriqi and his Khaksar Movement.
d) Translate all Khaksar material into English and other languages and properly index and catalogue it.
e) Make Khaksar material available at public libraries within Pakistan and outside the country.
f) Publish a biography of Allama Mashriqi.
g) Produce film(s) and documentary (ies) on his life and times and the Khaksar Movement.
h) Arrange seminars and lectures on his life and works.
i) Establish Allama Mashriqi University.
j) Establish Allama Mashriqi Museum.
k) Ensure the inclusion of Mashriqi and the Khaksar Tehrik's role in the academic curriculum.
l) Ensure the availability of all Khaksar materials in libraries and academic/research institutions within and outside the country.

If forming of the Allama Mashriqi Research Academy (AMRA) is not in the jurisdiction of the HEC, please take appropriate steps towards my requests/suggestions, thanks.

I have made these proposals because the preservation and publication of documents related to Mashriqi and the Khaksar Movement are vital to Pakistan's history. I am confident that with your able guidance, the necessary steps shall be taken to ensure that people learn from the unparalleled life of this distinguished personality.

May God bless Pakistan and its people.

With best wishes and warm regards,

Allah Hafiz.

Nasim Yousaf

Grandson of Allama Mashriqi & nephew of Dr. Akhtar Hameed Khan"

Acknowledgement:

Prof. Dr. Atta-ur-Rahman sent a letter number 1-1/CHR/HEC/-4/2766 dated November 11, 2004 thanking me for the suggestion and stated, "We will of course try to do what we can to assist you in this valuable endeavour."

Letter to the Minister for Education

"Fax Message: Page 1 of 2

November 08, 2004

Lt.Gen (Retd) Javed Ashraf Qazi
Minister for Education
Government of Pakistan, Islamabad, Pakistan

Subject: Allama Mashriqi and the Academic Curriculum.

Mohtarram Javed Ashraf Qazi sahib,

Assalam-u-Alaikum,

I would like to bring to your attention an extremely important matter related to the history of Pakistan, one, which has been neglected in the past due to political controversies. In Pakistan, a culture of tolerance has not yet been developed and this needs to change. This is extremely important for the progression of any nation.

Please note, anyone with even a nodding acquaintance with Indo-Pak history can recognize the names of Allama Mashriqi (Inayatullah Khan) and his Khaksar Tehrik (also known as the Khaksar Movement). However, most people lack detailed knowledge of the Khaksar Tehrik and Mashriqi's exemplary personality, his academic and scholarly accomplishments, his religious outlook, his adoption of a simple lifestyle as a leader of a poor nation, and his struggle for freedom. Allama Mashriqi was not only a world-renowned mathematician and scholar but also a superb visionary and courageous freedom fighter. Indeed, his life is a beacon for humanity to follow.

It is unfortunate that the majority remains ignorant of this giant among men and has little or no idea of his services to the nation. It is of the utmost importance that people today understand the purpose of the Khaksar Tehrik and Mashriqi's historic role in rebuilding the nation and mobilizing the masses toward independence. In addition to his active role in the freedom movement, Mashriqi was an internationally recognized mathematician and scholar. His monumental book *Tazkirah*, (nominated for Nobel Prize), equally deserves utmost attention of the scholars. In *Tazkirah*, Mashriqi scientifically examines the Holy Quran. It is extremely important that scholars are encouraged to carryout studies on this unprecedented book.

Keeping in mind the importance of the subject, I have been conducting independent research on Allama Mashriqi and the Khaksar Tehrik for many years. I have already documented some of the unexplored facts regarding Mashriqi's role and the Pakistan Movement in my recently published books in the USA. These are listed here:

1) *Allama Mashriqi & Dr. Akhtar Hameed Khan: Two Legends of Pakistan.*
2) *Pakistan's Freedom & Allama Mashriqi: Statements, Letters, Chronology of Khaksar Tehrik (Movement), Period: Mashriqi's Birth to 1947.*

In view of the importance of this subject matter, I request you to take immediate steps. I would like to bring to your attention the fact that highly important and extensive Khaksar materials are missing. These materials, taken by the Government from the Khaksar headquarters and other offices during raids in the pre- and post- partition period, should be recovered and published. Much time has already been lost. Many important members of Mashriqi's family, his party lieutenants, and followers have passed away. Keeping the urgency of the situation in mind, a drive needs to be launched to collect these materials from all sources.

In my humble view, the Ministry of Education, with its extensive resources, needs to establish an Allama Mashriqi Research Academy (AMRA) to enlighten the nation about Mashriqi's scientific interpretation of the Holy Book and the role of Mashriqi and the Khaksar Movement.

The Allama Mashriqi Research Academy (AMRA) would accomplish the following:

    a) Carry out studies on *Tazkirah* and arrange its translation in English and other international languages.
    b) Collect Khaksar material from all sources including Quaid-e-Azam Muhammad Ali Jinnah's archives, Khaksars' and the Khaksar Tehrik's archives, India Office (U.K.), Cambridge University, the archives of

Mahatma Gandhi, Jawaharlal Nehru, and other leaders of the time.
c) Provide research facilities, including scholarships on Allama Mashriqi and his Khaksar Movement.
d) Translate all Khaksar material into English and other languages and properly index and catalogue it.
e) Make Khaksar material available at public libraries within Pakistan and outside the country.
f) Publish a biography of Allama Mashriqi.
g) Produce film(s) and documentary (ies) on his life and times and the Khaksar Movement.
h) Arrange seminars and lectures on his life and works.
i) Establish Allama Mashriqi University.
j) Establish Allama Mashriqi Museum.
k) Ensure the inclusion of Mashriqi and the Khaksar Tehrik's role in the academic curriculum.
l) Ensure the availability of all Khaksar materials in libraries and academic/research institutions within and outside the country.

If forming of the Allama Mashriqi Research Academy (AMRA) is not in the jurisdiction of the Ministry of Education, please take appropriate steps towards my requests/suggestions, thanks.

I have made these proposals because the preservation and publication of documents related to Mashriqi and the Khaksar Movement are vital to Pakistan's history. This information is part of Pakistan's national heritage and is an asset to the country. I am confident that with your able guidance, the necessary steps shall be taken to ensure that people learn from the unprecedented works and life of their distinguished leader. Your efforts in this direction shall enable the present and the future generations to get guidance and inspiration from this giant among men.

May God bless Pakistan and its people.

With best wishes and warm regards,

Allah Hafiz.

Nasim Yousaf

Grandson of Allama Mashriqi & nephew of Dr. Akhtar Hameed Khan"

Letter to the Minister for Information & Broadcasting

"Fax Message: Page 1 of 2

November 08, 2004

Mr. Sheikh Rashid Ahmad
Federal Minister for Information and Broadcasting
Government of Pakistan, Islamabad,
Pakistan

Subject: The Media and Allama Mashriqi and Dr. Akhtar Hameed Khan's services to the nation

Mohtarram Sheikh Rashid Ahmad sahib,

Assalam-u-Alaikum,

Please accept my belated congratulations on your appointment as Federal Minister for Information and Broadcasting.

I would like to bring to your attention the services of two important personalities of Pakistan, Allama Mashriqi and Dr. Akhtar Hameed Khan, whose works are a beacon for the nation and need to be highlighted in the public media.

Allama Mashriqi (Inayatullah Khan):

Allama Mashriqi was the founder of the Khaksar Tehrik (Khaksar Movement) and one of the greatest leaders of the 20th century. Anyone with even a nodding acquaintance with Indo-Pak history can recognize the names of Allama Mashriqi and his Khaksar Tehrik. However, most people lack **detailed** knowledge of the Khaksar Tehrik and Mashriqi's exemplary personality, his academic and scholarly accomplishments, his religious outlook, his adoption of a simple lifestyle as a leader of a poor nation, and his struggle for freedom. Allama Mashriqi was not only a world-renowned mathematician and scholar but also a superb visionary and courageous freedom fighter. Indeed, his life is a beacon for humanity to follow.

It is unfortunate that the majority remains ignorant of this giant among men and has a vague or no idea of his services to the nation. This is because of the political controversies surrounding the independence of Pakistan. In Pakistan, a culture of tolerance has not yet been developed and this needs to change. This is extremely important for the progression of any nation.

It is of the utmost importance that people understand Mashriqi's historic role in rebuilding the nation and mobilizing the masses towards independence. Keeping in mind the importance of the subject, I have been conducting independent research on Allama Mashriqi and the Khaksar Tehrik for many years. I have already documented some of the unexplored facts regarding Mashriqi's role in the Pakistan Movement in my recently published books in the USA. These are listed here:

1. *Allama Mashriqi & Dr. Akhtar Hameed Khan: Two Legends of Pakistan.*

2. *Pakistan's Freedom & Allama Mashriqi: Statements, Letters, Chronology of Khaksar Tehrik (Movement), Period: Mashriqi's Birth to 1947.*

In view of the significance of this subject, I request you to take the following steps to **enlighten the nation about the role of Allama Mashriqi and the Khaksar Movement**:

Proposals In Regards To Allama Mashriqi:

I propose the following:

1. National media should be directed to allocate adequate time to enlighten the public on Allama Mashriqi and the Khaksars' services to the nation.

2. Relevant government agencies under your Ministry should be directed to hold scholarly discussions on television, etc. about the ideology of the Khaksar Movement and the monumental work, *Tazkirah*, authored by Allama Mashriqi. This book was nominated for the Nobel Prize and presents the teachings of the Holy Quran from a scientific perspective.

3. Funds should be allocated or recommended to relevant agencies for making film on the life and times of Allama Mashriqi and the Khaksar Movement.

Dr. Akhtar Hameed Khan:

Dr. Akhtar Hameed Khan's services are well known and the President of Pakistan General Pervez Musharraf and the new Prime Minister Mr. Shaukat Aziz have praised them at symposiums in Dr. Khan's honor at different times. I am positive you are equally familiar with his contributions toward Pakistan.

Proposals In Regards To Dr. Akhtar Hameed Khan:

I propose the following:

1. National media should be directed to allocate adequate time to enlighten the public on Dr. Khan's services.

2. Seminars should be held and broadcasted on his birth and death anniversaries (July 15, 1914 and October 09, 1999, respectively).

I have made the above proposals because Mashriqi and Dr. Khan's personalities are a source of inspiration and learning for all of us and educating the masses about them is very important. I am confident that with your able guidance, the necessary steps shall be taken.

Your efforts in this direction shall be long remembered by the present and future generations.

May God bless Pakistan and its people.

With best wishes and warm regards,

Allah Hafiz.

Nasim Yousaf

Grandson of Allama Mashriqi & nephew of Dr. Akhtar Hameed Khan"

Letters to the Speaker of the National Assembly and the Chairman of the Senate of Pakistan

Fax and email message:

"August 23, 2005

Mr. Chaudhary Amir Hussain
Speaker, National Assembly of Pakistan
Parliament House, Islamabad, Pakistan.

Mohatrram Chaudhary Amir Hussain sahib,

Assalamu Alaikum,

I am pleased to attach an open letter addressed to All Members of the National Assembly of Pakistan. I would indeed be indebted to you, if this letter is read in the Assembly and a copy of it is given to each member when the National Assembly is in full session.

With best wishes and warm regards,

Allah Hafiz,
Nasim Yousaf
Grandson of Allama Mashraqi

Author:
1) *Pakistan's Freedom & Allama Mashriqi: Statements, Letters, Chronology of Khaksar Tehrik (Movement), Period: Mashriqi's Birth to 1947*
2) *Allama Mashriqi & Dr. Akhtar Hameed Khan: Two Legends of Pakistan*
3) *Pakistan's Birth & Allama Mashraqi: Chronology & Statements, Period: 1947-1963 (Under Print)*
4) *Import & Export of Hand Knotted Oriental Rugs Part I: Export to USA, Part II: Import from Pakistan*
5) *Import & Export of Apparel & Textiles, Part I: Export to the USA, Part II: Import from Pakistan*
6) *Export Housewares, Gifts & Decorative Accessories to the United States of America (Under Print)*
7) Other works

To All Honorable Members of the National Assembly of Pakistan

Subject: Pakistan Movement and the Role of Prominent Leaders and Political Parties

Honorable Ladies & Gentlemen!

Assalamu Alaikum,

I would like to bring to the attention of all Members of the National Assembly of Pakistan the shortcomings in the writing and documentation of the history of Pakistan.

It is sorrowful to note that there is not much attention paid to enlighten the nation about the role of many political leaders and parties, such as the Khaksar Tehreek, Red Shirts, Ahrars, in the freedom movement for independence. It is again sad and distressful to observe that the role of these parties and their leaders has virtually been eliminated from the history of Pakistan due to political controversies, particularly with the Muslim League. Pakistan's educational curriculum and books on these political parties and their leaders are either imprecise or have completely ignored their part.

Another sad part is that original material of each party, though a national heritage, is missing from the public and many research libraries at home as well as abroad. Without these each individual's or party's role can never be properly projected. In the absence of original material of these organizations, many authors end up using other material / sources, and this leads to the distortion of facts and figures.

The issue of many missing facts of Pakistan's history is of national importance. It requires immediate attention and needs to be raised at the National Assembly so that the attention of relevant authorities is drawn to do the needful.

I remind the honorable Members of the National Assembly of Pakistan that this material is fast vanishing or decaying, and if necessary and immediate steps are not taken, the history of Pakistan will remain incomplete and distorted. The coming generations will hold all of us, particularly the ones with authority, responsible for this negligence.

Keeping in view the urgency and importance of the subject matter, the following steps need to be taken:

1) Relevant government agencies should be directed to collect and make the material of each party / leader available in the public and research libraries in Pakistan as well as outside the country.

2) National media should be directed to allocate adequate time, particularly on national days such as March 23 and August 14, to enlighten the public on the role of various parties and leaders towards independence.

3) Separate research academies or at least departments need to be formed to collect material on specific parties and leaders.

4) Funds should be allocated to relevant agencies for making films/documentaries on the life and times of these parties and their founders.

At the end, I would say, in Pakistan, a culture of tolerance needs to develop, and we must rise above controversies and vindictiveness. This is extremely important for the progression of any nation.

May God bless Pakistan and its people.

With best wishes and warm regards to everyone,

Allah Hafiz,
Nasim Yousaf
Grandson of Allama Mashraqi
August 23, 2005
http://www.nasimyousaf.info

Author:
1) *Pakistan's Freedom & Allama Mashriqi: Statements, Letters, Chronology of Khaksar Tehrik (Movement), Period: Mashriqi's Birth to 1947*
2) *Allama Mashriqi & Dr. Akhtar Hameed Khan: Two Legends of Pakistan*

3) Pakistan's Birth & Allama Mashraqi: Chronology & Statements, Period: 1947-1963 (Under Print)
4) Import & Export of Hand Knotted Oriental Rugs Part I: Export to USA, Part II: Import from Pakistan
5) Import & Export of Apparel & Textiles, Part I: Export to the USA, Part II: Import from Pakistan
6) Export Housewares, Gifts & Decorative Accessories to the United States of America (Under Print)
7) Other works"

NOTE: A similar letter was sent to the Chairman of the Senate Mohammad Mian Soomro on August 24, 2005.

Press Release

From the Office of Mr. Nasim Yousaf
November 19, 2004

"Allama Mashriqi Research Academy Demanded"

"Mr. Nasim Yousaf, grandson of Allama Mashriqi (Inayatullah Khan) has been conducting research on Allama Mashriqi for a decade now, and has demanded the Government of Pakistan to establish the Allama Mashriqi Research Academy (AMRA), as such an academy is vital to the nation's history. Mr. Nasim Yousaf traveled to London recently to continue his research on Allama Mashriqi and the Khaksar Tehrik (Khaksar Movement). After returning to USA, he states that a tremendous amount of material on the Khaksar Tehrik is lying unexplored at the India Office of the British Library. He urges that researchers must visit the India Office and The Centre of South Asian Studies at Cambridge University where they can find materials related to Allama Mashriqi and the Khaksar Tehrik. He refers particularly to the files on the Khaksar Movement and correspondence (from the late 1930's and 1940's) between the Viceroy of India and the Governors of various provinces in British India. Mr. Yousaf states that this correspondence shows the efforts of the Government of British India to crush the Khaksar Movement. The correspondence also reflects their concern and alarm regarding the Khaksar Movement, which endangered their rule in India. Mr. Yousaf deplores the fact that the material has not been properly indexed and catalogued, thus causing difficulties in accessing it quickly and efficiently. He points out that the Khaksar Tehrik's material is also available at the National Document Center (Cabinet Division, Government of Pakistan, Islamabad), yet even there, the material is not properly indexed or catalogued.

Mr. Yousaf expresses sorrow that the Government of Pakistan has done nothing in regards to the substantial material on Allama Mashriqi and the Khaksar Tehrik. The Government has not put forth an attempt to make Khaksar material available in the public or in research libraries due to political controversies between the Khaksar Tehrik and the Muslim League. He places emphasis on the fact that a culture of tolerance has not yet been developed in Pakistan and that this needs to change. This is extremely important for the progression of any nation.

Keeping in mind the importance of this material to Pakistan's national history, Mr. Yousaf recently sent a letter to the Prime Minister of Pakistan, Shaukat Aziz. A portion of the letter is as follows:
"...Mashriqi's unprecedented services, pre and post creation of Pakistan, should not be transgressed and disregarded. It is greatly deplorable that the Pakistani nation is unaware of the truth that Allama Mashriqi founded the Khaksar Tehrik (Khaksar Movement) in 1930 with a definite purpose. Its objective was to revive the people from their deep slumber in order to bring independence to the subcontinent, uplift the suffering masses, and restore the glory of the Muslims. This Movement created history and successfully mobilized the people that led to freedom, but unfortunately the Khaksar Tehrik's services have been completely ignored, which is unjustifiable from the nation's point of view. The role of Allama Mashriqi and the Khaksars in mobilizing the public for independence needs to be made public. It is highly deplorable that many history books have distorted and misquoted Allama Mashriqi's role. The nation needs to be apprised of the historical facts that are unknown to a vast majority. I am certain that my books that have been published (in the USA) will surely be of source of information to everyone interested in the struggle towards liberty of the nation...I would like to stress with great concern that a lot of Khaksar materials have already disappeared for various reasons and many important people from Allama Mashriqi's time have died. Time is running out and many of the above steps [that Mr. Yousaf suggested in the letter to the Prime Minister] need to be taken at once to secure Pakistan's national heritage and history. If action is not taken soon, Pakistan's history will forever remain incomplete."

To apprise the Prime Minister of Allama Mashriqi's contributions, unparalleled services, and sufferings during the struggle for independence, Mr. Yousaf also sent the following books to Mr.Shaukat Aziz. Mr. Yousaf is the author of these works and according to him, these are just a drop in the ocean as to what could be written on Mashriqi and the Khaksar Tehrik:

1. *"Allama Mashriqi & Dr. Akhtar Hameed Khan: Two Legends of Pakistan."*

2. *"Pakistan's Freedom & Allama Mashriqi: Statements, Letters, Chronology of Khaksar Tehrik (Movement), Period: Mashriqi's Birth to 1947."*

In his letter, Mr. Yousaf requested to the Prime Minister Shaukat Aziz to immediately issue a directive to establish the Allama Mashriqi Research Academy (AMRA). This Research Academy (AMRA) should be entrusted to perform various functions, such as collection of Khaksar materials from all sources including Quaid-e-Azam Muhammad Ali Jinnah's archives, Khaksars' and the Khaksar Tehrik's archives, India Office (U.K.), Cambridge University, as well as the archives of Mahatma Gandhi, Jawaharlal Nehru, and other leaders of the time. The AMRA should also be responsible for various functions such as the acquisition and translation of all Khaksar materials, including "Tazkirah" (a monumental work of Allama Mashriqi) into English and other international languages, and to ensure easy accessibility of such materials for everyone. If this is not done, research on Allama Mashriqi and Khaksar Movement will always remain incomplete and biased.

The Media and Allama Mashriqi

Mr. Yousaf also comments on the poor knowledge the nation is kept under. He regrets that the media has also not made any efforts to enlighten the nation on the role of Allama Mashriqi and the Khaksars in mobilizing the nation toward independence. For example, although it is a historical event and extremely important to Indo-Pak history the Khaksar massacre of March 19, 1940 in Lahore has virtually been ignored in the history books as well as in the media. People are unaware of what happened on that day and following that day. Quaid-e-Azam Muhammad Ali Jinnah's statement, that he issued on March 20, 1940 with regard to the Khaksar tragedy, speaks of this event's significance. He stated: "I am deeply grieved to hear the tragic account of the incident in Lahore last evening regarding the clash between the Police and the Khaksars resulting in terrible loss of life...As one who has always been so kindly treated by the Khaksars, I appeal to them most earnestly to keep peace and not precipitate matters by defying law and order..."[2] It is also consequential to note that when Quaid-e-Azam Muhammad Ali Jinnah was traveling to Lahore to attend the historic Muslim League Session (March 22-24,

---

[2] Yousaf, Nasim. 2004. *Pakistan's Freedom & Allama Mashriqi: Statements, Letters, Chronology of Khaksar Tehrik (Movement), Period: Mashriqi's Birth to 1947.* New York, USA: AMZ Publications.

1940), wherever his train stopped and he came out to talk to the public, they raised slogans in support of the Khaksars. The media (print, electronic, and the television) has entirely disregarded the public's sympathy and support for the Khaksars that was evident during the entire Muslim League Session. Mr. Yousaf regrets that even on Pakistan Day, the media does not talk of this tragic occurrence nor the Khaksar Resolution, which was passed on the same day that the Pakistan Resolution was adopted by the Muslim League. He urges that the media should inform the nation of the events surrounding the Khaksar massacre — the circumstances and the truth on what led to the Khaksar tragedy and passing of Khaksar Resolution on that momentous day. He also points out that the nation needs to know that the ban on the Khaksar Movement after March 19 was severely resisted by the Khaksars. The rulers left no stone unturned to exterminate the Movement but it prevailed and continued to mobilize the masses to rise for freedom. The fact of the matter is that, as actions by the Government to crush the Khaksar Movement grew stronger, the desire for freedom grew even greater.

Mr. Yousaf requests to journalists to conduct independent research and let the nation know of the facts of Pakistan's history and contributions of Mashriqi and the Khaksars toward liberty. He also emphasizes that people need to read the Khaksar Tehrik's own material to understand their perspective. People who have used non-Khaksar material in their books and writings will automatically reflect the anti-Khaksar point of view. This deflects the public from the truth.

A Reminder on Allama Mashriqi's Contributions

Mr. Yousaf reminds journalists that Allama Mashriqi and the Khaksars' services to the nation undoubtedly stand out when you study historical documents and Khaksar Tehrik's material. He reiterates that during the struggle movement, Mashriqi, his family, and a large number of Khaksars heavily suffered monetarily, physically, and mentally, and many Khaksars even lost their lives. Mashriqi's life story and that of the Khaksar Movement is extremely exhilarating and moving. Indeed, Mashriqi's life guides and inspires readers, instilling a spirit of patriotism and love for the common man. It also influences leaders to adopt simplicity, provide selfless service to the nation, and uplift the masses. It also suggests to leaders to refrain from leading high profile lifestyles while huge populations live below the poverty line and are deprived of basic necessities. In his lifetime, Mashriqi was offered various high posts, but he turned them down, as he believed in principled politics; he would not compromise his beliefs. Mashriqi set various examples in life that we can learn from.

Those who think Allama Mashriqi's Khaksar Movement was primarily disruptive are unknowing of the truth. Mr. Yousaf does not blame people from this school of thought because the nation is kept ignorant. He points out that the military component of the Movement was for not merely seeking freedom, but also for discipline, unity, physical fitness, punctuality, community service and last but not least, character building. The Khaksar Tehrik's basic ideology and commandments direct people to serve humanity and eradicate social prejudices. The Khaksars were to be indifferent to one's beliefs, color, creed or caste. It was mandatory for every Khaksar to wear the badge of Akhuwat (brotherhood) on his/her shoulder; this in itself preached love, affection, and fraternity. Its noble ideology of lifting the masses and bringing a sense of brotherhood among all communities, regardless of religion, are some of the features that need to be publicized. After he was released from prison, Allama Mashriqi made a public address on January 02, 1943. As reported in the "The Hindustan Times", Delhi of January 05, 1943 "He [Mashriqi] pleaded with the Muslims for religious tolerance, broadmindedness and magnanimity. The Muslims ruled for 1,000 years only because they treated non-Muslims with consideration, loved them and shared their sorrows and troubles, he observed. The Muslim Empire showed signs of decay when Muslim Rulers became intolerant towards non-Muslims and conservatives in their religious outlook..." ? Mashriqi was not only a great philosopher but a visionary; whatever he said and did has a lesson to be learnt from.

Mr. Yousaf states that there are a lot of misconceptions that exist about the Khaksar Tehrik's ideology and its role toward independence. Thus, it is an obligation of the media to provide equal opportunity and give coverage to all those who struggled for freedom and let nation know of each party's contributions. Remember! All those who mobilized the nation to rise for freedom are part of Pakistan's history and each one's role has to be adequately highlighted. Mr. Yousaf emphasizes that the history of any nation is an important part of learning and this process must not be stopped. It is important to make every party's point view known, as this can serve as a source of learning. In this way, the nation can learn from the rights and wrongs of different ideologies.

Mr. Yousaf vows to continue his effort to let the nation know of the services of Allama Mashriqi and the Khaksars. He is currently working on his third book, a sequel to his most recently published book, "Pakistan's Freedom & Allama Mashriqi"; his new work will also be a great source of information for those interested in Pakistan's history. Extracts from Mr. Yousaf's research have also been published on the following web sites dedicated to Allama Mashriqi. Mr. Yousaf says that the web sites, listed below, dedicated to Allama Mashriqi have become an immense source for researchers, historians, authors, professors, and students, and thus far thousands of people have visited them to seek information on this great personality of the sub-continent.

http://www.allamamashriqi.info
http://www.allama-mashriqi.8m.com

Mr. Yousaf laments that, in Pakistan, those leaders get more coverage in the media who are corrupt, have looted the country with both hands, and have done nothing to uplift the masses in the past 60 years of its creation. If Pakistan is to advance, we need to highlight those with a clean record so that the youth is inspired by morality and ethics and not by corruption, immorality, deceit, falsehood, and to say the least hypocrisy. He says that true leaders like Allama Mashriqi are born once in centuries and Pakistan needs more people like them.

Mr. Yousaf Praises Dr. Akhtar Hameed Khan

Keeping in view the services of Dr. Akhtar Hameed Khan, in his letter to the Prime Minister, Mr. Yousaf thanked the Prime Minister Shaukat Aziz for speaking at the seminars arranged in memory of Dr. Khan after his death. Mr. Yousaf also made some suggestions in respect to Dr. Khan, so that people continue to seek inspiration from his personality and his works. Mr. Yousaf suggested that a road leading to Orangi Town and the Orangi Town in Karachi be named after Dr. Akhtar Hameed Khan, where he rendered unprecedented services to the poor people of that area.

Those who are interested in learning more about Dr. Khan are advised to visit a web site dedicated to Dr. Khan. This site is serving as a great source to researchers, students, and others who are seeking information on Dr. Khan and his works:

http://www.akhtar-hameed-khan.8m.com"

Bibliography & Index

"Allama Mashraqi's life
is a valuable guide"

– Nasim Yousaf

Works Cited/Bibliography

Abbreviations
n.d. - No Date

BP - *Business Post*
C&MG - *The Civil & Military Gazette*
DT - *The Dacca Times*
EE - *The Eastern Examiner*
ET - *The Eastern Times*
FPJ - *The Free Press Journal*
HT - *The Hindustan Times*
KM - *Khyber Mail*
MN - *Morning News*
MNK - *Morning News*
PO - *The Pakistan Observer*
PT - *The Pakistan Times*
SI - *The Star of India*
TI - *The Times of India*
TS - *The Statesman*
TT - *The Tribune*

Works Cited

Al-Islah (Khaksar weekly).

Bhatti, Mohammad Azmat Ullah. n.d. *Al-Mashriqi*. Lahore, Pakistan: Al-Mashriqi Research Academy Gujrat, Pakistan.

BP (*Business Post*) (Karachi, Pakistan).

Chitan (Lahore, Pakistan).

C&MG (*The Civil & Military Gazette*) (Lahore, Pakistan).

Dawn (Delhi, India).

Dawn (Karachi, Pakistan).

DT (*The Dacca Times*).

EE (*The Eastern Examiner*) (Chittagong).

ET (*The Eastern Times*) (Lahore, Pakistan).

FPJ (*The Free Press Journal*) (Bombay, India).

The Hindu (India).

HT (*The Hindustan Times*) (New Delhi, India).

Hussain, Syed Shabbir. 1988. *The Muslim Luminaries*. Islamabad, Pakistan: National Hijra Council.

Hussain, Syed Shabbir. 1991. *Al-Mashriqi: The Disowned Genius*. Lahore, Pakistan: Jang Publishers.

Hussain, Syed Shabbir. 1994. *Kashmir Aur Allama Mashriqi*. Islamabad, Pakistan: World Affairs Publications.

Imroze (Lahore, Pakistan).

Jang (Karachi, Pakistan).

KM (*Khyber Mail*) (Peshawar, Pakistan).

Mashraqi, Allama (Khan, Inayat Ullah). [1931] 1997. *Isha'arat*. Lahore, Pakistan: Khaksar Hameed ud Din Ahmed (son of Allama Mashriqi) c/o Al-Tazkirah Publications.

MN (*Morning News*) (Dacca).

MNK (*Morning News*) (Karachi, Pakistan).

PO (*The Pakistan Observer*) (Dacca).

PT (*The Pakistan Times*) (Lahore, Pakistan).

SI *(The Star of India)* (Calcutta, India).

TS (*The Statesman*) (Calcutta, India).

TI (*The Times of India*) (Bombay, India).

TT (*The Tribune*) (Lahore, Pakistan).

Yousaf, Nasim. 2003. *Allama Mashriqi & Dr. Akhtar Hameed Khan: Two Legends of Pakistan*. New York, USA: Nasim Yousaf.

Yousaf, Nasim. 2004. *Pakistan's Freedom & Allama Mashriqi: Statements, Letters, Chronology of Khaksar Tehrik (Movement), Period: Mashriqi's Birth to 1947*. New York, USA: AMZ Publications.

Zaman, Sher. 1987. *Khaksar Tehrik Ki Jiddo Juhad Volume 2*. Rawalpindi, Pakistan: Khaksar Sher Zaman c/o Al-Tazkirah Publications.

Zaman, Sher. 1988. *Khaksar Tehrik Ki Jiddo Juhad Volume 3*. Rawalpindi, Pakistan: Khaksar Sher Zaman c/o Al-Tazkirah Publications.

Bibliography

Editor's Collection.

Mashriqi, Allama (Khan, Inayat Ullah). n.d. *Khitabat Au Muqalaat*. Compiled by Ghulam Qadeer Khawaja. Lahore, Pakistan: Al-Faisal Nashiran Au Tajaran Kutab.

Mashriqi, Allama (Khan, Inayat Ullah). n.d. *Qaul-i-Faisal: Yani Khaksar Tehrik Kay Gharz Au Maqqasid Ki Muqammal Tashrih*. Rawalpindi, Pakistan: Farog-e- Islam Foundation.

Mashriqi, Allama (Khan, Inayat Ullah). 1952. *Armughan-i-Hakeem*. Lahore, Pakistan: Al-Tazkirah Publications.

Mashriqi, Allama (Khan, Inayat Ullah). 1952. *Dahulbab*. Lahore, Pakistan: Al-Tazkirah Publications.

Mashriqi, Allama (Khan, Inayat Ullah). 1955. *Human Problem (A Message to the Knowers of Nature)*. Lahore, Pakistan: Al-Tazkirah Publications.

Mashriqi, Allama (Khan, Inayat Ullah). 1977. *Muqalaat Aur Doosri Tehreerain Volume 3*. Lahore, Pakistan: Idarah-i-Talimat-i-Mashriqi.

Mashriqi, Allama (Khan, Inayat Ullah). 1979. *Maulvi Ka Ghalat Mazhab*. Reprint, Lahore, Pakistan: Al-Tazkirah Publications.

Mashriqi, Allama (Khan, Inayat Ullah). [1924] 1980. *Tazkirah Volume 2*. Lahore, Pakistan: Al-Tazkirah Publications.

Mashriqi, Allama (Khan, Inayat Ullah). 1980. *God, Man, and Universe*. Edited by Syed Shabbir Hussain. Rawalpindi, Pakistan: Akhuwwat Publications.

Mashriqi, Allama (Khan, Inayat Ullah). 1987. *Quran and Evolution: Selected Writings of Inayat Ullah Khan Al-Mashriqi*. Edited by Syed Shabbir Hussain. Islamabad, Pakistan: El-Mashriqi Foundation.

Mashriqi, Allama (Khan, Inayat Ullah). 1993. *Man's Destiny*. 2nd ed. (Revised and Enlarged). Edited by Syed Shabbir Hussain. Islamabad, Pakistan: El-Mashriqi Foundation.

Mashriqi, Allama (Khan, Inayat Ullah). [1924] 1997. *Tazkirah Volume 1*. Lahore, Pakistan: Al-Tazkirah Publications.

Mashriqi, Allama (Khan, Inayat Ullah). [1926] 1997. *Khitab-e-Misr*. Lahore, Pakistan: Al-Tazkirah Publications.

Mashriqi, Allama (Khan, Inayat Ullah). [1960] 2001. *Beh Baha Takmillah Volume 1*. Lahore, Pakistan: Al-Tazkirah Publications.

Saleemi, Safdar. 1967. *Khaksar-i-Azam Aur Khaksar Tehrik*. Lahore, Pakistan: Bab Al-Ishaat Khaksar Tehrik.

The Sind Observer (Karachi, Pakistan).

Zaman, Sher. 1986. *Khaksar Tehrik Ki Jiddo Juhad Volume 1*. Rawalpindi, Pakistan: Khaksar Sher Zaman c/o Al-Tazkirah Publications.

Zaman, Sher. 1992. *Sir Syed, Jinnah, Mashriqi*. Rawalpindi, Pakistan: Khaksar Sher Zaman c/o Al-Tazkirah Publications.

Index

1
1970, 145, 146
1971, 146

2
20 kanals, 203, 227

A
A Class, 182
A.B.A Awan, 169
A.H Qureshi, 208
A.R. Changez, 197
Aafaaq, 73
Abdul Ghaffar Khan, 141, 181, 199, 204
Abdul Hamid Khan Bhashani, 141
Abdul Huq Jehanzeb, 258
Abdul Jabbar Dehlvi, 148, 153, 168
Abdul Rasheed, 101
Abdul Wadood, 77, 88, 126
Abdul Waheed Khan, 252
Abdullah Malik, 250
Abdus Sami Pal, 221
Abid Hussain, 135, 188, 200
Academic Curriculum, 315, 319
acquittal, 174, 229
acquitted, 160, 170, 210, 212, 229, 232, 270
Additional District Magistrate, 177, 183, 217, 224
address, 32, 39, 58, 81, 90, 91, 109, 110, 111, 112, 129, 134, 150, 154, 155, 159, 194, 200, 219, 222, 333
ADM, 175, 177, 179, 182
Advocate-General, 90, 91, 92, 167, 168
Aerodrome, 112
Agha Mansabdar Khan, 72
Agra, 35, 37
Ahmed Hassan Quraishi, 252
Ahmed Khan Langa, 146
Ahrar, 36
Aikman Road, 226
ailments, 209, 211, 212
Air Forces, 48
Akhora Police Station, 222
Akhri Umeed, 61, 91, 94
Akhtar, 18
Akhtar Hameed Khan, 251, 309, 310, 311, 312, 316, 318, 320, 321, 322, 323, 324, 330, 334, 339
Akhtar Qureshi, 178
Akhter Hameed Khan, 17
Alam Chishti, 51
Albert Victor Hospital, 245, 246
Alhaj Alla Dad Khan, 169
Ali Mohammad, 169, 179, 184, 232
Al-Islah, 40, 61, 62, 146, 147, 258, 338
All Parties, 252
Allah, 149, 182, 313, 318, 321, 324
Allama, 3, 5, 17, 18, 19, 23, 25, 29, 30, 31, 32, 33, 34, 36, 37, 39, 40, 41, 42, 50, 51, 52, 57, 58, 62, 63, 64, 65, 71, 72, 73, 74, 75, 76, 77, 78, 82, 83, 84, 85, 92, 93, 98, 99, 100, 101, 102, 103, 106, 108, 110, 111, 112, 113, 114, 115, 116, 117, 118, 119, 120, 125, 126, 127, 128, 129, 133, 134, 135, 136, 137, 138, 139, 140, 141, 142, 145, 146, 147, 148, 149, 150, 153, 155, 156, 159, 160, 162, 163, 167, 169, 171, 172, 173, 175, 176, 178, 179, 181, 182, 183, 185, 186, 187, 188, 189, 191, 192, 193, 194, 195, 196, 199, 200, 201, 203, 206, 207, 209, 210, 211, 212, 213, 216, 217, 218, 219, 220, 221, 222, 224, 225, 226, 227, 228, 229, 230, 231, 237, 245, 246, 247, 248, 249, 250, 251, 252, 253,

254, 255, 256, 257, 301, 309, 310, 311, 312, 313, 315, 316, 317, 318, 319, 320, 321, 322, 323, 324, 329, 330, 331, 332, 333, 334, 338, 339
Allama Alauddin Siddiqi, 125
Allama Inayat Ullah Khan Mashriqi, 103, 150, 167
Allama Inayatullah Khan Al-Mashraqi, 255
Allama Inayatullah Khan al-Mashriqi, 125
Allama Inayatullah Khan Mashriqi, 75, 82, 106, 110, 113, 116, 117, 118, 126, 135, 137, 140, 153, 212, 257
Allama Iqbal, 227
Allama Mashraqi, 9, 17, 21, 55, 73, 85, 93, 99, 100, 143, 167, 173, 182, 186, 187, 188, 191, 217, 220, 222, 227, 230, 233, 259, 263, 264, 267, 268, 271, 279, 280, 297, 298, 335, 362
Allama Mashriqi, 75, 83, 93, 94, 95, 98, 106, 112, 118, 137, 213, 246, 303, 304, 305, 306, 307, 310, 313, 315, 319, 322, 329, 330, 331, 333, 334
Allama Mashriqi Museum., 317, 321
Allama Mashriqi Research Academy, 314, 329
Allama Mashriqi University, 312, 317, 321
All-Jammu and Kashmir, 135
All-Party, 112, 114
Alnaj Muhammad Ashraf, 169
Altaf Hussain, 114
amalgamate, 89, 146, 148, 186
Ambala, 58
American, 109, 117, 129, 250
Aminuddin Sehrai, 146
Amir, 51, 112, 169, 185, 195, 199, 201, 222, 247, 248, 249, 252
Amir Habibullah Khan, 51, 248
Amir Habibullah Khan Saadi, 248
Amiran Bibi, 197, 222

AML&M, 311
AMRA, 311, 317, 320, 321, 329, 331
Amritsar, 158
Anglo-American, 116
Anglo-Americans, 117
announcement, 90, 142, 160, 183, 216
Ansar Ali, 252
anti-Mashraqi, 133, 174, 188
Anti-Mashraqi, 154
anti-Pakistan, 75
Apparel, 18
appealed, 70, 111, 121, 125, 126, 127, 138, 162, 171, 246
appeasement, 126
application, 53, 57, 113, 163, 167, 175, 180, 184, 193, 194, 197, 207, 208, 209, 210, 211, 213, 214, 222, 224, 226, 240
approver, 175, 180, 185, 186, 187, 189, 190, 191, 196, 202, 218, 219, 220, 224, 226, 228, 229, 232
archives, 311, 317, 320, 331
armed, 48, 49, 65, 69, 90, 137, 156, 176, 177, 178, 180, 184, 198, 216, 221
arms, 47, 48, 90, 91, 145, 196, 246
Armughan-i-Hakeem, 271, 298, 340
arrested, 30, 31, 36, 37, 38, 39, 41, 42, 51, 62, 66, 69, 70, 71, 72, 75, 81, 83, 84, 85, 88, 91, 92, 98, 99, 100, 106, 107, 148, 153, 158, 160, 161, 162, 163, 168, 169, 170, 171, 172, 173, 178, 180, 188, 189, 196, 201, 217, 235, 237, 240
Articles, 18
Asghar Ali, 178, 190, 196
Asghar Haider, 184, 232
Ashiq Hussain, 77
Ashraf Khan, 157
Ashraf Sandow, 69
Aslam Tariq, 240
Assam, 201
assasin, 226

assassinate, 228
assassinated, 75, 169, 190
assassination, 75, 133, 134, 171, 201
assemble, 30, 37, 39, 40, 41, 153, 155, 202, 216
assembling, 156
Assembly, 48, 70, 81, 83, 87, 91, 139, 140, 174, 217, 236, 238
Assistant Inspector General, 169, 170, 171, 181, 182, 184, 198, 199, 200, 225
at Metro Hotel, 220
Ata Mohammad, 169, 184, 187, 192, 195, 205, 222, 223, 226, 228
Ata Mohammed, 169, 170, 171, 173, 184, 188, 193, 200, 203, 205, 206, 207, 216, 225, 226, 227, 228, 229
Atta Mohammad Butt, 240
Atta Mohammed, 169, 172, 173, 181, 186, 205
Atta-ur-Rahman, 315
Attock, 146
Attorney General, 208
Awami League, 81, 99, 163
Ayub Khan, 174, 197, 235, 237, 238, 245, 247, 248, 249, 250, 255, 257
Azad Kashmir, 141
Azam Garh, 221
Azam Khan, 258
Azamgarh, 198
Azhar, 250

B

B Class, 182
Bahadur Shah Day, 31, 36, 37
Bahawalpur, 120, 163
bail, 62, 84, 148, 158, 162, 163, 167, 175, 178, 179, 180, 197, 207, 208, 209, 210, 211, 213, 214, 217, 230, 232, 240
Balram Dubey, 36
ban, 39, 49, 61, 64, 65, 85, 86, 90, 91, 176, 178, 179, 181, 215, 219, 238, 239, 332

Bangladesh, 141, 146
Banqipur, 31
bans, 84, 162, 176
Baptist Perara, 170
Barrister Ijaz Hussain Batalvi, 173, 174, 186, 190, 192, 196, 210, 215, 221, 228
Barrister Mian Ahmad Shah, 263
Bashir Ahmed Siddiqui, 254, 257
BBC, 251
beaten, 35, 42, 175, 189, 196, 220
belcha, 238
belchas, 30, 38, 90
Bengal, 30, 31, 33, 35, 36, 48, 49, 186, 201
Bengal Bratachan Society, 48
Bengal Ordinances Temporary Enactment Act, 48, 49
Bengal Special Powers Ordinance, 48, 49
Bharat, 113, 139, 146, 155, 156, 195, 230
Bharat-Pakistan Muslim League, 146
Bhatti Gate, 164, 236
Bihar, 30, 31, 32, 33, 34, 35, 37, 38, 39
Biharis, 33, 35
bill, 99
biography, 311, 312, 317, 321
Biography, 17
blessing, 120, 121
Bombay, 29, 96, 253, 310, 338
Borstal, 174, 175, 185, 186, 192, 197, 215, 216, 217, 220, 222, 229, 231
Borstal Jail, 192
branch, 179, 220
branches, 146, 179
British, 32, 40, 49, 75, 76, 83, 104, 105, 107, 133, 134, 174, 257, 329
brotherhood, 25, 40, 333
bullets, 137
buried, 251, 255, 256
buttons, 224

C

C.I.D., 43, 52, 61, 66, 69, 88, 98, 158, 222, 223, 225
C.W. U'ren, 133
Calcutta, 50, 201, 339
Cambridge University, 311, 317, 320, 329, 331
Camp, 32, 33, 37, 155, 224
campaign, 78, 117, 142, 214
Campbellpur, 178
Canadian High Commissioner, 110
canal, 112, 126, 127, 128
caste, 25, 127, 333
cause, 49, 64, 76, 84, 87, 89, 125, 127, 134, 135, 136, 139, 140, 239, 257, 315
Central Office, 178, 179
Central Safety Act, 97
Ceon, 133
Ch. Ghulam Abbas, 140, 239
Ch. Gul Nawaz, 180
Ch. Karam Dad, 180
Ch. Mohammad Ali, 137, 263
Ch. Mohammed Zafar Yasin, 185
Ch. Muhammad Sharif, 199
Ch. Nazir Ahmed Khan, 207, 208, 209
Ch. Qadir Bakhsh, 222
Ch. Sultan Khan, 232
challaned, 184, 198, 222
character, 136, 216, 231, 239, 333
Charges, 160
Chaudhary Amir Hussain, 325
Chaudhary Muhammad Rafi, 164
Chaudhry Hamidullah, 140
Chaudhry Khaliquzzaman, 141
chest, 182, 184, 191, 193, 203, 207, 208
Chief Minister, 169, 174
China, 115, 117
Chiniot, 147, 194, 222
Chittagong, 250, 253, 254, 255
Chowk Yadgar, 153, 252
CID, 77, 188, 224
citizens, 36, 61, 81, 126, 239
Clarification, 15
class system, 20
cloak, 153
coalition, 103, 104, 105, 106
cock and bull, 206, 229
colour, 127
coma, 245, 246, 249
comments, 15, 29, 30, 35, 40, 43, 49, 50, 51, 52, 57, 61, 62, 64, 66, 69, 71, 73, 74, 75, 77, 78, 81, 82, 83, 85, 99, 100, 101, 102, 107, 108, 110, 121, 128, 129, 133, 134, 136, 140, 141, 145, 146, 147, 149, 153, 154, 155, 158, 159, 160, 161, 162, 163, 167, 168, 169, 170, 172, 173, 175, 177, 178, 179, 180, 181, 182, 185, 188, 189, 190, 192, 193, 196, 197, 201, 205, 206, 207, 208, 209, 210, 211, 214, 215, 217, 218, 221, 222, 225, 226, 227, 228, 229, 231, 232, 235, 236, 238, 239, 240, 246, 247, 248, 255, 257, 258
Committee, 17, 32, 34, 38, 82, 83, 118, 119, 121, 139, 146, 252
communal, 29, 47
communique, 47, 48
Communist, 115, 116, 117, 121
condition, 6, 33, 205, 212, 213, 245, 246, 247, 248, 249, 250
condolence, 253, 256
Condolence, 254
conference, 50, 61, 64, 65, 86, 90, 91, 99, 100, 106, 121, 137, 140, 141, 145, 184, 236, 239
Conference, 50, 51, 61, 64, 86, 114, 115, 118, 135, 138, 139, 140, 141, 142, 145, 174, 252
confinement, 42, 101, 185
confiscate, 61, 164, 170, 177
confiscated, 62, 63, 169, 176, 178, 180, 182, 199, 211, 212, 213, 225
Congress, 6, 37, 38, 47, 89, 121
conscience, 64, 113, 125, 220
conspiracy, 43, 113, 133, 134, 171, 175, 197, 204, 206, 208, 213, 220, 226, 228, 229, 235

constituency, 150
constitution, 83, 114, 148, 156
Convener, 114, 252
Convention, 135, 136, 252
convict, 219
cordoned, 161, 184
Costi, 133
creed, 25, 127, 333
Criminal Investigation Department, 43, 61, 77, 98, 158, 224
Criminal Law, 238
Criminal Law Amendment Act, 176, 237, 238
Criminal Procedure Code, 97
crops, 112
cross-examination, 90, 91, 92, 188, 192, 219, 224
cross-examined, 93, 190, 200, 219
cross-examines, 100, 187, 188, 194, 196, 199, 223
crowd, 31, 63, 64, 114, 179, 180, 185, 195, 268, 284
curriculum, 49, 312, 317, 321
Curriculum, 302
custody, 35, 134, 169, 170, 171, 179, 181, 182, 189, 200, 217, 219, 229

D

D.C. Smith, 250
Dacca, 114, 246, 247, 248, 249, 253, 254, 255, 256
dam, 113
Danagar Zai village, 221
dars, 195
daughter, 199, 241, 259
Day, 70, 73, 76, 81, 114, 115, 157, 332
Declaration, 13
Defence, 206
Deh al' baab, 115
Delhi, 30, 35, 36, 37, 38, 39, 40, 41, 42, 47, 148, 153, 156, 161, 168, 186, 201, 202, 216, 254, 255, 333, 338
deliberations, 34, 120, 141, 157

democracy, 50, 70, 78, 104, 181, 218
democratic, 70, 75, 78, 106, 150, 167, 177, 181
demonstration, 101, 157
demonstrations, 36, 39, 84, 85, 156
deputation, 37, 38, 74, 77
Deputy Commissioner, 53, 95, 161
Deputy Commissioners, 161
detention, 66, 72, 74, 75, 81, 85, 92, 93, 101, 102, 103, 134, 161, 167, 168, 175, 203, 213, 214, 220, 230, 237
detenu, 77, 93, 97, 98
deterioration, 103, 104, 106, 121, 125, 208, 212
dictated, 175, 220
dictator, 119, 167, 187, 188, 221
dignitaries, 241, 301
Dignitaries, 301
Din Mohammad, 110
diplomatic missions, 141
disappeared, 312, 330
disband, 39, 40, 41, 202, 216
disbanded, 47, 105, 216, 255
disbandment, 40, 41, 42, 202
Discard, 218
discrimination, 25, 61
Division Bench, 167, 215
doctor, 169, 189, 207, 209, 213, 217, 220, 245, 247, 248
documentary, 317, 321
documents, 63, 164, 169, 170, 178, 180, 317, 321, 332
Dost Mohammad Khan, 30
Dr. Akhtar Hameed Khan, 334
Dr. Graham, 103
Dr. Khan Sahib, 170, 172, 173, 181, 184, 187, 196, 197, 198, 199, 200, 206, 210, 211, 219, 221, 222, 223, 226, 227, 228
Dr. Sadiq, 209, 211
Dr. Wadood, 88
Dr. Wadud, 83
drill, 48, 49, 84
durra, 196

E

East Pakistan, 141, 147
economic, 41, 103, 111, 112, 114, 120
economic development, 111
editor, 6, 17, 18, 39, 183, 186, 224
Editor, 17, 29, 30, 35, 39, 40, 43, 49, 50, 51, 52, 53, 57, 61, 62, 64, 66, 69, 71, 72, 73, 74, 75, 77, 78, 81, 82, 83, 85, 99, 100, 101, 102, 107, 108, 110, 114, 119, 121, 128, 129, 133, 134, 136, 140, 141, 145, 146, 147, 153, 154, 155, 158, 159, 160, 161, 162, 163, 167, 168, 169, 170, 172, 173, 175, 177, 178, 179, 180, 181, 182, 185, 188, 189, 190, 192, 193, 196, 197, 201, 205, 206, 207, 208, 209, 210, 211, 214, 215, 217, 218, 221, 222, 225, 226, 227, 228, 229, 231, 232, 235, 236, 238, 239, 240, 246, 247, 248, 255, 257, 258
editorial, 41, 106, 112, 117, 136, 141, 253, 254, 256
education, 134
Egypt, 52, 76, 82, 83
Ehsan Qadir, 30
Ehsanullah Khan Aslam, 188, 189, 222, 297
elected, 51, 82, 167, 186, 202, 217, 221
election, 71, 82, 85, 89, 91, 98, 99, 129, 167, 217
elections, 69, 70, 71, 76, 77, 78, 83, 85, 87, 88, 89, 92, 98, 99, 100, 125, 173, 176, 177, 179, 182, 186, 190, 203, 204, 214, 217
El-Mashriqi, 15
Embassy of Pakistan, 302, 314
emergency, 50, 65, 111, 112, 128
Emergency, 63, 128
escort, 179
Europe, 108, 109
European, 52, 107, 108, 109, 133, 250
exploiter, 59
Export, 18

F

F.K. Abra, 29
fabricated, 19, 20, 102, 175, 181, 182, 203, 232, 240, 269, 270
Faisalabad, 58, 137, 147, 194, 222
Fakir of Ipi, 155
fast, 78, 83, 105, 114, 127, 136, 145, 181, 230
Fateh Mohammad, 181, 184, 200, 202
Fateh Mohammed Awan, 200
Fazlul Haq, 135
Federal Minister for Information and Broadcasting, 322
film, 98, 311, 317, 321, 324
fine, 185, 188, 198, 216
fire, 35, 36, 42, 156
flag, 39, 153, 198, 221
food, 74, 75, 103, 104, 109, 111, 175, 230
foundation, 118, 202, 210, 312
founder, 47, 64, 65, 69, 70, 90, 110, 111, 112, 115, 118, 119, 120, 125, 137, 256, 315, 322
four million, 155
freedom, 19, 20, 21, 23, 40, 49, 61, 107, 125, 126, 139, 156, 161, 185, 201, 252, 301, 304, 305, 310, 316, 319, 322, 326, 330, 332, 333
French, 83, 133
Frontier Crimes Regulation, 70
Frontier Province, 148, 172
funeral, 33, 36, 52, 84, 241, 251, 253, 255, 256, 257, 279, 281, 283, 284, 285, 291, 297, 307

G

G.M. Syed, 81
Gandhi, 30, 32, 34, 37, 38, 39, 42, 43, 311, 317, 321, 331

garlanded, 229
Gazette, 47, 50, 51, 52, 58, 63, 64, 65, 76, 78, 82, 84, 98, 99, 100, 101, 103, 104, 106, 107, 110, 111, 112, 115, 117, 118, 120, 121, 125, 126, 127, 128, 129, 135, 136, 137, 138, 140, 141, 149, 157, 162, 167, 168, 169, 171, 173, 181, 187, 194, 196, 200, 207, 209, 211, 213, 214, 216, 218, 223, 225, 226, 228, 229, 231, 232, 235, 236, 238, 246, 247, 249, 250, 253, 255, 256, 337, 338
General Pervez Musharraf, 301, 302, 303, 324
genocide, 153, 201
Ghaus Muhammad, 198, 221
Ghazi Mohammed Ishaq, 84
Ghiasuddin, 91, 92, 93
Ghiasuddin Ahmad, 91
Ghias-Ud-Din Ahmad, 93, 94
Ghulam Jilani Barq, 252
Ghulam Qadir, 185
Gibb, 133
Gillaume, 133
glimpse, 179, 180
Gloom, 254
Golam Azam, 181
Governor, 48, 49, 50, 57, 58, 63, 71, 85, 87, 88, 92, 110, 120, 121, 141, 249
Governor of Punjab, 57
Governor-General, 120
grandson, 17, 329
grenade, 297
guilty, 47, 113, 215, 216, 228
Gujranwala, 63, 72, 74, 76, 113
Gujrat, 78, 84, 160, 240
Gulberg, 226

H

habeas corpus, 77, 85, 101
Habeas Corpus, 77, 85, 86, 93, 98, 99, 100, 101
Hadees-ul-Quran, 72, 120
Hafiz Jalundhari, 252
Haj, 103, 107, 108, 110, 111, 112
Haji Ashraf, 182
Haji Maula Baksh, 81
Haji Mohammad Ashraf, 88
Haji Mohammed Ashraf, 69
Hakim, 35, 81, 247
Hakim Muhammad Ahsan, 81
Hakim-i-A'la, 35
Hameed, 18
handcuffed, 180, 181, 186, 188, 189, 213, 216, 217
harassed, 158, 161, 173
Hareem-e-Ghaib, 115, 297
hartal, 139, 140
Hasan Abdal, 73
Hasanat Ahmad, 175, 176
Hashim Gazdar, 114
Hashim Raza, 65
Hassan Mohammed, 169, 174, 199, 200
Hatim Alvi, 81
headquarters, 37, 112, 157, 225, 297, 316, 320
Headquarters, 189, 251
health, 73, 74, 75, 78, 81, 82, 83, 102, 121, 167, 173, 193, 205, 208, 210, 211, 212, 213, 214, 230, 237, 238, 245, 246, 247, 248, 250
hearing, 41, 85, 86, 93, 98, 99, 100, 160, 167, 174, 183, 185, 186, 188, 197, 201, 208, 209, 215, 229, 240
heavy guard, 185
heroes, 153
Higher Education Commission, 315, 317
Hindu, 29, 30, 37, 66, 104, 105, 127, 158, 254, 255
Hindu-Muslim, 29, 30, 37
Hindus, 30, 35, 38, 40, 65, 89, 104, 105, 116, 127, 202
Hitti, 133
holiday, 107, 312
holocaust, 201
hoodwink, 139, 147
hospital, 36, 37, 213, 245, 247, 248, 249, 250, 253

hostile, 57, 118, 156, 159, 178, 187, 191, 192, 196, 197, 207, 218, 225, 226, 228, 229, 232
house, 34, 61, 62, 69, 163, 169, 170, 172, 173, 174, 178, 182, 183, 189, 194, 195, 199, 205, 221, 225, 226, 241
Human Problem, 133
Human Rights Commission, 58
humanitarian, 33, 35, 50, 117, 158
humanity, 127, 143, 259, 304, 306, 307, 313, 316, 319, 322, 333
Hussain Shaheed Suhrawardy, 57, 58, 65, 70, 85, 86, 93, 98, 99, 100, 140, 141
Hyderabad, 126, 127, 145, 180, 252

I

Ibraheem Jalees, 81
Ibrahim, 172, 174
Ichhra, 32, 61, 69, 168, 169, 178, 186, 190, 191, 197, 199, 229, 312
Idara-i-Aliya, 37, 186
ideologies, 120, 121, 125, 333
Iftikhar Hussain Khan, 141
Ijaz Hussain, 173, 174, 186, 190, 192, 194, 196, 197, 206, 207, 210, 211, 212, 213, 215, 221, 228
Ilahi Bakhsh, 209, 211, 212, 213
ill, 42, 145, 156, 169, 212, 213, 214, 217, 245, 246
imam, 221
Imam, 112
imperialism, 82
imprisonment, 70, 162, 185, 188, 216, 232
Inamullah Khan Akram, 174, 266
Inayatullah Akhtar, 178, 191, 192, 194, 197
Inayatullah Hassan, 163
India, 23, 29, 30, 35, 37, 38, 40, 43, 47, 48, 49, 50, 51, 52, 57, 58, 64, 66, 87, 89, 91, 92, 99, 100, 101, 103, 104, 113, 115, 116, 126, 134, 136, 139, 141, 145, 146, 147, 153, 154, 155, 156, 158, 159, 160, 161, 162, 168, 186, 201, 202, 203, 204, 210, 214, 217, 230, 232, 245, 246, 250, 251, 253, 254, 255, 310, 311, 315, 317, 320, 329, 331, 337, 338, 339
Indian Congress, 20
Indian National Congress, 23, 153
Indo-Pak, 251, 319, 322, 331
Indo-Pakistan, 23, 116, 252, 257
industrialize, 111
Inpector General of Police, 169
Inspector General of Police, 174, 184, 191, 220, 221, 225
interview, 29, 103, 115, 116, 118, 129, 173, 175, 211
interviews, 37, 38, 115, 173
invitees, 138, 141
Iran, 82
Ishaq Zafar, 182
Iskandar Mirza, 141, 148, 199, 204, 225, 263
Islam, 43, 50, 51, 52, 61, 63, 64, 65, 69, 70, 71, 72, 73, 74, 75, 76, 77, 78, 81, 82, 83, 84, 86, 87, 88, 89, 90, 91, 92, 98, 99, 100, 101, 102, 103, 104, 105, 106, 107, 108, 109, 110, 111, 112, 113, 114, 115, 116, 117, 118, 119, 120, 121, 125, 126, 127, 133, 135, 136, 137, 140, 142, 145, 146, 147, 148, 149, 154, 155, 156, 157, 186, 190, 194, 201, 202, 216, 220, 222, 236, 238, 252, 256
Islam League, 43, 51, 52, 61, 63, 64, 65, 69, 70, 71, 72, 73, 74, 75, 76, 77, 78, 81, 82, 83, 84, 86, 87, 88, 90, 91, 92, 93, 94, 95, 98, 99, 100, 101, 103, 104, 105, 106, 107, 108, 110, 111, 112, 113, 114, 115, 116, 117, 118, 119, 120, 121, 125, 126, 127, 135, 136, 137, 140, 142, 145, 146, 147, 148, 149, 154,

155, 156, 157, 186, 194, 201,
202, 216, 220, 222, 236, 238
Islamia College, 257
Islamic State, 104, 105, 125
isolationist, 114
ita'at-i-amir, 112
Izhar-i-Haqiqat, 94

J

Jacobabad, 128
Jafar Imam, 33, 35
Jail, 42, 71, 72, 73, 74, 75, 77,
78, 81, 82, 83, 88, 107, 162,
163, 167, 168, 174, 177, 182,
184, 185, 186, 189, 190, 191,
192, 193, 197, 205, 207, 208,
211, 215, 216, 217, 219, 220,
222, 229, 230, 231, 235, 237
Jalal pur Jatan, 84
Jalapur Jatan, 76
Jamaat-i-Islami, 99, 176, 195,
199
Jamia, 43
Jammu, 135, 139, 245, 252
Jammu and Kashmir, 139
Javed Ashraf Qazi, 319
Jawaharlal Nehru, 37, 43, 159,
311, 317, 321, 331
Jeddah, 103, 109
jehad, 116, 126, 171
Jehad, 116, 155
Jehangir Park, 135, 136, 139
jihad, 47, 50
Jihad, 117
Jinnah, 30, 32, 36, 50, 52, 81, 89,
99, 110, 114, 263, 305, 310,
311, 317, 320, 331, 341
Jinnah Awami Muslim League,
114
Jinnah Faces An Assassin, 310
jirga, 221
journalists, 126, 332
Jubilee, 257
Judge, 162, 163, 173, 183, 184,
185, 188, 190, 197, 207, 208,
209, 210, 214, 215, 216, 218,
219, 221, 222, 223, 224, 225,
226, 227, 228, 229, 231, 232

judgement, 101, 160, 163, 185,
188, 222, 229, 231, 232
judicial lockup, 177, 179
judicial lock-up, 160, 172 , 179,
181, 240
Jullundur, 37
Julsa, 252
Jumma, 102
Justice, 85, 89, 92, 100, 101, 102,
167, 174, 197, 207, 208, 210,
211, 212, 213, 215, 310

K

K. N. Islam, 147
Karachi, 52, 61, 64, 65, 75, 81,
86, 90, 99, 100, 102, 108, 110,
113, 125, 127, 129, 134, 135,
136, 137, 138, 139, 140, 141,
146, 148, 149, 171, 175, 176,
178, 179, 180, 181, 182, 183,
184, 191, 192, 194, 196, 199,
200, 201, 203, 204, 211, 215,
226, 229, 232, 237, 245, 246,
247, 248, 249, 250, 252, 253,
254, 255, 256, 257, 258, 312,
334, 338
Karam Bibi, 192, 194, 197
Karamat un Nisa, 197
Kashmir, 19, 29, 43, 51, 52, 65,
66, 72, 73, 103, 108, 111, 113,
114, 115, 116, 117, 120, 126,
127, 128, 134, 135, 136, 137,
138, 139, 140, 141, 142, 145,
146, 154, 155, 156, 157, 158,
161, 162, 168, 170, 175, 185,
186, 201, 202, 216, 236, 239,
245, 252, 255, 257, 301, 338
Kashmir chalo, 136
Khadim Mohy-ud-Din, 63
Khairpur, 162, 252
Khaksaar, 15
Khaksar, 15, 17, 18, 19, 21, 29,
30, 32, 33, 34, 36, 37, 38, 39,
40, 41, 42, 47, 49, 50, 51, 52,
62, 65, 73, 75, 86, 90, 94, 96,
100, 101, 105, 112, 115, 118,
129, 134, 136, 145, 148, 150,
153, 154, 155, 156, 157, 159,

162, 163, 167, 168, 170, 171, 172, 175, 176, 177, 178, 179, 180, 181, 182, 183, 184, 186, 187, 188, 189, 190, 191, 196, 197, 202, 208, 215, 216, 217, 219, 220, 221, 222, 224, 225, 232, 236, 237, 238, 239, 240, 249, 251, 254, 256, 257, 258, 304, 305, 306, 309, 310, 311, 312, 315, 316, 317, 319, 320, 321, 322, 323, 324, 325, 326, 327, 329, 330, 331, 332, 333, 338, 339, 340, 341
Khaksar Movement, 15, 17, 41, 202, 216, 221, 238, 310, 315, 319, 322, 329, 330, 331, 332
Khaksar Mujahid Corps, 50
Khaksar Tehreek, 51
Khaksar Tehrik, 18, 19, 49, 202, 304, 305, 306, 310, 315, 319, 322, 329, 330, 340, 341
Khaksar Volunteers, 164
Khaksars, 17, 23, 29, 30, 31, 32, 33, 35, 36, 37, 38, 39, 40, 41, 42, 47, 50, 51, 61, 62, 65, 69, 75, 85, 90, 96, 133, 134, 136, 145, 158, 161, 162, 170, 171, 180, 182, 186, 188, 190, 191, 192, 198, 199, 202, 203, 204, 212, 216, 219, 221, 235, 236, 237, 238, 239, 240, 257, 258, 304, 305, 306, 310, 311, 315, 317, 320, 323, 330, 331, 332, 333, 334
Khalid Jamil, 252
Khalid Mehmood, 192
Khalid Memorial School, 180
Khalifa, 112
Khan Abdul Qaiyum Khan, 171, 188, 220, 221
Khan Abdul Qayyum Khan, 168, 171, 172, 183, 184, 187, 188, 191, 200, 258
Khan Habibullah Khan, 248, 258
Khan Jalal Baba, 169
Khan Mohammed Niaz Khan, 77
Khan Mushtaq Hussain Khan, 207
Khan of Mamdot, 88
Khan Saad Ullah Khan, 199, 223
Khan Saadullah Khan, 181
Khan Sahib, 141, 148, 169, 170, 171, 172, 173, 174, 178, 180, 181, 183, 184, 186, 187, 188, 189, 190, 191, 192, 193, 194, 195, 196, 197, 198, 199, 200, 202, 203, 204, 205, 206, 207, 208, 210, 211, 212, 213, 215, 216, 217, 218, 219, 220, 221, 222, 223, 224, 225, 226, 227, 228, 229, 230, 231, 232, 269, 270, 271
Khawaja Abdul Ghafoor, 252
Khawaja Abdul Rahim, 85, 86
Khawaja Abdur Rahim, 167
Khawaja Afzal, 77
Khawaja Nazimud Din, 77, 114, 252
Khawaja Nazimuddin, 82, 125, 127
Khawaja Samin Jan, 200
Khawaja Wali Muhammad, 185, 221, 224
Khawaja Yasin Butt, 61
Khilafat, 41
Khitab-e-Lahore, 62, 63, 99
Khitab-i-Aam, 194
Khitab-i-Lahore, 61, 63, 91, 93, 94
Khuda Bakhsh, 198
Khuda Baksh, 170
Khurshid Khalid, 160, 177, 180, 189, 190, 192, 193, 196, 200, 202, 219, 220, 224, 226, 236, 238, 239, 240
Khutbai-am, 222
Khwaja Wali Mohammad, 172, 207
King Abdul Aziz Ibn-us-Saud, 108
King Edward Medical College, 208, 209, 211, 212
Kitab Ghar, 61
Kohistan, 296
Krishak Sramik Party, 181
Kunwar Saadatullah, 146

L

Lahore, 29, 30, 31, 36, 37, 38, 39, 40, 47, 50, 51, 52, 53, 58, 61, 62, 63, 64, 65, 69, 70, 71, 72, 73, 74, 76, 78, 81, 82, 83, 84, 85, 86, 90, 91, 93, 94, 95, 98, 99, 100, 101, 102, 103, 104, 105, 106, 107, 108, 110, 111, 112, 114, 115, 117, 118, 120, 125, 126, 127, 128, 129, 136, 138, 139, 140, 141, 149, 150, 153, 154, 155, 157, 158, 159, 160, 161, 162, 163, 167, 168, 169, 170, 171, 172, 173, 174, 175, 176, 177, 178, 179, 180, 181, 182, 183, 184, 185, 186, 187, 188, 189, 190, 191, 192, 193, 194, 195, 196, 197, 198, 199, 200, 201, 202, 203, 204, 205, 207, 208, 209, 210, 211, 212, 213, 214, 215, 216, 217, 218, 219, 220, 221, 222, 223, 224, 225, 226, 227, 228, 229, 231, 232, 235, 236, 237, 238, 239, 240, 245, 246, 247, 248, 249, 250, 251, 252, 253, 255, 256, 257, 304, 305, 306, 312, 331, 338, 339, 340, 341
Lahore District and Sessions Judge, 208, 209, 216, 219, 221, 222, 223, 224, 225, 226, 227, 228, 229, 232
Lahore Fort, 169, 172, 177, 188, 190, 191, 219
lakh, 33, 103, 201
land, 30, 36, 40, 99, 103, 110, 120, 200, 203, 222, 227, 238
langra, 36
languages, 311, 313, 317, 320, 321, 331
Larkana, 257
lathis, 35, 198, 216, 221
law, 48, 49, 62, 63, 74, 77, 91, 93, 99, 100, 105, 113, 162, 176, 177, 179, 199, 208, 237, 238, 239, 241, 331
Law, 85, 105, 176, 179, 198, 223, 237
lectures, 107, 311, 312, 313, 317, 321
letter, 33, 37, 38, 42, 52, 53, 57, 71, 88, 90, 108, 113, 127, 133, 156, 157, 199, 204, 225, 227, 228, 238, 302, 303, 313, 314, 318, 330, 331, 334
letters, 83, 136, 301
Liaquat Ali Khan, 43, 62, 66, 71, 72, 73, 75, 76, 95, 133, 134, 171, 204, 208, 263
Liaquat Bagh, 115
Liaquat Garden, 157
liberate, 30, 43, 113, 126, 140, 142, 145, 216, 236
liberated, 72, 155
liberation, 43, 70, 117, 136, 137, 155, 170, 239, 255, 257
liberties, 61, 67, 70, 107, 108
libraries, 311, 317, 321, 329
lifestyle, 218, 316, 319, 322
lifestyles, 64, 332
Lodikatra, 36
Lok Sabha, 203, 204
Lucknow, 30
lungs, 213
luxury, 59, 64, 75, 218
Lyallpur, 58, 137, 147, 194, 222

M

M. Anwer, 207
M.A. Khuhro, 141
M.A.K. Chaudhri, 198
M.A.K. Chaudhry, 200, 221
M.H. Qureshi, 76
M.M. Shaheed, 252
M.N. Rizvi, 183, 184, 186, 188, 189, 192, 195, 196
M.Yunus, 32, 33
Magistrate, 69, 160, 161, 162, 163, 170, 171, 172, 173, 174, 175, 177, 178, 179, 180, 182, 183, 185, 186, 187, 188, 189, 190, 191, 192, 193, 194, 195, 196, 197, 198, 199, 200, 201, 205, 206, 207, 210, 212, 215, 217, 220, 223, 224, 229, 240
Mahboob Ahmed, 36

Mahmood Hassan, 133
Mahmud Ali Qasuri, 118
Majlis-e-Nafiza, 95
Majlis-e-Shura, 217
Maliha Lodhi, 302
Malik Akram, 88, 146
Malik Amir Muhammad Khan, 249
Malik Firoz Khan Noon, 182, 219
Malik Habib Ullah, 181, 199, 225
Malik Habibullah, 169, 170, 171, 182
Malik Habibullah Khan, 169
Malik Mehmood, 178
Malik Mohammed Aslam Khan, 197
Malik Noor Muhammad, 200
Malik Sahib, 220
Maluana Abdus Sattar Niazi, 248
Mamdot, 141
Manzil, 163
Manzoor Qadir, 174
Manzur Elahi, 147
Manzur Qadir, 197
March 19, 1940, 85, 189, 201, 312, 331
Margoliouth, 133
Mashraqi, 3, 5, 15, 17, 18, 19, 20, 21, 23, 25, 27, 29, 30, 31, 32, 36, 37, 38, 39, 40, 41, 42, 43, 44, 49, 51, 52, 57, 58, 62, 63, 64, 65, 66, 69, 71, 72, 73, 74, 75, 76, 77, 78, 81, 82, 83, 84, 85, 86, 93, 98, 99, 100, 101, 102, 103, 104, 105, 106, 107, 108, 110, 111, 112, 113, 114, 115, 119, 120, 121, 125, 126, 128, 129, 133, 134, 135, 139, 141, 142, 145, 146, 147, 148, 149, 153, 154, 155, 158, 159, 160, 161, 162, 163, 167, 168, 169, 170, 171, 172, 173, 174, 175, 177, 178, 179, 180, 181, 182, 184, 185, 186, 187, 188, 189, 191, 192, 193, 194, 195, 196, 197, 199, 200, 201, 202, 203, 204, 205, 206, 207, 208, 209, 210, 211, 212, 213, 214, 216, 217, 218, 219, 220, 221, 222, 223, 225, 226, 227, 228, 229, 230, 231, 235, 237, 238, 241, 245, 246, 247, 248, 249, 250, 251, 252, 253, 254, 255, 256, 257, 259, 263, 264, 266, 268, 269, 270, 271, 273, 274, 275, 276, 277, 278, 279, 280, 281, 282, 283, 284, 285, 286, 289, 291, 292, 293, 294, 295, 296, 297, 298, 301, 325, 327, 328, 339
Mashraqi's death, 256, 289
Mashraqi's son, 174
Mashraqui, 15
Mashriqi, 15, 18, 19, 29, 31, 32, 33, 34, 41, 43, 50, 52, 53, 57, 58, 61, 63, 64, 69, 70, 72, 74, 75, 78, 81, 82, 83, 86, 87, 88, 89, 90, 91, 92, 93, 101, 102, 103, 106, 108, 110, 111, 112, 113, 114, 115, 116, 117, 118, 119, 120, 125, 126, 127, 128, 129, 133, 134, 135, 136, 137, 138, 139, 140, 146, 147, 148, 149, 150, 153, 154, 155, 156, 158, 159, 160, 161, 162, 163, 167, 169, 170, 171, 174, 175, 176, 177, 178, 179, 180, 181, 182, 183, 184, 185, 186, 188, 189, 191, 196, 197, 200, 201, 202, 203, 209, 211, 212, 213, 214, 219, 220, 221, 224, 225, 226, 227, 228, 235, 237, 238, 241, 245, 246, 247, 248, 249, 250, 251, 252, 253, 254, 255, 256, 257, 259, 301, 309, 310, 311, 312, 313, 315, 316, 317, 318, 319, 320, 321, 322, 323, 324, 329, 330, 331, 332, 333, 334, 338, 339
Mashriqui, 15, 42, 51, 111
massacre, 37, 103, 312, 331
masses, 20, 29, 43, 51, 64, 69, 77, 100, 129, 147, 149, 167, 188, 193, 310, 313, 316, 319, 323, 324, 330, 332, 333, 334
Masuda Yousaf, 241, 259

material, 52, 120, 148, 176, 228, 311, 317, 320, 321, 329, 330, 332
materials, 61, 99, 176, 177, 178, 180, 312, 316, 317, 320, 321, 329, 330, 331
Maulana Abul Ala Maududi, 188, 195, 199, 222
Maulana Fazal Hussain Dilawar, 73, 77, 82, 83, 84, 107, 127
Maulana Maudoodi, 88, 182, 247
Maulana Maududi, 141
Maulvi Nasiruddin, 61
Mayo Hospital, 213, 245, 246, 248, 249, 265, 278
Mazdoor Organisation, 88
Mazdoor Organization, 69
measures, 31, 36, 39, 50, 69, 70, 137, 162
media, 312, 313, 322, 323, 324, 331, 333, 334
medical report, 208, 209, 210, 213
Mehman Khana, 202
Mehmankhana, 191
memorandum, 156, 157
memorize, 187
Mere Weather Tower, 139, 140
merger, 146, 149, 186, 221
message, 41, 89, 110, 113, 121, 148, 153, 155, 245, 246, 257
Mian Iftikhar-ud-Din, 88
Mian Inayatullah, 146
Mian Mehmood Ali Kasuri, 85, 86, 100
Mian Mohammad, 171, 232, 252
Mian Mumtaz Mohammad Khan Daultana, 82, 141
Mianwali Jail, 72, 73, 81
Middle East, 133
militarise, 127
military, 48, 49, 65, 84, 90, 104, 118, 127, 194, 215, 216, 238, 239, 241, 333
Military, 47, 48, 50, 51, 52, 58, 63, 64, 65, 76, 78, 82, 84, 98, 99, 100, 101, 103, 104, 106, 107, 110, 111, 112, 115, 117, 118, 120, 121, 125, 126, 127, 128, 129, 135, 136, 137, 138, 140, 141, 149, 157, 162, 167, 168, 169, 171, 173, 181, 187, 194, 196, 200, 207, 209, 211, 213, 214, 216, 218, 225, 226, 228, 229, 231, 232, 235, 236, 238, 246, 247, 249, 250, 253, 255, 256, 337, 338
million-man march, 158, 161, 170, 185, 216, 232
Million-Man March, 156
Minister, 77, 82, 85, 87, 92, 108, 133, 135, 136, 140, 141, 147, 148, 161, 168, 169, 171, 172, 174, 197, 199, 200, 202, 203, 208, 214, 221, 222, 223, 227, 248, 252, 258, 315, 319, 322, 334
Ministry of Education, 302, 320, 321
Minto Park, 149, 153, 154, 155, 186, 194, 222
Mir Afzal, 170
Mir Ali Ahmed Talpur, 252
Mir Manzoor Mohammad Warsi, 202
Mir Muhammad Riaz, 175, 192
Mir Zafarullah Khan Jamali, 303, 308
Miraj Din, 164, 257
Mirpurkhas, 126
Mirza Azam Beg, 212
Mirza Bashir Ahmed, 188
Mirza Shamsul Haq, 172
mischief, 171
misquoted, 311, 330
Mochi Gate, 64, 81, 89, 110, 149, 164, 195, 223
Mohammad Ali Bogra, 236
Mohammad Asghar, 170
Mohammad Hussain, 149
Mohammad Mian Soomro, 328
Mohammad Rafi, 180, 184, 186, 200
Mohammad Sadiq, 162
Mohammad Yousaf Khan, 241, 266
Mohammed Anwar, 186

Mohammed Khursheed Khalid, 154, 168, 174, 175, 180, 186, 187, 188, 218, 219, 221, 228, 229
Mohammed Khurshid Khalid, 160, 190, 219, 220
Mohammed Mirza, 223
Mohammed Rafi, 197, 207, 212
Mohammed Siddique, 212
monument, 312
moral fiber, 135
Morocco, 82
mosque, 42, 113, 198, 221
Mountbatten, 30, 35, 36, 43
Mountbatten Plan, 30
Movement, 18, 19
Mubarak Saghar, 81
Muhammad Akram, 69, 172
Muhammad Ali Jinnah, 310, 331
Muhammad Ayub Khan, 265, 278, 286
Muhammad Ayyub Khuhro, 114
Muhammad Bashir, 222
Muhammad Khursheed Khalid, 169, 170, 172, 175, 177, 185, 187, 188, 219, 220, 224, 240
Muhammad Khurshid Khalid, 167, 189, 190, 191, 192, 216, 217, 220, 224, 232, 239, 240
Muhammad Latif, 183, 237
Muhammad Munir, 93, 101
Muhammad Shamaz Khan, 198
Muhammad Zakria, 237
Muhammed Sadiq, 314
Mujahadeen-e-Islam, 69
Mujahadeen-i-Islam, 88
Mujibur Rahman, 141
mullaism, 89, 116
Multan, 63, 64, 81, 98, 237, 252
Multan Bar Association, 252
murdabad, 145
murder, 20, 37, 75, 76, 133, 134, 169, 170, 171, 172, 173, 174, 175, 178, 180, 181, 183, 184, 185, 186, 187, 188, 189, 191, 192, 193, 194, 195, 196, 197, 198, 199, 200, 201, 203, 204, 205, 206, 207, 208, 209, 210, 211, 212, 213, 214, 215, 216,
217, 219, 220, 221, 222, 223, 224, 225, 226, 227, 228, 229, 230, 231, 232
Musalman, 116, 202
Musalmans, 108, 116, 201
Musawat-e-Islam, 69
Musawat-i-Islam, 88
Mushtaq Ahmad Gurmani, 141
Mushtaq Ahmed Qureshi, 164
Muslim, 23, 29, 30, 31, 32, 35, 36, 40, 41, 42, 47, 48, 49, 50, 51, 52, 63, 64, 65, 66, 69, 71, 86, 87, 88, 89, 91, 98, 99, 100, 102, 103, 104, 105, 106, 107, 108, 109, 111, 112, 114, 120, 139, 145, 146, 147, 148, 149, 150, 153, 154, 155, 156, 157, 159, 162, 163, 167, 168, 170, 171, 172, 176, 177, 178, 180, 181, 182, 183, 184, 186, 187, 190, 191, 200, 201, 202, 208, 214, 215, 216, 217, 220, 232, 236, 238, 250, 252, 253, 258, 310, 329, 331, 333, 338
Muslim League, 20, 30, 35, 41, 51, 71, 87, 95, 96, 98, 105, 114, 145, 146, 147, 148, 153, 154, 155, 164, 168, 170, 172, 176, 180, 186, 187, 190, 214, 215, 216, 217, 220, 304, 305, 326, 332
Muslims, 30, 35, 37, 38, 40, 41, 42, 43, 47, 50, 51, 57, 58, 64, 82, 87, 89, 92, 99, 100, 101, 104, 105, 109, 112, 116, 118, 121, 128, 133, 145, 147, 153, 193, 201, 202, 310, 330, 333
Mussalmans, 37, 58, 205

N

N.W.F.P., 81, 202
Nasim Yousaf, 5, 6, 9, 13, 17, 27, 45, 55, 59, 67, 79, 123, 131, 143, 151, 165, 218, 233, 243, 261, 283, 299, 307, 313, 314, 318, 321, 324, 325, 327, 329, 335, 339, 362
Nasir Ahmad Sheikh, 146

Nasir Ahmed Shaikh, 146
Nasiruddin Kamran, 77
nation, 23, 25, 36, 40, 43, 49, 59, 64, 67, 72, 76, 106, 107, 112, 115, 119, 123, 125, 126, 127, 134, 135, 136, 141, 145, 147, 205, 214, 218, 239, 245, 246, 301, 310, 312, 315, 316, 317, 319, 320, 322, 323, 329, 330, 331, 332, 333, 334
National Assembly, 325, 326
National Assembly of Pakistan, 325, 326
National Guard, 35, 41
National Institute of Historical and Cultural Research, 302
Naushera, 198
Naval, 48
Nawab Muhammad Hussain Khan, 37
Nawab Muzzafar Ali Khan, 252
Nawab Yameen Khan, 252
Nawabshah, 126
Nawai Waqt, 296
Nawa-i-Waqat, 184
Naya Payam, 168
Nazim-e-Aala, 238, 240
Nazim-i-Nashr-o-Isha'at, 73
negotiations, 34, 52, 127, 137, 156
Nehru, 37, 39, 42, 63, 66, 72, 73, 89, 113, 114, 127, 128, 137, 154, 156, 158, 159, 175, 186, 201, 202, 216, 227
Noakhali, 31
Noorul Amin, 252
North-West Frontier Province, 81, 222
notification, 48, 49, 63, 179, 203
notifications, 48

O

oath, 196, 226
obituary, 254
office, 62, 69, 82, 87, 119, 147, 170, 177, 178, 180, 183, 199, 202, 217
one million man march, 19
one million march, 154
one million men, 162
operated, 239, 246, 247
Opposition, 71, 87, 88, 90, 96, 98, 106, 114, 120, 121, 174
Orangi Town, 312, 334
Ordinance, 48, 49, 99, 215, 216, 235, 240
Orientalists, 133

P

P.I. Syed Fayyaz Hussain, 185
Pakistan, 3, 5, 17, 18, 19, 23, 29, 30, 31, 35, 36, 40, 41, 42, 43, 50, 51, 52, 57, 61, 63, 64, 65, 69, 70, 71, 72, 75, 76, 78, 81, 82, 83, 85, 86, 87, 89, 91, 95, 96, 98, 99, 100, 102, 103, 104, 105, 106, 107, 108, 110, 111, 112, 113, 114, 115, 116, 117, 118, 119, 120, 121, 125, 126, 127, 128, 133, 134, 135, 136, 137, 138, 139, 140, 141, 145, 146, 147, 148, 150, 153, 154, 155, 156, 157, 158, 159, 161, 163, 167, 168, 169, 171, 172, 174, 175, 176, 179, 181, 182, 183, 184, 186, 188, 191, 194, 195, 197, 198, 200, 201, 202, 203, 204, 207, 208, 209, 210, 211, 212, 213, 214, 215, 216, 217, 218, 219, 223, 225, 226, 227, 228, 230, 231, 232, 235, 236, 237, 238, 239, 240, 245, 246, 247, 248, 249, 250, 251, 252, 253, 255, 256, 257, 301, 302, 303, 304, 305, 307, 308, 309, 310, 311, 312, 313, 314, 315, 316, 317, 318, 319, 320, 321, 322, 323, 324, 329, 330, 331, 332, 333, 334, 337, 338, 339, 340, 341
Pakistan Commercial Exporters of Towels Association, 17
Pakistan Socialist Party, 81
Pakistani, 73, 104, 105, 106, 116, 232, 301, 310, 330

pamphlet, 61, 62, 63, 89, 90, 91, 93
Pandit, 37, 38, 39, 114, 127, 159
parade, 31, 48, 84, 139, 157, 190, 220, 236, 238
parades, 37, 84, 90, 159, 161
parading, 30, 162
partition plan, 19, 40
Partition Plan, 36, 43, 52
party politics, 85, 86, 125
passport, 52, 53, 57, 58, 103, 107, 108
passports, 58, 116
Patiala, 50
Patna, 31, 32, 33, 34, 36, 37, 38, 39, 41
patriotic, 106, 217
patriotism, 137, 253, 256, 332
Peshawar, 30, 77, 129, 153, 155, 171, 173, 178, 181, 201, 221, 252, 257, 258
petition, 58, 77, 85, 86, 93, 98, 99, 100, 101, 102, 167, 197, 208, 215
Petition, 77, 86, 101
petitioners, 197
photographers, 184
pickets, 31
pilgrimage, 108
Pilgrimage, 103, 107, 111
pilgrims, 112
Pir Alhan Shah, 163
Pir Elahi Buksh, 81
Pir Ilahi Baksh, 108
Pir of Manki Sharif, 88
poem, 271, 297, 298
police, 35, 36, 38, 39, 48, 49, 61, 62, 66, 69, 77, 109, 158, 160, 161, 168, 169, 170, 171, 172, 173, 175, 176, 177, 178, 179, 180, 181, 182, 183, 184, 187, 188, 189, 190, 191, 192, 193, 194, 196, 197, 200, 201, 203, 204, 206, 210, 213, 215, 216, 217, 219, 220, 221, 224, 227, 229, 235, 237, 240, 245
political, 20, 29, 30, 61, 65, 66, 70, 71, 81, 84, 99, 103, 111, 112, 113, 114, 119, 125, 128, 133, 134, 137, 140, 141, 142, 145, 147, 149, 155, 159, 176, 177, 179, 181, 190, 211, 212, 213, 214, 216, 218, 219, 230, 235, 236, 238, 239, 310, 315, 319, 323, 329
politicians, 116, 126
poor, 63, 81, 83, 107, 116, 121, 129, 150, 154, 193, 208, 211, 214, 230, 237, 238, 246, 309, 313, 316, 319, 322, 331, 334
posters, 47, 217
poverty, 59, 64, 100, 218, 312, 313, 332
power, 40, 64, 71, 105, 107, 114, 118, 120, 125, 176, 177, 188, 197, 210, 214
prayers, 102, 195, 198, 221, 249, 256, 257
Prediction, 145
predicts, 145
President, 21, 35, 51, 71, 76, 84, 86, 121, 135, 146, 147, 148, 154, 155, 164, 167, 168, 170, 171, 174, 180, 181, 182, 183, 186, 199, 200, 202, 204, 216, 217, 218, 220, 225, 230, 235, 236, 237, 238, 239, 240, 245, 247, 248, 249, 250, 252, 253, 254, 255, 257, 258, 263, 265, 278, 286, 301, 302, 303, 324
President General Pervez Musharraf, 301, 302, 303
Press, 29, 34, 37, 44, 52, 62, 63, 74, 75, 77, 82, 83, 84, 103, 105, 106, 108, 117, 120, 125, 127, 147, 149, 161, 163, 171, 173, 174, 183, 184, 236, 237, 239, 329, 337, 338
Press Note, 52, 74, 161, 237
Press statement, 44, 147
pressure, 41, 73, 74, 75, 101, 193, 217, 219, 239
Prime Minister, 57, 62, 63, 71, 72, 73, 75, 77, 82, 85, 86, 87, 95, 112, 114, 125, 127, 133, 134, 137, 138, 139, 140, 141, 146, 147, 148, 156, 159, 182, 208, 217, 219, 252, 263, 264,

301, 303, 304, 308, 309, 313, 314, 324, 330, 331, 334
Principal, 208, 209, 211, 212, 257
priority, 134
procession, 36, 37, 72, 73, 74, 112, 126, 139, 140, 158, 159, 161, 229, 251, 283, 285
processions, 39, 84, 156, 161, 162
projects, 113, 239
property, 47, 62, 102, 178, 179, 188, 204, 211, 212, 213
proposal, 104, 120, 129, 154, 204
Proposals, 311, 312, 323, 324
public meeting, 31, 63, 64, 66, 70, 71, 73, 74, 76, 81, 91, 110, 111, 114, 127, 135, 137, 139, 140, 142, 153, 155, 159, 194, 219, 222, 223, 236, 256
Public Safety Act, 52, 69, 70, 71, 81, 91, 92, 99, 103, 107, 163, 167
published, 6, 18, 61, 63, 72, 75, 99, 115, 119, 120, 159, 217, 227, 235, 251, 252, 311, 312, 316, 320, 323, 330, 334
Punjab, 30, 35, 36, 52, 57, 58, 61, 63, 66, 69, 70, 71, 72, 73, 74, 75, 77, 81, 82, 83, 84, 85, 86, 87, 88, 89, 91, 92, 93, 99, 100, 103, 107, 112, 115, 121, 125, 128, 160, 167, 176, 186, 201, 257
Punjab University, 125
purdah, 36
Purnea City, 36
Putna, 31

Q

Qaid-e-Azam, 50, 96
Qaiser Mustafa, 77, 84
Qamar ud Din, 121
Qazi Hafizullah, 174, 178, 189, 190, 191, 196
Qazi Khail, 170
Qazi Muhammad Hafiz Ullah, 217

Qazi Muhammad Hafizullah, 177, 224
Qazi Sabahuddin, 77
Qizilbash, 169, 214
Quaid-e-Azam, 52, 227, 258, 263, 305, 310, 311, 317, 320, 331
Quaid-i-Azam, 32, 105, 110, 201
Quetta, 177
Quran, 109, 113, 116, 118, 136, 195, 201, 316, 320, 323

R

Radcliffe Award, 42
Rafiq Sabir Mazangavi, 258
Raids, 164
Raja Mohammad Afsar Khan, 266, 283
Raja Mohammad Akbar Khan, 266
Rajhasthan, 96
rally, 39, 47, 65, 112, 153
Ramzan Khokhar, 240
Randhawa, 174, 190, 193, 199, 200, 217, 219, 224, 226
Rashid Kamal, 163, 171
Rawalpindi, 69, 72, 75, 77, 91, 95, 98, 114, 116, 117, 134, 155, 156, 157, 159, 167, 177, 182, 205, 215, 235, 236, 237, 239, 240, 241, 252, 256, 259, 339, 340, 341
Razakar, 155, 157, 158, 160, 237, 238
Razakars, 65, 73, 74, 75, 90, 91, 133, 136, 137, 142, 146, 153, 156, 157, 158, 160, 161, 162, 185, 188, 202, 237, 238
Red Shirts, 198, 199, 202, 221, 222
refugees, 31, 32, 33, 34, 37
rehabilitation, 31, 32, 33, 34, 38, 138
Rehabilitation, 32, 35
Rehan Shah, 169, 180, 184, 215
rejected, 101, 102, 148, 186, 209
Relief Camp, 35

religion, 47, 109, 113, 127, 195, 333
Republican Party, 148, 190, 203
research, 17, 311, 315, 316, 317, 320, 321, 323, 329, 331, 332, 334
Research, 18
resolution, 70, 74, 76, 82, 137, 139, 141, 156, 237, 256
revolution, 32, 230
Riaz Qadeer, 245
rich, 107, 150, 167, 188
rights, 6, 47, 57, 58, 61, 64, 71, 77, 100, 102, 119, 238, 333
riots, 30, 40
river, 128, 146
Rizvi, 183, 187, 194, 195, 197, 198, 199, 200, 201, 205, 206, 207, 210, 229
Russia, 115, 116, 117

S

S.A. Mahmud, 167, 168
S.A. Rehman, 167
S.A. Saeed, 77
S.M.Nasim, 185
Sabzibagh, 36
sacred mission, 226
sacrifice, 50, 51, 135, 136, 137, 139, 141
Saddar ud Din Ansari, 252
Saeed Ahmed, 222, 223
Safdar Saleemi, 88, 112
Safety Act, 70, 72, 83, 194
Safia Saad Ullah Khan, 199
Said Akbar, 134
Sajjanpur, 232
Salar, 41, 101, 164, 198, 221
Salar-e-Suba, 101
Salar-i-Ala, 41
Salars, 50
Sameen Jan, 184, 197
Sameen Khan, 181
Sami Khan, 177
Samin Khan, 169
Sardar Abdul Hameed Dasti, 135
Sardar Abdul Qayyum, 135, 141

Sardar Abdur Rab Nishtar, 114, 146, 187
Sardar Ibraheem, 140
Sardar Mohammad Alam, 252
Sardar Mohammed Ibraheem, 140
Sardar Nishtar, 146
Sardar Patel, 42
satyagraha, 136, 137, 138
Saudi, 103, 108, 109, 110, 112
Saudi Arabia, 103, 108, 109, 110, 112
scholar, 113, 229, 254, 316, 319, 322
scholarship, 133, 257
scholarships, 311, 317, 321
science, 134
scientific development, 134, 315
scientific institute, 134
scuffle, 224
sealed, 62, 177, 178, 179, 180
Secretary, 51, 57, 58, 63, 73, 77, 81, 82, 83, 84, 86, 91, 93, 100, 101, 107, 110, 111, 112, 126, 156, 163, 170, 171, 172, 176, 181, 215, 225, 252, 253
Section 144, 39, 99, 161, 162
secularism, 153
Security Council, 29, 66, 103, 141, 157
seized, 157, 178
self-help, 313
selflessly, 142, 239
semi-military, 215, 216
seminars, 311, 317, 321, 334
Senate, 325, 328
sentence, 162, 185, 190, 198, 232
sentenced, 162, 185, 188, 229
session, 36, 114, 136, 137
Sessions, 162, 163, 185, 188, 190, 197, 207, 208, 209, 210, 215, 216, 217, 218, 219, 221, 222, 223, 224, 225, 226, 227, 228, 229, 231, 232
Shabbir Ahmed, 208, 210, 211, 213, 215
Shafaat Ahmed Khan, 29, 32
Shah Alam, 163, 170
Shah Gharib, 160

Shah Muhammad Suleman, 201
Shah Nawaz, 36, 141
Shah Uzair Munimi, 36
Shahab-ud-Din, 88, 89
Shahbaz, 227
Shahi Mosque, 129
Shahnawaz, 140
Shaikh Anwar-Ul-Haq, 209, 218
Shaikh Fazal-e-Elahi, 164
Shaukat Aziz, 301, 309, 313, 324, 330, 331, 334
Shaukat Tarar, 172, 175, 193, 223, 224
Shaukatullah, 39
Sheikh Abdul Majid, 81
Sheikh Anwar ul Haq, 208, 209, 215, 216, 217, 218, 219, 221, 222, 223, 224, 225, 226, 227, 228, 229, 231, 232
Sheikh Anwar-ul Haq, 207
Sheikh Fazal Elahi, 186
Sheikh Fazal Ilahi, 76
Sheikh Mohammad Nasim, 207
Sheikh Qamar-ud-Din, 118
Sheikh Rashid Ahmad, 322
Sher Bahadur Khan, 198
Sher Zaman, 40, 129, 236, 339
shirt, 184, 224
Shoaib Sultan Khan, 312
Sialkot, 82, 89, 101, 160, 162, 171, 208, 232
Sikhs, 40
Sind, 33, 81, 110, 126, 127, 139, 140, 145, 171, 252, 257
Sindh, 81
Sir Zia ud Din, 263
Sirdar Abdur Rab Nishtar, 58
slogan mongers, 136
Slogans, 72, 160, 229
snatched, 184, 193, 203, 224
social, 109, 112, 137, 256, 333
soldier, 127
soldierly, 153
solidarity, 113, 118, 125, 126, 140, 145
son, 42, 169, 174, 175, 178, 179, 180, 181, 188, 189, 192, 193, 194, 197, 198, 199, 200, 204, 205, 211, 223, 241, 256, 266, 269, 297, 339
son-in-law, 241
Sound Diagnosis, 136
sovereignty, 49, 145
Soviet, 156
speakers, 70, 138, 139, 145, 256, 310
speech, 61, 66, 92, 99, 102, 116, 120, 129, 137, 140, 154, 155, 159, 195, 222
St. John Ambulance Brigade, 48
starvation, 113, 127
State, 47, 105, 106, 112, 117, 125, 126, 149, 183, 210, 235
statement, 31, 32, 37, 40, 43, 62, 65, 73, 75, 81, 82, 83, 89, 101, 106, 107, 112, 118, 120, 127, 128, 129, 136, 149, 154, 159, 160, 168, 171, 172, 173, 174, 175, 176, 177, 178, 181, 183, 184, 186, 187, 189, 190, 191, 193, 195, 196, 199, 200, 201, 202, 203, 204, 205, 206, 208, 216, 217, 219, 220, 221, 224, 226, 228, 230, 258, 331
stooges, 117
story, 36, 38, 192, 194, 197, 206, 219, 228, 229, 332
strike, 72, 139, 140
struggle, 40, 52, 64, 76, 115, 116, 117, 119, 136, 137, 311, 319, 322, 330, 332
studies, 316, 317, 320
study, 17, 30, 185, 332
sub-continent, 40, 49, 116, 201, 252, 257, 310, 330, 334
suffer, 136, 193, 217, 218
Suhrawardy, 70, 86, 87, 88, 92, 93, 94, 95, 96, 97, 98, 99, 100, 156, 182, 264
Sukker, 178
Sukkur, 126, 252
Superintendent of Police, 49, 169, 189, 221, 225, 226
supporters, 69, 71, 74, 154, 158, 177, 184, 229, 231, 237
Swat, 258
Switzerland, 247, 248

Syed Abdul Aziz, 33, 35
Syed Abdul Wadood, 69
Syed Abdul Wadud, 82, 101, 111, 115
Syed Abid Husain, 136
Syed Akbar Ali Shah, 81
Syed Aziz-ul Huq, 181
Syed Ejaz Hussain, 192
Syed Fayyaz Hussain, 207
Syed Hasnat Ahmed, 173, 177, 180, 193, 217, 223, 224
Syed Makhdoom Shah Banori, 36
Syed Nur Ahmed, 100, 101
Syed Younus Ali Shah, 266
symposium, 125

T

Takmillah, 163, 235
Tameer, 252, 296
Tazkara, 116
Tehreek, 15, 17, 51
Tehrik, 15, 17, 39, 40, 41, 47, 49, 50, 73, 75, 129, 147, 189, 202, 236, 238, 239, 240, 251, 252, 257, 309, 310, 311, 312, 315, 316, 317, 319, 320, 321, 322, 323, 329, 330, 331, 332, 333, 339
Tehrique, 15
telegram, 42, 72, 73, 107, 114, 128, 248, 254
thanks, 33, 105, 248, 256, 309, 317, 321
tonga, 188, 275
tongawala, 189, 220
topple, 235
torn, 182, 184, 224
torture, 175, 182, 189, 190, 191, 197, 200, 217, 218, 219, 220, 224, 230, 237
tortured, 170, 175, 178, 188, 191, 201, 203, 204, 213, 217, 224, 227
travel, 52, 57, 58, 64, 108
treacherously, 186
treason, 102

treatment, 38, 42, 182, 205, 207, 208, 209, 210, 212, 213, 218, 230, 247, 248
tribute, 251, 253
tributes, 153, 251, 252, 253, 255, 256, 284, 289, 307
Tributes, 256
Tritton, 133
troops, 73
trumpet blowing, 118
truncated, 30, 35, 36, 43
Truth, 23
Trygve Lie, 57, 58
Tufail Mohammad, 176
Tunisia, 82, 83

U

U.N., 58, 66, 104, 114, 139
Ulema, 113
ul-ul-Amr, 112
ummat, 120, 121
unconscious, 247
uniform, 49, 238
uniforms, 179, 216, 238
United Nations, 29, 57, 58, 103, 115, 116, 139, 156, 157
unity, 29, 37, 51, 65, 112, 119, 126, 147, 236, 239, 333
University of Dhaka, 133
unlawful, 47, 50, 176, 179, 215
UNO, 116
USA, 6, 17, 18, 246, 311, 313, 316, 320, 323, 329, 330, 331, 339
USSR, 117

V

Vallabhbhai Patel, 42
Vellore Jail, 297
vested, 40, 75, 117, 121, 149, 158, 185, 214, 239, 310
veto, 156
Vienna, 121
violence, 47, 48, 100, 189, 192, 197, 200, 224, 225
volunteers, 39, 98, 136, 137, 153, 157, 158, 216, 219, 232, 239

W

Wagah, 127, 203
Wahdat Colony, 203, 222, 227
Wahgah, 158, 160, 161, 185, 224
Walton Airport, 110
Waqt, 61, 183, 186, 224
war, 115, 116, 117, 127, 153
Warning, 117
Warrants, 182
Warsi, 202
water, 66, 109, 112, 113, 127, 128, 189, 203, 220
Wazirabad, 172, 190, 220
Waziristan, 155
wealth, 138
web site, 334
Web site, 18
web sites, 18, 334
weight, 73, 74, 189, 212, 213, 230
West Pakistan, 103, 115, 127, 137, 141, 146, 174, 181, 201, 208, 215, 240
West Punjab Government, 52
West Punjab Public Safety Act, 167
Western Powers, 115, 117
wife, 83, 195, 197, 222, 223, 241, 256, 259

Y

Yaqub Ali, 167
Yasin Butt, 183, 186, 224
Yusaf Khattak, 88
Yusuf Haroon, 136

Z

Zafar Haider, 170, 184, 186, 232
Zakir Husain, 42
Zawar Haider, 266
Zia Ambalvi, 112
Zindabad, 41, 145, 160, 185, 230
Zurayk, 133
Zwemer, 133

"Allama Mashraqi's life — his message to the world"

-Nasim Yousaf

www.ingramcontent.com/pod-product-compliance
Lightning Source LLC
Chambersburg PA
CBHW030400100426
42812CB00028B/2784/J